emphasis ART

Animals in the Jungle, *a group mural by primary-grade schoolchildren. The background is composed of two 4 × 8-foot sheets of hardboard painted with black latex. Black construction paper stapled to corrugated cardboard may also be used. Each youngster in class contributed one cutout construction-paper animal that was stapled to the background. Children who completed their assignment early created additional details: trees, shrubs, clouds, and birds.*

FOURTH EDITION

emphasis ART

FRANK WACHOWIAK
University of Georgia

A Qualitative Art Program for Elementary and Middle Schools

HARPER & ROW, PUBLISHERS, New York
Cambridge, Philadelphia, San Francisco,
London, Mexico City, São Paulo, Singapore, Sydney

Sponsoring Editor: Louise Waller
Cover Photos: Frank Wachowiak
Production Manager: Jeanie Berke
Compositor: York Graphic Services, Inc.
Printer and Binder: Kingsport Press

EMPHASIS ART, *Fourth Edition*

Library of Congress Cataloging in Publication Data

Wachowiak, Frank.
  Emphasis art.

  Includes index.
  1. Art—Study and teaching (Elementary) 2. Art—
Study and teaching (Secondary) I. Title.
N350.W26 1985   372.5′044   84-27892
ISBN 0-06-046871-8

   87 88 9 8 7 6 5 4

Book design and color photography by the author. Supplemental photography by Theodore K. Ramsay, David Hodge, W. Robert Nix, Jimmy Morris, Baiba Kuntz, Shirley Lucas, and Michael F. O'Brien. Robert D. Clements assisted with the proofreading and indexing of the book.

To children everywhere who make the teaching of art a never-ending, forever-rewarding adventure, and to their teachers, in both elementary and middle schools, who share in the wonder and discovery. With special thanks to my former students, now teachers and professors of art, who have been so generous in sharing the results of their teaching to help make this book a colorful treasury of child art.

This delightful print is by an upper-elementary-grade youngster from Japan. Known as paper etching, it employs a laminated shiny-surfaced cardboard as the plate. Parts of the cardboard surface are scratched or peeled off producing the white or light areas in the final print. Oil-based printing ink is used to coat the cardboard plate. Moistened paper and a printing press are employed.

Self-portrait in black crayon, 12 × 18 inches. A first-grade child draws herself combing her hair and brushing her teeth at the same time, for which she needs four eyeballs, two for one task and two more for the other. **Facing page:** *The author and one of his young charges at a Saturday art class.*

CONTENTS

PREFACE

By the time this fourth edition of *Emphasis Art* reaches its audience, I will have completed a half-century of teaching art to children. As I look back to my first elementary-school art classes in rural Minnesota, through two decades at the laboratory school of the University of Iowa, culminating in my present Saturday morning classes for youngsters at the University of Georgia, I treasure those creative encounters with children that have enriched and colored my life. In the happy, charged environment of children searching, discovering, and creating, it has been easy to stay young at heart.

In planning this revision of *Emphasis Art*, I had two major concerns: to make the book's content more comprehensive by including middle-school art projects that I had described in my earlier text *Art in Depth*, now out of print; and, in light of current proposals by some art educators to make *talking about art* rather than *making or doing art* the paramount activity in school art classes, to emphasize and reaffirm the importance of the qualitative art-studio experience in the art programs of our country's schools. In my 50 years of teaching art to youngsters, I have never had cause to question the intrinsic worth or the learning potential of the elementary- and middle-school art-studio experience. In all instances the children's critical faculties in appreciating art were sharpened and enhanced because of their intense, purposeful studio involvement. Through richly planned art motivations that included original works of art, reproductions, films, tapes, and color slides, the youngsters' creative efforts flowered, and their art awareness thrived.

Art making and art appreciating are most successful and most meaningful when they complement each other in an orchestrated, coordinated endeavor. Whether in the classroom or the art room, every studio project can incorporate vital aspects of art appreciation if the teacher is armed with the appropriate visual resources and a basic knowledge of art history and art fundamentals.

I know teachers who have added to the children's insight regarding African and American Indian art motifs through studio projects in mask making, who have coordinated the study of Egyptian tomb friezes with the making of group murals, and who have introduced students to the diverse painting styles of Diego Velasquez, Albrecht Dürer, Hans Holbein, Rembrandt Van Rijn, Amedeo Modigliani, Pablo Picasso, and Andrew Wyeth during studio classes in figure and portrait painting. Every phase of world art through the centuries can be brought to life and given immediacy in an art-studio environment, whether it be the mosaics of Ravenna in Italy, the T'ang ceramics of China, the illuminated manuscripts of medieval Europe, the glories of Greek sculpture, the ukiyo-e woodblock prints of Japan, or the fascinating mobiles of Alexander Calder. The best teachers of art have created exciting comprehensive programs for both elementary and middle schools in which art studio and art appreciation are imaginatively combined to provide the child with a growing treasury of knowledge about art, artists, art styles, and art's permeating influence in our everyday lives.

To help the teacher become more knowledgeably effective in the area of art criticism, I have expanded the chapter "Avenues to Art Appreciation" to include current thought on understanding the visual arts. Two new chapters have been added to make the book indispensable to teachers seeking aid in the critical areas of art-class management and the evaluation of student work. They are Chapter 5, "Teaching Strategies," and Chapter 7, "Evaluating Children's Art."

Another new chapter requested by teachers is "Art for Children with Special Needs." Because of *mainstreaming* federal legislation, the task of teaching the physically handicapped and the mentally retarded child is becoming more and more the responsibility of the classroom teacher and the art teacher. This chapter provides teachers with guidelines needed to enhance both their repertoire and expertise in this critical area, as well as some suggestions useful in identifying and guiding the artistically talented or gifted child. An addition to the Appendixes includes a brief historical outline detailing the growth of art education in the United States.

The response of educators at all levels to the third edition of *Emphasis Art* has been gratifyingly positive. The book's clarity, brevity, structure, and wealth of colorful illustrations have found universally enthusiastic endorsement. The present edition is once more the result of continuing involvement and research with children in busy classroom and studio situations. The art teaching strategies, motivations, techniques, and evaluative procedures described are based on actual experiences and observations of outstanding elementary- and middle-school art practices both in this country and abroad.

The intent of *Emphasis Art*, as envisioned years ago, has not been altered. The qualitative character remains. This revised edition again concerns itself with the adventures, joys, responsibilities, problems, and rewards of teaching art to children, with the strategic, guiding role of the teacher; with projects based on perennial, universal art principles; and with those recurring evaluative design and composition clues that can help the teacher identify and encourage the art in children's art.

In addition to providing the supplemental material on middle-school art, the expanded chapter on art appreciation,

and the new chapters on teaching strategies, evaluation of student art, and mainstreaming, this edition offers a profusion of new illustrations in color, as well as in black and white, from worldwide sources.

Emphasis Art is designed foremost for elementary- and middle-school teachers of art who want to augment and enrich their art programs. It is also proposed as a text for the college or university student in search of a candid and documented blueprint of high-caliber elementary- and middle-school art practices. It offers a lucid description of a proven, dynamic program for those veteran teachers who seek continuing challenges, new techniques, and classroom-tested art projects for their instructional repertoire.

The importance of the instructor's dedication, preparation, and influence is emphasized throughout the book. A creative, confident, enthusiastic teacher with a love of children and a growing understanding and appreciation of art fundamentals is *sine qua non* the prime catalyst in the development of a promising, productive, and qualitative art program. Constant planning, imagining, organizing, researching, experimenting, motivating, evaluating, and resource building are the challenging and often enervating responsibilities of the successful teacher of art. The privilege, however, of sharing the contagious, exuberant, magical world of children and young adolescents, as they explore, search, discover, and invent, compensates beyond measure for the extra effort required.

Children from the first through the eighth grades respond and grow in a program in which art fundamentals and techniques are not left to chance but are taught sequentially, purposefully, and imaginatively. Debate concerning process versus product has needlessly clouded the picture. Perceptive teachers are aware that wherever and whenever the process of discovery and creation is founded on a knowledge, appreciation, and use of art and design principles, the product always reflects this understanding. Mounting evidence, exemplified and corroborated by contemporary child art creations, many illustrated herein, suggests that we have been underestimating the expressive capabilities of children and, in many instances, have not even begun to tap their true artistic potential.

The philosophy and the strategy of guiding youngsters as they visually express their ideas, responses, and feelings, documented in this text, are the hallmark of those schools where the *emphasis is on art*—art as an adventure; a flowering; a celebration; and a discipline with its own singular demands, unique core of learnings, and incomparable rewards. Whatever compelling features this book may possess is in no small measure due to the expressive magic of those children whose creations sparkle across the pages and to the commitment of those imaginative and devoted teachers who help make the art class a dynamic, productive experience for them.

I am pleased to acknowledge the assistance and contributions of the following colleagues: W. Robert Nix, professor of art, University of Georgia, photographic consultant; Theodore K. Ramsay, professor of art, University of Michigan, Ann Arbor, coauthor of the first and second editions of *Emphasis Art*; David Hodge, professor of art, University of Wisconsin, Oshkosh, coauthor of *Art in Depth*; Claire B. Clements, professor of education, University of Georgia; Robert D. Clements, professor of art, University of Georgia; Mary Hammond, professor of art, George Mason University, Virginia; Jimmy Morris, fine arts coordinator, Athens, Georgia; Patrick Taylor, professor of art, Kennesaw College, Kennesaw, Georgia; Baiba Kuntz, art instructor, Winnetka, Illinois; James McGrath, coordinator, arts and humanities, U.S. Department of Defense, Dependents Schools, Pacific Region; Michael F. O'Brien, art instructor, American High School, Seoul, Korea; Shirley Lucas, art instructor, Oshkosh, Wisconsin; Mary E. Swanson, art instructor, Nashua, New Hampshire; Diane Turner, art instructor, Laurens, South Carolina; Linda Riddle, art instructor, Heidelberg, West Germany; Carolyn Shapiro, art instructor, Brookline, Massachusetts; Michihisa Kosugi, art instructor, Saga, Japan; Alison Schneider, art instructor, Athens, Georgia; Julianne Hutto, art instructor, Athens, Georgia; Jean Grant, coordinator, arts and humanities, DODDS, Atlantic Region; Norihisa Nakase, artist-art instructor and art education liaison, Tokyo, Japan; Eric Ma Presado, artist-art instructor, Manila, Philippines; Federico Moroni, artist-art instructor, Santarcangelo, Italy; and Chen huei-Tung, artist-art instructor, Tainan, Taiwan. I also want to thank the following persons for giving permission to use published material: Masachi Shimono, Editor, *Nihon Bunkyo Suppan*, Osaka, Japan; and Professor Osamu Muro, executive director, *Art Education Magazine*, Tokyo, Japan.

To the members of the editorial and production staff at Harper & Row, Publishers, my grateful acknowledgment for their contributions, especially those of Louise Waller, executive editor, and Ronni Strell, project editor.

Frank Wachowiak

Pet in a Garden, *oil pastel on 12 × 18 inch violet-colored construction paper. Preliminary drawing was made in school chalk, which was then reinforced with a black permanent-ink, large-sized, felt-nib pen. Color was then applied up to, but not covering, the black lines. Children were encouraged to use color imaginatively and to repeat colors for unity. The animal (pet) was drawn first and the garden environment added afterward. The time employed was approximately three 50-minute class periods. See the child at work on this painting in the circle illustration on the facing page. Grade 2, Athens, Georgia.*

1

INTRODUCTION

The teaching of art in elementary and middle schools is a richly rewarding and highly fulfilling experience when it is undertaken with conviction, purpose, imagination, and love. It is a privilege, a revelation, and a joy to observe and guide children as they create in pencil, pen, crayon, paint, pastel, clay, wood, yarn, cloth, paper, wire, metal, and found materials. Their imagination and inventiveness know no bounds. Their designs and configurations are excitingly unpredictable. Their naiveté delights us. No wonder, then, that their spontaneous and intuitive visual expressions have entranced and even influenced noted artists such as Henri Matisse, Pablo Picasso, Paul Klee, and Karel Appel. To observe children developing in drawing, painting, modeling, and constructive skills and to see them grow year after year in artistic expression is to witness a significant and fascinating aspect of their emerging personalities. Yet these same youngsters, deprived of the guidance and encouragement of a sympathetic, knowledgeable teacher, may lag on the same creative plateau for years. Their cognitive and affective growth, their employment of visual resources, their command of the vocabulary and language of art, and their use of line, shape, form, color, pattern, design, and composition may remain static or even retrogress, leading eventually to discouragement, frustration, and apathy.

Enriched and stimulated by a teacher's varied and challenging motivations, children learn to see more, sense more, recall more, and become more vitally aware of their changing and expanding environment. Consequently, they are more able to express their ideas visually with a growing confidence. The teacher of art in the elementary school can begin very early to talk to the young child about the exciting wonders and uses of design and color. Today's children are more inquisitive, more informed, and often more discerning than their predecessors. Teachers of art in the primary grades may have to rely on simpler teaching strategies, providing more easily absorbed art terminology for their students, but they will soon discover that the children readily understand the ideas of using dark and light values or dull and bright colors for contrast, of creating big and little shapes for variety, of repeating a shape or color to achieve pattern, of drawing things large to fill the composition, and of overlapping shapes to create distance and space. It is the teacher's responsibility to help build the children's creative confidence by guiding them as they progress from one art learning stage to another toward the attainment of color and design awareness, repeating when necessary those art principles that can bolster their visual expressiveness and add quality to their performance.

Teachers have been misled too often by the false assumption that anything a child draws, paints, or constructs is *art*. It may be, indeed, a child's visual statement, but it is not necessarily a work of art. To be art it must, as much as possible, be expressed in the language, structure, and form of art. Children who express their ideas, responses, and reactions to experiences with honesty, sensitivity, and perceptiveness in a framework of compositional principles and design create art. For the majority of youngsters this sense of design and art structure must come from the many planned art-life experi-

---

These paintings by children from the Orient illustrate that the artists were not content with stereotyped or shorthand versions of a place or an event; instead, they combined perception and recall with art skills to document their experiences so vividly. **Top: Hong Kong; Center: Philippines; Bottom: Taiwan.**

ences and happenings provided by the resourceful teacher. This awareness and knowledge can be augmented and reinforced by visits to art centers, galleries, and museums and by exposure to selected art books, reproductions, films, slides, and periodicals. (See Appendixes C and D.)

Very often what some observers call "art" in a child's drawing is not art at all but simply a visual report that relates to factual writing. Art, on the other hand, is more akin to poetry, which, like all fine art, comes to life when it distills the essence of an experience in highly expressive and discriminative choices. A basic statement such as "I live in a house" might be compared, for example, to a stereotyped drawing of a box-shaped house resting on a baseline in the middle of a page. If we ask a child to tell us where she lives in poetic style, she might say:

> My house is sunny white with a red tile roof.
> It peeks through two big willow trees,
> and a blue door in front says "Come in."
> A green bush hedge surrounds my house,
> and a row of red and yellow tulips hugs the porch,
> where I sit on a swing and say "Come in."

In much the same manner poetic form enlivens and enriches children's visual expression as they call upon their store of perception, imagination, and awareness for their drawing. The house then metamorphoses from the impoverished boxlike stereotype to a highly personal dwelling, individual and unique. It may be transformed to a structure of textured brick, rough stone, clapboard, cedar shingles, or cast cement featuring chimneys; cornices; shutters; iron railings; breezeways; porches; carports; weather vanes; TV antennas; trellises; creeping vines; lantern posts; picture, bay, and dormer windows; awnings; pierced screens; picket fences; flower boxes; mailboxes; and cobblestone walks.

Imaginative underwater themes intrigued the Japanese children who painted these fantastic interpretations of oceanic exploration and adventure. When youngsters are capable of producing such rich visual statements, why allow them to settle for stereotyped, minimal results?

sizing the teacher's responsibility to keep youngsters engaged in worthwhile experiences so that they may have something meaningful to express, draw, paint, print, model, or construct. Typically, we find them helping the children recall a past event or happening. Often they provide new visual enrichments through a field trip, model brought to class, dramatization, film, dance, musical recording, story, or poem. But for qualitative teaching in art this initial stimulation is not enough. The teacher must also learn to guide and counsel the children as they continue to express their reactions and responses in a developing artistic framework from preliminary drawing to finished product.

Every time children create a work of art—painting, collage, print, sculpture—they should be encouraged to evaluate their efforts from stage to stage in the studio process, beginning with the initial sketch or drawing. If nothing is said to the growing youngsters about design, structure, composition, line, value, color, contrast, pattern, and other aspects of

Children who are challenged to a keen awareness of their environment and encouraged to be "noticers" draw their homes in a personal, individual way, emphasizing those features that make each house unique. Upper-elementary-grade youngsters devoted at least 2 hours to these felt-nib-pen drawings.

In poetry one discovers that the quality of the verse often depends on the choice use of an expressive word, phrase, or couplet and on effective alliteration, meter, rhythm, and sometimes rhyme. In the most evocative, colorful art creations of children, one discerns a corollary employment of art principles and fundamentals resulting in a unity and rich design that distinguishes them from the ordinary, often impoverished, expressions.

In practically every art guide we find references empha-

the visual-art form, it is presumptuous to assume they will develop in aesthetic awareness and artistic potential.

Children who persevere when they draw, paint, print, and construct create more fulfilling, rewarding, and exciting art when they are guided to see more and become more fully aware of their environment. If their contact with the world, the people in it, and nature is superficial; if they only half sense life's possibilities; and if their identification with and their response to visual stimuli are minimal, they are apt to be content with a hasty, casual, lazy, noncommittal, shorthand statement of an experience or event. Stereotyped interpretations such as stick figures, lollypop trees, box houses, and two curved lines for a bird are seldom based on a truly perceived, richly observed experience.

The teacher of art must be constantly resourceful and prepared to help the child respond more sensitively, to distinguish identifying characteristics effectively, and to note differences in things that provide the contrast good design often demands. This aspect of teacher support and guidance is only one facet of the complex job of art-project motivation, but without it the average child's art production, limited by abbreviated time schedules, tends to be cursory and sterile.

Qualitative art experiences should have a regularly scheduled and undisputed place in the curriculum of elementary and middle schools. When art is not alloted sufficient time in the school week, when it plays a role subordinate to every other subject in the classroom and consists mainly of peripheral activities such as making maps, stereotyped holiday decorations, and endless posters, it is presumptuous to expect it to perform a vital role in the creative growth of the child.

Art experiences in the elementary and middle schools are justified when they contribute to the aesthetic, percep-

Animals are a favorite drawing subject for young children. Here primary-grade youngsters used oil pastel on colored construction paper to depict cats frolicking in a garden. Preliminary drawings were made in the felt-nib pens employing black permanent ink.

tive, discriminative, and expressive development of every child. Art taught effectively and purposefully has a body of knowledge and skills to be mastered. It has unquestionable merit as a unique avenue to mental, social, and individual growth and should be recognized, lauded, and embraced as a living and learning experience in its own right. Indeed, *art is education,* because every art lesson, every art project, if taught purposefully, imaginatively, and qualitatively, augments and enhances the youngsters' skills in basic learnings and in perceiving, reading, analyzing, and building a vocabulary.

Consider, for example, a project on imaginary animals. A discussion of creatures such as the dragon, unicorn, griffon, winged horse, and mermaid might reveal their variety and their appellations in addition to the myths and legends associated with them. The creation of an imaginary monster that is part animal, part bird, part fish, and part insect may require a knowledge of a host of special body characteristics with the words that describe them: bills, horns, tusks, whiskers, beaks, fins, crests, gills, antennas, tails, hooves, paws, claws, wings, antlers, scales, fangs, snouts, wattles, manes, feathers, and plumage. Think what a boon to vocabulary building can be achieved through an exciting art experience in which the effective use of the chalkboard and the written word play an important role!

An unfortunate handicap in the implementation of an imaginative, qualitative school art program is the continued employment of duplicated patterns and misguided correlation practices wherein art is exploited to make other school subjects more palatable. In this process, although other disciplines may benefit, the youngster's interest and delight in art can be jeopardized.

Teachers who are familiar with the examples of

Illustrated on this page are line drawings by children depicting imaginary animals. Note how the complex creatures fill the picture plane. **Top and bottom:** *Upper elementary grades.* **Middle:** *Grade three.*

children's art in *Emphasis Art* often inquire how long it takes the children to complete projects of the quality illustrated. They no doubt sense that the art works enriching this text are not the result of a single art period and most certainly not of the abbreviated 45-minute art lesson so commonly scheduled. In most instances the motivation and the preliminary drawing alone take one period. A completed project may take three to four art periods, depending on the age of the child or the grade level. When art is scheduled only once a week, classroom teachers of art are concerned that they cannot hold the child's interest in a project that extends over such a long period. Among the alternatives suggested to counteract the time factor and still produce a qualitative work of art is limiting the size of the paper used in the art lessons—for example, using 6 × 9-, 9 × 12-, or 12 × 12-inch surfaces instead of 12 × 18 inches for detailed compositions or designs and 12 × 18-inch paper instead of 18 × 24 inches for expressively free tempera paintings. In many countries teachers find 9 × 12-inch sheets an adequate size for making pictures. The results I have seen by children from Taiwan, Italy, and India are especially delightful.

Teachers are frequently advised to "teach the child, not the subject" and are reminded that "it's the process, not the product, that is important." Teachers of elementary- and middle-school art need more than general admonitions today. They need specific help. Instructors faced with today's overloaded classes and limited time schedules do well if they simply keep the youngsters under control. Permissive philosophies will not solve their problems. Teachers can maintain an effective, positive, and productive atmosphere in their classes as long as they can alert the students to an awareness of the objectives of the project and the satisfaction to be achieved in a purposeful art endeavor.

Illustrations on this page are by elementary schoolchildren from Tainan, Taiwan. They depict traditional festivals and pageants. **Top and bottom: Dragon dance. Middle: River festival.**

*Inspiration for children's drawings is as near as the school library, the view from a classroom window, a butterfly collection shared. Encourage looking, comparing, and imagining from the first grade on. **Above:** Another example of the "pet-in-a-garden" theme, which is universally popular with children. This example is by a nine-year-old child attending the author's summer art class in Cortona, Italy. Medium is oil pastel on red-orange construction paper.*

2

FUNDAMENTALS OF ART: A REVIEW

Teachers of art in the elementary and middle schools today are often handicapped by a limited background in art fundamentals. One reason for this inadequacy can be found in the minimal art experiences that these teachers have had during their own elementary, middle, and secondary school years. However, a portion of the blame must rest with those college and university art-education instructors who allow their students to compromise, to settle for less than they are capable of achieving in art, and who permit their students to dissipate valuable time and energy in activities that call for little more than step-by-step manipulation of tools and materials.

A high-quality methods course, whether directed to the classroom teacher or the special-art teacher, should provide students with aesthetically significant, in-depth *art-doing* and *art-appreciating* experiences. Fundamentally valid art concepts based on recurring compositional principles employed in the visual arts, both past and present, should color and permeate the college or university art-education program. The studio content should be characterized by a deliberate and continuing emphasis on sensitive and expressive drawing experiences. Preliminary sketches or drawings, evaluated in an art context, should be the rule in the majority of studio projects. In essence, the students' inquisitive investigation of their environment, their continuing experimentation with new materials and techniques, their multisensual perceptual development, and their oft-hidden, untapped artistic potential should be encouraged and rewarded at every stage.

Which Is Earth No. 57 *Ink and acrylic with collage on paper. Liu Kuo-sung, 1970, 33½ × 23¼ inches.*

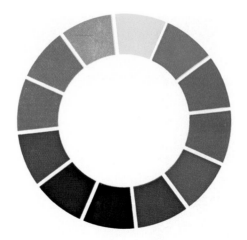

Teachers of art in our elementary and middle schools can grow creatively and professionally if they continue to study and review the increasing number of publications devoted to art and artists. As they read contemporary essays and reviews on painting, sculpture, printmaking, architecture, and crafts, they will discover recurring references to the basic elements or components of art: point, line, shape, color, value, pattern, form, and space. They will also find repeated mention of art's fundamental principles or laws: balance, rhythm-repetition, variety, emphasis, domination-subordination, radiation, and unity. The creation of art, they will discover surprisingly, is a continually challenging adventure, a constantly changing odyssey, providing relatively few shortcuts to successful composition or design, and although they may borrow ideas and inspiration from art's rich past, they must reinterpret their findings in the context of the present. The computerized future may demand new approaches, new strategies, and new techniques; yet there are some significant guideposts, some constant avenues to design and composition that teachers can always turn to in their search for a viable, workable teaching blueprint to use with confidence in counseling and instructing the children in their art classes.

Line in art is a human invention, a unique method of perceiving and documenting the visible world. Therefore, a primary concern of teachers of art should be an understanding and implementation of the linear image. The line drawing is the basic, structural foundation of all graphic composition and pictorial design. Expressive, sensitively drawn lines vary in weight, width, and emphasis. They may be delicate, bold, static, flowing, rhythmic, ponderous, hesitant, violent, or dynamic. They are achieved through freedom and spontaneity or through thoughtful and deliberate action. They may converge, radiate, run parallel, meander, twist, skip, and crisscross to create confusion, flow, rhythm, order, or chaos. An object or image is usually more visually exciting when deline-

ated in a variety of expressive lines. Lines sensitively drawn can create and define shapes, values, and paths of motion. Teachers and students should turn to nature and selected constructed objects for limitless sources of line variety: frost, tree branches, roots, spider webs, water ripples, lightning, veins in leaves, feathers, seashells and coral, grain in wood, cracks in ice and dried mud, bark of trees, interstices in insect wings, bridge spans, road maps, TV antennas, shopping carts, bird cages, and wicker furniture. Children should be provided with many opportunities to study and express their ideas in line and pattern in their myriad forms.

A study of pictorial design, of composition in painting, prints, and posters, eventually centers on the *shape* of things. The shapes created by lines merging, touching, and intersecting one another take many forms. They may be square, rectangular, round, elliptical, oval, triangular, or amorphous. They may emerge as nonobjective, figurative, or freeform. Shapes can also be created by other means such as ink or color washes, charcoal smudges, paint pourings, object printing, and paper cutouts. The achievement of varied, expressive shapes in a developing composition provides youngsters with one of art's most stimulating challenges and rewards.

Nature is, by far, the richest source of inspiration for the study of variety in shapes. Natural forms and configurations such as those found in tree branches, leaves, seashells, eggs, nuts, petals, berries, and feathers are usually much more varied and subtle than those based on measured or mathematical formulas. Perhaps that is why artists turn to aging, dilapidated buildings for their drawing inspiration instead of the coldly geometric shapes of most contemporary architecture. There is a subtly illusive quality in old, disintegrating forms that endows them with a special magic in the artist's eyes.

There is far too much reliance on geometric formula and perspective rules in the rendition of table tops, cabinets, doors, windows, fences, façades, roofs, and sidewalks. Teachers should encourage students to use artistic license to give vitality to static imagery through meaningful distortion, omission, exaggeration, and free-form interpretation.

The shapes of objects or figures in a composition such as trees, houses, people, animals, furniture, and vehicles are generally called "positive shapes." The empty area around them is referred to as "negative space," even though this space may include ground, water, and sky. In most instances, when the positive shapes are varied in size and shape, the negative spaces or shapes are consequently just as varied and as interesting, thereby enhancing the composition.

Value, especially the contrast produced by juxtaposing a variety of values, plays a very important role in pictorial design. *Value*, simply stated, refers to the light and dark elements in a composition. Every shade (dark value) and tint (light value) of every color or hue has a place on the value scale. Teachers and students must learn to perceive a color in terms of its value to create effective and exciting color con-

---

Guide the children to turn often to nature and her myriad shapes, forms, patterns, textures, and colors for continuous inspiration in their art endeavors. Nowhere else are the elements of variety within unity so constantly and beautifully exemplified. Build a resource file of photographs and color slides of nature as motivational aids.

trasts. Value analyses of master paintings and prints can help students understand and appreciate the principles employed in achieving successful light and dark orchestration. Compositions with sharply contrasting values are generally more dramatic and dynamic in their visual impact. Values when repeated create movement in a painting, leading the viewer from one part of the composition to another.

Can you imagine a world without color? How dull it would be. *Color* has three properties or components: *hue*, the name of the color, *value*, the lightness or darkness of the color, and *intensity* (saturation), the brightness or dullness of the color. Unfortunately, its most amazing property is often ignored. Color has *magic!*

Color in painting is a continuing challenge to art students, teachers of art, and, often, artists. It is not uncommon to observe students performing with confidence and success when they draw or compose in line or in black and white values only; yet they find themselves completely frustrated when they tackle color. All color theories, wheels, and schemes offered to date cannot help them solve their dilemma. Yesterday's academic formulas no longer prevail. What were once identified as receding colors now may glow as advancing hues. Colors that simply did not harmonize according to the traditionalists now are juxtaposed audaciously. Artists Henri Matisse, Pablo Picasso, and Hans Hofmann are acclaimed pioneers in liberating painting from naturalistic color restrictions.

To both elementary- and middle-school teachers of art these conclusions may suggest chaos and confusion in the realm of color orientation and expression. Fortunately there are some guidelines that can lead a youngster to an understanding of color, to both its limitations and its potential. *Limitation* definitely plays an important role in the mastery of

---

These colorful depictions of fish in the sea or fish in an aquarium are oil pastels on colored construction paper created by upper elementary grade youngsters. No two are exactly alike although the children had the same motivational material—color photos of fish, seashells, and seaweed.

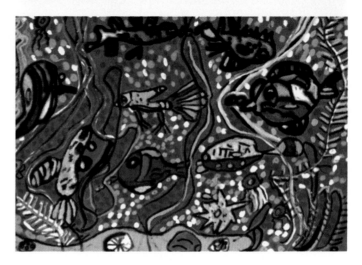

The Shapes of Time: Iowa City, *mixed-media collage, Ted Ramsay, 1964, 18 × 24 inches, collection of the author. Dilapidated, weathered buildings often reveal a unique, characteristic visual appearance to which artists respond. Here Ted Ramsay, professor of art, University of Michigan, Ann Arbor, captured the complex, varied* *design in a tenement cul-de-sac. In his preliminary sketch for the completed collage shown on the facing page, notice how he deployed a variety of line and pattern, at the same time balancing his light and dark areas for contrast. Observe, too, the subtle changes that have taken place in the transition from drawing to collage.*

color orchestration. Sometimes students may be advised to limit their palettes to black, white, and one color in all of its various tints and shades. Another suggestion offered is to employ analogous or related colors, those adjacent to one another on the color wheel, for example, blue, blue-green, green, and yellow-green. To avoid pitfalls of clashing color or strident chromatic relationships, students should be counseled to minimize the intensity of colors in a composition. This process, sometimes referred to as "neutralization" or "dulling" of a color, involves the mixing or combining of a color with its complementary hue, which can be found opposite to it on the color wheel. Examples of complementary colors are red and green or blue and orange. Many colors now available in crayon, oil pastel, and tempera are already neutralized, for example, sienna, brown, umber, ochre, and chrome green.

Although many outdated theories have been questioned and even discarded, some successful strategies in color usage persist. A fraction of bright, intense color will hold its own against a more generous employment of neutralized colors. Colors can be repeated to create movement and unity in a composition, but it is recommended that the size and shape of the repeated color be varied for effectiveness. Dark and cool colors generally recede; bright warm colors usually advance. Complementary colors such as red and green in their fullest intensities create vibrant contrasts when juxtaposed. Black, grey, and white can be combined with any color scheme without creating any harmonic conflicts. Often, as in the case of black outlining, the dark linear accent gives a contrasting sharpness and sparkle to the composition. Both teacher and student should be aware that the character, identity, and impact of a color depend a great deal on the colors adjacent to or surrounding it; for example, a green shape on a turquoise

The young child in the illustration above left, absorbed in her work, is using the felt-nib watercolor markers now available in small or large sizes and in a variety of colors. Be sure these markers are capped after each art session to prevent them from drying out. One

color can be used over another to create new hues and neutralizations. Smaller-sized background paper 9 × 12 inches and 12 × 12 inches is recommended when children use the small, fine-nib markers.

background may be relatively unnoticed, but intense orange against an intense blue will vibrate and arrest the eye.

The painters of the postimpressionist era including Wassily Kandinsky, Franz Marc, Marc Chagall, and Odilon Redon and contemporary colorists such as Josef Albers, Karel Appel, Mark Rothko, Paul Jenkins, Helen Frankenthaler, and George Vasarely have provided the art world with eye-opening creations in color, resulting in surprises such as blue horses and multihued people. Teachers and students should turn, too, for inspiration in color usage to the luminous stained-glass windows of Gothic cathedrals, the jewel-like miniatures of India and Persia, the shimmering mosaics of Byzantium, and the fascinating ukiyo-e color woodcuts of Japan.

Space is an element in pictorial composition and in abstract design that can often confuse the student. In two-dimensional art expression *space* is sometimes designated as the negative area between positive objects. This kind of space is often referred to as "decorative" or "surface" space. Another category of space to be considered is space-in-depth, often described as "plastic space." Common pictorial devices for achieving the illusion of space-in-depth on a two-dimensional plane, as in a painting, are diminishing sizes of objects

as they recede in distance; sharp, clear details in the foreground and blurred, indistinct elements in the background; overlapping of shapes or forms; objects farther away from the observer drawn higher on the picture plane; bright, intense colors in the foreground, neutral or dulled colors in the background; and the employment of traditional perspective-creating techniques such as converging lines and horizon levels.

As children move into middle school they discover other means of creating space through shading and foreshortening. Some of this expertise in space handling comes intuitively, but most children must be guided in mastering the intricacies of perspective and space-in-depth. Rules of perspective should not be imposed on children unless they indicate a need for them. One cannot guarantee the success of a composition by simply applying the canons of perspective.

An important avenue to effective picture making is the sensitive exploitation of *balance* or *symmetry*. Both teachers and students should be familiar with the two types of compositional balance: symmetrical or formal balance and asymmetrical or informal balance. Although formal balance was employed in many master paintings of the past, the contemporary artist has, for the most part, avoided the rigid, sometimes static, demands of formal juxtaposition. Strictly sym-

metrical compositions, where objects or figures on the right balance similarly weighted components on the left, usually lack the open-ended orchestration and variety that give excitement to a work of art.

A common misconception about composition in art is that emphasis can be achieved by drawing something very large and placing it in the center of the picture. Size and placement in the composition by themselves do not ensure domination. The object to be noticed must exhibit other attributes as well; contrasting value, color, and detail will usually attract the viewer's attention.

Despite the reminder that there are no hard and fast rules in composing, teachers and students usually discover that a pictorial creation is much more interesting and attractive when the principal subject or figure is not placed exactly in the center of the composition. As teachers and students study the works of painters, printmakers, and collagists, they become aware of the subtle and successful employment of asymmetry or informal balance in their compositions.

Variety in composition and design has always played a significant role. A study of the recurrence of variety or diver-

Upper-grade youngsters employ felt-nib watercolor markers to portray their conceptions of a "dream car," "dream boat," or "dream bike." Class discussion before the drawing began focused on the ideal vehicle of the future that would incorporate all gadgets and conveniences desired as well as an imaginative, colorful design.

sity in great works of art, past and present, will prove of inestimable value to both teachers and students. Analyses of masterpieces of drawing, painting, and printmaking reveal the artists' reliance on, and constant use of, a variety of shapes and forms in their compositions. Seldom does one discover two shapes that are alike. Look at a score of multi-figure paintings by recognized artists throughout the centuries and you will discover variety in composition fully exploited: No two heads are on the same level, no two figures are in the same position, and no two figures stand on the same levels in the foreground.

Although humans are nature's children, unlike the embodiments and creations of the natural world, they must learn to employ variety in their graphic imagery. Youngsters might do well to look once more at the wings of a butterfly, the stripes on a zebra, the spots on a leopard, the feathers on a bird, the scales on a fish, the web of a spider, the cracks in an ice flow, or the frost on a windowpane.

Variety as a vital element in pictorial design can be exploited in many ways and in many instance. It can be employed in every facet of a composition—line, shape, value, color, pattern, texture—to give excitement and interest to a work of art, but it must be counterbalanced by a repetition of those art elements if the desired unity is to be achieved. Emphasis, too, must be considered. Generally, the most successful compositions employ both major and minor areas of emphasis. The principle of variety can aid in the placement of objects, figures, or shapes in a composition. They may vary in size and shape, begin on different planes, terminate at different heights, touch the boundaries of the picture plane at different points creating multiple avenues into the composition, and strategically overlap one another to create even more varied shapes and negative spaces.

Illustrations on this page are by upper-grade elementary school-children. They took turns modeling in the middle of the room and added backgrounds to complement the figures. Oil pastel on colored construction paper. **Facing page:** *Scene by a young child from Greece depicting the countryside and seaport village.*

In this age of jets, rockets, computers, video games, and space exploration, it is difficult for youngsters not to be caught up in the feverish rush of events. That may be the reason why so many students race through their assignments and why the facile, the instant, and the minimal appeals to them. So much of what we see in art today reveals a lack of sustained and persevering effort. We are misled if we equate speed of execution with freedom of expression. A genuinely spontaneous and sparkling quality in a work of art is not achieved easily. It is usually the result of many years of mastering a technique, developing a keen perceptiveness, and integrating mind, heart, eye, and hand.

The basic art principles or laws reviewed in this chapter are not new or improved formulas, but implemented wisely and consistently they can provide elementary- and middle-school art teachers and their students with a practical and dynamic color and design foundation on which to build a qualitative art program. There will always be exceptions to every rule, but in most instances and in most classrooms or art studios, a fundamentals approach as described here, based on a knowledge of composition and design principles as exemplified in the world's art masterpieces, enhanced by a growing appreciation of design in nature, will prove to be the most successful and rewarding.

3

CHILDREN AND THEIR ENVIRONMENT

Children everywhere have much in common. They react in similar ways to their environment. They laugh and cry, playact, sing, and dance. They delight in seeing and manipulating bright, colorful objects, games, machines, and vehicles. They respond to sympathetic, supportive voices and to loving, nurturing hands.

Children the world over draw in very much the same manner at similar developmental stages. They begin with random, haphazard scribbles, gradually acquiring more control; then move to simple, geometric, schematic symbols, confidently and proudly giving names and titles to their drawings; and finally, progress to characteristic and semirealistic interpretations. Their natural graphic responses are generally instinctive and intuitive; yet these basic representations do not necessarily mean that they are making artistic choices. What they express so spontaneously, so ingenuously, is usually done with unconscious naiveté.

No two children are alike. Even twins, who may confuse their teachers with surface similarities, have different personalities, different feelings and reactions, and different mental and creative abilities. These uniquely individual characteristics of children and young adolescents present teachers with some of their most critical guidance challenges. Teachers of art soon learn that they cannot expect the same responses, skills, or art interpretations from any two children, even those of identical ages and backgrounds.

Children often live in a special world halfway between reality and make-believe. Their art is the happy result of seeing, knowing, and imagining. Teachers can help youngsters grow in perceiving and analyzing skills by providing a variety of visually stimulating resources and experiences. The teacher's sympathetic support is a crucial factor in the success children achieve in art. Be responsive. Be appreciative. Applaud. Above: Children as noticers. Illustration courtesy of the University of Georgia Museum of Art, Athens, Georgia. Facing page: oil pastel; upper elementary grade.

Children in the same class may have diverse interests and needs. They should be provided with opportunities to participate in a variety of art experiences and to use a number of art materials to achieve a rewarding measure of satisfaction and success in a particular technique. The youngster who excels in clay manipulation may respond less enthusiastically and perform less ably during drawing and painting sessions. The child who confidently tackles brush and paint may sometimes need more supportive guidance when faced with three-dimensional construction problems.

The fact that children are inquisitive and highly impressionable has been documented in countless reports. They are susceptible to sight, sound, and smell influences every waking moment of their lives but are not always discriminative in the choices they make. Often the trite and tasteless wares in their environment make as strong an impact on them as the qualitative, well-designed products. It is a major responsibility of the teacher to guide children in their quest for the best, toward more aesthetic choices, and to provide them with daily experiences to create and appreciate art.

Children in all grades, one through eight, need the understanding, approbation, and love that a sympathetic teacher provides, but they also thrive on the friendship, approval, spirited competition, and intellectual rivalry of their classmates. To grow, mature, and build their self-worth, children must possess a certain measure of security and confidence, an inquiring nature, a heightened perceptual awareness, and a stimulating, supportive environment at home and at school.

Since no two children are alike, it is almost impossible to categorize them by grade or age. A teacher sees a wide range of personal and behavioral characteristics among students in any given grade. Youngsters in the same class may

For many youngsters, there is no greater satisfaction than building structures out of clay, as this illustration of a middle school student, intent on his ceramic creation, attests. Notice how a simple, basic pinch-pot form has been enriched by the addition of a foot, neck, handles, and embellishing relief pattern.

come from different backgrounds and economic levels and may have had totally different day-to-day experiences; their problems and needs are not the same. Yet to understand them and help them grow through art, the teacher must be aware of those characteristics that have been identified with certain age groups by researchers in educational psychology, sociology, and child study. For a more detailed, sequential description of children's growth and behavior patterns, refer to Appendixes A and B. But a word of caution is indicated here. The traits and characteristics described there are clues to understanding children in general and may not necessarily apply to a particular or individual child. For a description of the characteristics of mentally retarded and physically handicapped children and ways of helping them through art, refer to Chapter 9, "Art for Children with Special Needs."

It is important that teachers have a basic understanding of the natural graphic abilities of the children in their classes to appreciate their developmental possibilities and limitations. The elementary- and middle-school art program that emphasizes quality, however, demands more of the students than what they do naturally. It is true that some children and young adolescents perceive, draw, and compose sensitively with special skills in using line, color, pattern, and space, but the majority of youngsters in our schools today must be guided, stimulated, and motivated toward richer use of design and compositional fundamentals, toward a fuller awareness of their environment in its varied aspects.

What do youngsters really see? To what do they respond? If teachers can bring children to notice something they have never noticed before, to become aware, to see with the inner eye, they will have started them on an endless, exciting, rewarding journey of a thousand discoveries. The teacher can help children expand their horizons and their

Children around the world respond to similar environmental motivations for the themes and subject matter of their art. Their creative endeavors are influenced by their culture, their country's history, their family ties, education, religion, geographic location, climate, economics, and political structure.

visual repertoire by calling their attention to the countless wonders in the world around them, for example:

The intricate pattern of a spider's web
The varied shapes created by cracks in mudflats, ice, and cement walks
The subtle, pale colors of shadows on fallen snow
The variety of grain pattern in wood
The space breakup and design of a jungle gym
The flaming colors of autumn woods and leaves
The complex design of a honeycomb
The varieties of green in summer foliage
The varied textures and patterns of tree bark
The shadows of tree branches on building walls
The graceful movements of a cat
The magnificent lines and patterns of bridges
The intriguing abstract design of torn billboard ads
The filigree pattern in leaf veins and insect wings
The pattern of frost on a windowpane
The ever-changing formations of clouds
The dew on early morning flowers and leaves
The reflections in water
The moody, misty colors of a foggy or rainy day
The flashing colors of stoplights, neon signs, and beacons
The rich luminosity of stained-glass windows
The subtle patina of peeling, deteriorating paint on aging doors and old metal
The patterns of fields, farms, forest, lakes, and rivers seen from the air
The oil-slick patterns on harbor waters
The fiery smoke of foundries
The tracks of animals in the snow
The linear grace of a jet stream
The pattern of TV antennas against a metropolitan sky
The strident colors and flashing light patterns of a rock show

Children and young adolescents are influenced constantly by environmental stimuli that teachers cannot always control. Television, the press, radio, the movies, video

The world of the future as illustrated in pen and ink by upper-elementary grade youngsters from Saga, Japan.

games, the theater, musical recordings, store-window displays, makeup, magazine illustrations, album covers, posters, cars, clothes, and package design clamor for their attention, shape their developing taste, and often influence and determine their cultural values. What a qualitative art program can do, in some measure, is to help the children become more selective, more discriminative, and more aesthetically sensitive in the many choices they must make as they seek to achieve a personal life-style.

The characteristics and needs of young adolescents require the attention and understanding of the teachers who instruct them in art. Teachers must remember that middle-school youngsters move into a changed academic world in which for the first time they may have a different teacher for each subject they take. If they come from the typical elementary-school situation where the classroom teacher taught art, it will be their first contact with a specialist art teacher. It is important that this initial contact be sympathetic yet stimulating. They should discover in their art teacher the same confidence, the same convictions regarding the worth of the subject, and the same enthusiasm that they see in the best science, math, or language teachers.

The middle-school youngster is experiencing a renaissance of awareness and self-consciousness, of sensitivity to differences in others, of identification with the peer group, of rediscovery and appreciation of the universe, of heightened emotional responses, and of intellectual inquisitiveness that in some ways may never be matched again. In many ways they are less inhibited than the upper-elementary-grade child, but they are still highly critical of their own performance. They are more willing to tackle new processes and new materials. They are technically more proficient; their ability to capitalize on suggestions is heightened, and they can enter into critical discussions on art design and structure with a keener sensitivity and with sharper argumentative skills. They are highly impressionable, their cultural horizons are expanding, and they may carry the preferences and prejudices they develop regarding art in these middle-school years for the rest of their lives.

It is in the middle school that the teachers really begin to see the personalities and idiosyncracies of their students reflected in their behavior and their art. There they find the extrovert, the loner, the risk taker, the methodical planner, the procrastinator, the idol seeker, the plodder, the perfectionist, the maverick, the dreamer, the braggadocio, the idealist, and the quiz whiz.

Teachers should remember that young adolescents are vulnerable emotionally. Direct criticism of their work in front of their classmates can be humiliating for them, and teachers should avoid sarcasm and belittling remarks at all costs. Teachers must not embarrass them, either, by praising their work too lavishly in front of their peers but should complement them, by all means, in private.

Middle-school youngsters are sometimes apathetic or cool in their response to art, especially if their art experiences in elementary school were not satisfying or rewarding. But once they are caught up in the exciting possibilities and results of a creative, productive, and qualitative art program, they become enthusiastic converts to the adventures and challenges of in-depth studio art.

These crayon and oil pastel resists are the creations of upper elementary grade art classes in Oshkosh, Wisconsin. The teacher provided stimulating motivations for the project including color photos, color slides, and color film.

4

THE TEACHER'S ROLE

Wherever art programs of quality and promise exist, whether in elementary or middle schools, in crowded cities or quiet farm communities, or in the United States or abroad, one always discovers in the wings an enthusiastic, resourceful, knowledgeable, imaginative, and gifted teacher. The teacher of the successful, productive art class is invariably a planner, an organizer, an expediter, a counselor, a dreamer, a goal setter, and, above all, a lover of life, children, and art.

Without a well-prepared, creative, and dedicated teacher at the helm, an art program can flounder in a sea of hasty, last-minute decisions, in trite and stereotyped activities, or in chaotic, pseudotherapeutic play sessions. The school that boasts a modern physical plant, a generous budget, and an administration sympathetic to art is fortunate,

but if it does not attract teachers who are prepared to teach art confidently, enthusiastically, developmentally, and qualitatively, it has little chance of establishing and implementing an art program of excellence and stature.

The reference to dedication is deliberate. Dedication is, and always will be, a vital teaching strength in a democratic society. It transcends teaching expertise. Nothing is written in the teaching contract about dedication, nor is there anything explicit in that agreement about the requisites of love, patience, and sympathetic support that go hand in hand with good teaching. But unselfish dedication and enthusiastic involvement are freewill gifts of a devoted teacher and cannot be measured except in terms of the inner fulfillment and satisfaction they bring.

Facing page: The ever-renewing cycle of life is all around us in exquisite and radiating forms. Teachers of art should turn to design in nature for constant motivational inspiration and be alert to guide their students to notice the subtle variations in the leaves and *petals of a flower, the feathers of birds, the interstices of a spider's web, the scales of a fish.* **Above in circle:** *A child absorbed in the study of a seashell, one of nature's infinite designs. Photo courtesy of Eastern Airlines.*

The best teachers of art, whether classroom teachers or special art instructors, believe wholeheartedly in the unique, spirit-enhancing, and rejuvenating powers of the art experience. They seek constantly to master the critically important motivations, the technical intricacies, and the evaluative strategies of every art project they teach. They take time to organize materials, tools, space, and time schedules to produce exemplary working conditions in the classroom or art room. They enrich the lives of their students through countless planned experiences in some learning or appreciating phase of the arts and crafts. They are constantly searching for inspirational stimuli that can renew the children's interest in a project when the initial excitement wanes. In their enthusiasm, which they display openly and generously, they encourage the youngsters to open their eyes to the design, color, form, rhythm, texture, and pattern in the world around them, in both natural and constructed wonders. They identify with their students. They are elated when a youngster makes a discovery or masters a skill; conversely, they are genuinely concerned when students encounter difficulties that defy resolution.

Experienced teachers plan the art-discussion period, the motivating question-and-answer session, and the preliminary show-and-tell segment with special care. They do not leave these vitally important parts of the lesson or project to chance or last-minute inspiration. In many instances they prepare a written outline of their strategy. Because the time allotted to art is often limited, they learn to phrase their questions to elicit the richest response in the shortest time. Their queries are primarily the leading kind, seldom calling for one specific right answer. They avoid dead-end questions, posing, instead, those that open up new avenues of exploration, invention, and discovery.

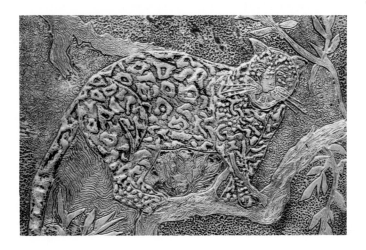

The aluminum-foil reliefs illustrated here are by university students majoring in art education. The technique is described fully in the section "Aluminum-Foil Relief." They exhibit the very rich and sophisticated results that can be achieved with easily obtainable materials and tools.

College and university students preparing to teach elementary- or middle-school art should explore the varied art materials and techniques they may be required to teach in order to build the confidence they need to guide the children's art endeavors. The illustrations above are by students from the author's university classes. **Left to right, beginning at the top:** oil pastel resist, plaster relief, tempera batik, oil pastel, yarn collage, crayon engraving, crayon resist, box construction, and vegetable print.

To keep the art program a vital, growing part of the school curriculum, today's top-notch teachers of art acquire and employ as many audiovisual aids as possible: original works of art, reproductions, films, photographs, color slides, filmstrips, tapes and loops, magazine articles, recordings, colorfully illustrated art books, and examples of student work.

Their confidence and effectiveness in art class is heightened immeasurably if they have had opportunities to explore and create successfully with the same art materials and tools available to their students. Experienced teachers often experiment with new art materials and tools before sharing them with their students. They do not assign a new, untried technique to their classes before exploring its possibilities and limitations.

Perceptive teachers of art learn to see differences as well as similarities in the graphic expressions of their students. They discover that no two interpretations of a shared experience by children in the same grade will look alike. In one instance they may find a bold, spontaneous rendering; in another case there may be a sensitive and deliberate delineation. One child may be fascinated with details and pattern. Another may revel in the imaginative and sparkling use of a rainbow of colors.

A positive, cheerful, and outgoing personality is a major asset for teachers of art. They must learn, too, in sometimes difficult and trying situations to be patient, calm, and resolute. Children want to believe in their teachers. They need the security of a teacher's abiding confidence in the worth of the subject being taught. Youngsters come to rely on their teachers for help with important choices, for possible resolutions to perplexing problems. They become skeptical of those teachers who confuse them with vague generalizations, who place all of the responsibility, all of the decision making, in their hands.

Teachers of art should learn to listen to the children's descriptions of their experiences, both real and imaginary, with sympathetic interest. They should avoid a desultory, keep-your-distance approach. Instead, their commitment, concern, and excitement for the project in process must be evident in their action, words, and faces. Veteran teachers learn to cultivate a ready sense of humor. It can help alleviate many a tension-fraught situation. Teachers who really care about children do not talk down to them; neither do they underestimate their potential to excel.

One result of the current confusion concerning goals and objectives in art education today is the false front some teachers of art erect to please their professional peers. In too many instances we find art teachers apologizing for making suggestions to children, for initiating projects, and for emphasizing art fundamentals. Let the truth be known! Where promising, sequential, imaginative, and qualitative elementary and middle school art programs exist, the classroom teacher of art or the special art teacher is on the job organizing, coaching, motivating, questioning, demonstrating, evaluating, approving, advising, and publicizing—in other words, *teaching*.

The initial warming-up strategies in teaching an art project are especially crucial for its ultimate success. Lessons introduced with adequate preparation, with preliminary experimentation in the particular material or technique involved, and with stimulating, motivational resources on hand add immeasurably to the quality of the art program. Experienced teachers of art are often able to envisage a project's potential in its entirety with all of its accompanying problems. This does not imply that they are not alert to innovative or unscheduled developments that may occur during the

---

This chapter is illustrated with the creative efforts of university students preparing to be art teachers and with the work of artist-teachers. It is vitally important that these students are provided with studio experiences in their university courses that emphasize the art techniques, materials, and tools they will need to be familiar with in their future teaching careers.

course of the lesson. It does mean, however, that they are continually aware of the significant long-range objectives or goals of the project.

Another crucial element in the ultimate success of every art project is the housekeeping involved. The teacher must organize classroom or art-room facilities so that there will be adequate working space, a sufficient supply of art materials and tools, varied storage facilities for both projects in process and those retained for exhibition purposes, a diversity of display spaces, and effective cleanup facilities. (See Appendixes E and F.)

Budgeting the time allotted to art is a vital consideration. The children should never feel that they are being rushed through any phase of a lesson or project. Wise teachers carefully plan the amount of time needed for the *three important stages of every art project—motivation, creation, and evaluation*. Indeed, the most qualitative teaching strategies and practices take more time, preparation, and concentration on the part of everyone involved. Teachers discover, too, that in many instances their young charges do not appreciate or enjoy a new art process or medium until they become deeply involved in it; once the youngsters become aware of the project's rich potential, their interest grows.

The subject or theme of every art project and its adaptability to the selected technique must be considered carefully by the teacher. It can prove frustrating for a student to make a preliminary sketch in pencil line and eventually lose the detailed interpretation in the bold brushwork of tempera application.

Since the teacher is the prime catalyst and bridge builder in the art class, it is the teacher's responsibility to help establish a positive learning climate in which purposeful inquiry, creativity, and individuality thrive. When teachers

The ever-changing art world continuously opens new creative avenues to explore. **Top:** *An interning elementary-school teacher took a clue from the San Blas Indian molas and, substituting colored felt, created her own adaptation.* **Center:** *Stichery with yarn and beads.* **Bottom:** *Yarn and felt applique.*

of art are truly concerned about the expressive growth of the children in their classes, they plan and implement activities that the youngsters may not always approve. They may ask their students to set higher standards of performance for themselves or demand a little more studio effort than the children have been accustomed to making. They are deeply aware that the best art is, in most instances, the result of purposeful, consistent, difficult, persevering, and time-consuming effort and not the product of an accidental, undemanding, trivial, or thoughtless activity.

Teachers of art will find their instructional effectiveness enhanced if they use the chalkboard to emphasize their motivational presentation and to outline the specific objectives or criteria for the project undertaken. In both instances the written word augments the spoken exposition and provides a ready, visual reference for the ongoing lesson. The chalkboard is, without a doubt, one of the best teaching tools available to an instructor. Its use provides a ready format for the identification and clarification of the various possibilities of an assigned project. For example, evaluative criteria in the form of questions offer a ready checklist of objectives, and when they are posted on a chalkboard or bulletin board, they provide the students with opportunities to make their own evaluations of work in progress, thereby minimizing their dependence on their instructor and discouraging the "Am-I-finished?" refrain.

Children in the primary grades who may have difficulty reading the chalkboard instructions will benefit more by the teacher's repetitions of the objectives. Wise teachers allow the children to work independently until they see that the youngsters are in need of more motivational fuel and then provide them with additional incentives to help them attain higher levels of artistic growth and achievement.

Fabric and crafted material from bazaars around the world combined with an assortment of old hats provided a colorful and challenging still-life arrangement for university art education classes. Two interpretations are illustrated, one cool and quiet, the other warm and vibrant.

A teacher's success in the art class is often based on the empathic rapport that can develop between instructor and students. The desired relationship may take a while to evolve, but once teachers build and establish a climate of cooperation and mutual understanding, their ability to guide and challenge their charges becomes the cutting edge of their teaching strength.

One can immediately sense the electric involvement, the purposefulness of endeavor, and the genuine rapport that exists between students and teacher when one visits a classroom or art room where art is considered important and where qualitative art learning is taking place.

The special quality that distinguishes high-caliber teachers of art from average instructors is their ability to respond intelligently, sympathetically, and purposefully to the children's creative efforts; to communicate with the youngsters knowledgeably and honestly regarding their progress in art; and to evaluate their studio production seriously and objectively, giving it importance and significance in the students' eyes by the concerned, critical attention paid to it.

*Illustrated on this page are two watercolors by artist-teachers. **Top:** Spring Bouquet, 10 × 16 inches, Cappy Page, Athens, Georgia. **Bottom:** Landscape 10 × 14 inches, Louis Rizzolo, professor of art, Western Michigan University, Kalamazoo.*

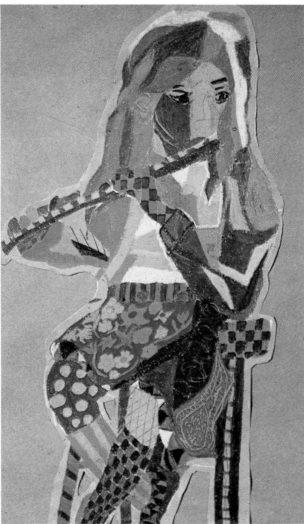

The colorful figures illustrated above were drawn from class models on large 24 × 36 inch colored construction paper, painted with oil pastels, and then cut out and mounted on a complementary colored sheet of construction paper. Two students cooperated on the coloring of each figure. The completed figures were displayed on the walls of the art room (see page 100). Grade 8, Campus School, University of Wisconsin, Oshkosh.

6

AVENUES TO MOTIVATION

Teachers everywhere agree that most children need some form of stimulating motivation, visual or verbal, to achieve qualitative results in their studio-art endeavors. In almost every school art textbook or guide published, repeated reference is made to the fact that youngsters must have something to say in order to express or delineate it in visual form.

Inspiration for children's art expression comes from varied sources. It may spring from their experiences at school and at home and in churches, temples, cathedrals, shrines, and synagogues; from their playground activities; from visits to aquariums, museums, art galleries, fairs, zoos, marinelands, botanical gardens, national parks, arboretums, historic sites, shopping malls, circuses, carnivals, parades, beauty contests, stock-car races, dog and cat shows, sports, and games; and from movies, television, funland rides, video arcades, theaters, festivals, pageants, books, comics, magazines, and musical recordings. The responsibility, however,

for reactivating these motivational experiences and giving them a significance and an immediacy to stimulate youngsters into art expression is primarily the teacher's.

Teachers must always be prepared to help enrich the children's store of knowledge, to tap their recall powers. Specifically, they might ask the thought-provoking, leading questions *Who? What? Where? When? Why? How?* concerning an event or experience. This avenue of questioning should be designed to encourage the children's remembering, seeing, and feeling, not just their verbal acuity. The important consideration here is the development of heightened awareness, of visual literacy and discrimination. The teacher must be ready to help the child clarify and graphically emphasize the significant aspects of an experience. One of the teacher's greatest challenges is to turn youngsters into *noticers*, avid noticers of color, structure, and design in their environment. Children who note the shapes of panes in win-

---

Facing page: Inspiration for children's art is often as near as the school yard. Teachers should take advantage of the immediate environment—the school playground, the cafeteria kitchen, the band room with musical instruments—as a visual motivational resource. Here the children are employing 18 × 24-inch sections of hard-

board as sketching pads for drawing. Notice in the circle illustration above that the child shown drawing in the foreground on the facing page has enhanced her composition, adding an encompassing sun whose rays reach almost every flower in the garden.

dows, the unique cornice on a door, the intricate latch on a cabinet, the subtle patina on aged sculpture, the moving reflections in water, the varied cracks in dry mud banks or ice flows, the shadow of a tree against a wall or on the snow, and the veins in a leaf or dragonfly's wing are youngsters who bring deeper insights and visual eloquence to their art expression and live a richer, discovery-charged existence. If teachers can bring their students to look intently at everyday images, to see the *unusual* in the *usual*, the youngsters will become inquisitive explorers for the rest of their lives.

In many instances the teacher will find it necessary to provide the children with supplemental motivating material through planned field trips and varied vicarious experiences in the classroom itself. That is why they should have on hand, or at close call, a rich fund of audiovisual resources such as color slides, filmstrips, films, color reproductions of paintings by established artists, artifacts, and examples of the students' own efforts in various techniques.

The most vital and successful art-project motivations are usually the result of vivid and meaningful personal experiences. Nothing replaces the actually perceived object, the direct contact, or the immediate observation for eliciting a detailed, richly expressive response. Sketching trips to a farm, factory, fire station, dairy, greenhouse, shipyard, bridge, or construction site are recommended. Live animals, birds, or pets brought to school will evoke stimulating and enthusiastic responses from the youngsters that may trigger individually colorful art expressions.

In the classroom or art room itself, the teacher can display nature's varied forms of fruits and vegetables, seashells, coral, driftwood, fossils, bark, rocks and pebbles, live and dried plants and flowers, gourds, collections of insects and butterflies, stones and minerals, mounted birds and animals, and fish in aquariums. Still-life objects such as bottles, lan-

Countless cultures around the world have created a variety of crafts and artifacts that can be introduced in class to whet the students' interest in art. **Top:** *Noh theatre mask from Japan.* **Center:** *Molas (reverse applique) San Blas Indians.* **Bottom:** *American Indian Kachina dolls and weaving.*

terns, clocks, musical instruments, lamps, and a variety of antique Americana can become the inspiration for a host of drawing and painting projects especially for upper elementary-school grades and the middle school.

At every opportunity teachers should tactfully discourage the student's dependence on, or use of, visual stereotypes. They should minimize the "draw-anything-you-want" assignments by emphasizing more drawing experiences based on things that can be immediately observed, touched, or studied.

Teachers should help children respond to nature's wonders in a number of ways by calling attention to both the biological phenomena and the compositional or design structure. This dual interpretation and description of nature in its myriad aspects should be encouraged in every art experience in which natural forms provide the source for the youngsters' expression.

The materials, tools, and techniques of the various art projects can become motivating devices, too, and in many instances may be the special catalyst that fires the students' efforts. In the primary grades the introduction of new, vibrant colors in oil pastel, tempera paint, watercolor felt-nib markers, crayon, and construction paper elicits enthusiastic response. Tissue paper in a host of colors delights upper-elementary-grade children who can handle it confidently in collage projects as they discover new colors through overlapping.

In the upper elementary grades and middle school, too, the teacher can whet the appetites of the youngsters by introducing them to melted crayon for encaustic painting, discarded tiles for mosaics, waxes and dyes for batiks, plaster for carving sculpture and bas reliefs, glazes for ceramics, and wire, plastic, wood, and boxes for construction projects.

In recent years critics of current art-education practices have called attention to the proliferation of media and techniques in the school art programs, citing their deleterious effects. Although some of this criticism is justifiable, it is not the new materials and techniques that are suspect but the manner in which some instructors exploit them. Teachers can testify that a student equipped with the newest, most expensive art materials and tools may produce a nonartistic monstrosity, whereas another youngster using only discarded remnants from an attic or junk heap may create an art object of singular beauty.

The introductory phase of an art lesson or project, if well planned, should kindle the spark that ignites the curiosity and interest of the students. It is unfair to expect youngsters to be challenged or excited by a series of art projects that begin simply with the teacher saying "Draw what you want today" or "Paint the way you feel." Elementary and middle school teachers of art should devote as much time to the presentation of an art lesson as the best teachers give to the preparation of a math or science unit.

There are many effective and successful ways to begin an art project. They include showing a film, filmstrip, or color slides on the theme selected; viewing slides or examples of previous work in related subject matter; guiding a class in a discussion of the theme objectives; conducting a field trip to enrich the students' know-how of the subject selected; playing recordings or tapes to create the mood of the particular visual theme chosen; demonstrating the technical process with student participation; calling attention to a bulletin-board or chalkboard presentation prepared for the art project; introducing a special guest who might speak, perform, or model for the students; and using selected poems, stories, songs, and instrumental music as motivational enrichment.

With a varied arsenal of motivational procedures planned well in advance by the teacher, students can look

forward to the art class as a unique and rewarding period of the school day. Each project and technique and, indeed, each age group demands its own pattern of motivation, and only the teacher with a rich repertoire of ideas and resources will be able to bring to the art program and art lesson the special ingredients that give it purposeful significance and excitement.

One of the most common problems the teacher of art faces is the lagging of student interest once the initial excitement of a new project or technique has waned. This is especially true in those situations in which youngsters do not set high enough standards for themselves and are satisfied with only a superficial effort and for those instances in which the children do not develop a real concern for, or identification with, the subject matter involved.

In almost every art class there are some children who find it difficult to persevere in a project. They insist that they are through with their work sooner than the others or feel that they have exhausted the possibilities of the project while their classmates are still busily involved in their creations. This situation poses a real challenge for the teacher, because it involves an interpretation of the fine balance between what children can honestly accomplish in art with intelligent and sensitive teacher guidance and what they are often willing to settle for. If at the outset of the project the teacher, in collaboration with the students, outlines specific, understandable goals and criteria of qualitative achievement in technique, composition, structure, and design, the recurring problem of children who rush through their work will not be so critical.

A criteria checklist could be posted on bulletin board or chalkboard for upper-elementary-grade and middle-school students as a reference as they proceed in their projects. This strategy could also alleviate one of the major quandaries facing the busy teacher, that of being able to provide guidance

A challenging drawing and painting project that appeals to children everywhere in the world is the chance to create their very own imaginary monster, which may be a combination of animal, bird, insect, and fish. Illustrated are make-believe animals by children from Hawaii, the Philippines, and Japan. Youngsters can add to the fun by naming their creations.

for each of the children effectively and still expedite the multiple responsibilities of classroom management. When questions pertaining to the project in process arise, the teacher can clarify and resolve them for the entire class by referring to the chalkboard or bulletin-board criteria, rather than repeating them orally for each student in a time-consuming procedure. Additionally, work in progress by youngsters can be shown to the class with appropriate constructive criticism to emphasize the objectives of a particular technique and to call attention to compositional requirements as well as possible variations in expression. A suggestion offered to one student will often trigger new ideas and fresh developments for others in class who may have reached a creative impasse or dead end.

At the upper-elementary-grade and middle-school levels the practice of writing brief, constructive remarks on the back of the student's work, or on slips of paper attached to the project, has proven beneficial in many instances and in a number of ways. It gives the teacher a chance to evaluate studio performance at a time relatively free of distractions and other responsibilities. It strengthens the possibility that every student in class will receive specific, individual help at some time during the project, and it provides the students with a definite working direction for the ensuing studio period that keeps them purposefully occupied. This strategy for project evaluation, although time consuming, can help the conscientious teacher implement individualized instruction that in turn results in a qualitative performance.

Because most children can absorb and retain only a few ideas at a time, the teacher should not overwhelm them with an avalanche of suggestions. Motivations should be provided in small doses, introducing, if possible, a new and exciting attention-getter each time the art class meets. The following motivational resources are suggested:

Reproductions of paintings, sculpture, prints, and crafts that can supplement, illuminate, and intensify the objectives of the lesson.

Photographs, in color or black and white, that can extend the students' visual repertoire of experiences.

Color slides of paintings, drawings, sculpture, prints, architecture, and crafts; of design elements in nature and constructed objects; of creative work by children worldwide; of examples illustrating technical stages in a project; of people in active work, in sports, and in costume; and of animals, birds, fish, insects, and flowers.

Filmstrips and cartridge tapes on artists, art history, and art techniques.

Films, TV films, and tapes that relate to the art project undertaken.

Books (stories, plays, poems, and biographies) and periodicals that can help both teachers and students toward a richer interpretation of the art project.

Recordings (disk or tape) of music, dramatizations, poetry, sounds of geographic regions—city and country, nature's forces, forest and jungle—and sounds of machines, planes, ships, trains, rockets, circuses, and amusement centers.

Guests invited to art class as inspiration, such as police officers, fire fighters and nurses; performers such as clowns, dancers, pantomimists, and musicians with their instruments; and scuba divers, pilots, athletes in uniform, and, if possible, models in space gear.

Resource and sketching trips to science, natural, and historical museums; art museums; university and college art studios; farms; factories; wharves; airports; observatories; bus and train stations; bridge and dam sites; national parks; zoos; shopping malls; boat marinas; air shows; amusement parks; and historical monuments. Be sure field trips are planned in advance. Visit the sketching site beforehand, if possible, to check on hazards and permits. Clear permission with the school principal so that parental approval can be obtained and travel arrangements can be expedited. If necessary, arrange for parent chaperones.

Models for art-class drawing projects may include animals, birds and fish, flowers and plant life, dried fall weeds, beehives, bird's nests, insect and butterfly collections, terrariums, pets, rocks and pebbles, fossils, coral, seaweed and seashells, skeletons of animals, and assorted still-life material: fruits and vegetables, including gourds; lanterns; kettles; teapots; vases; old clocks; bottles; fish net; old lamps; assorted fabrics for drapery; musical instruments;

Mixed-media collage by middle school youngster. The everyday interests of young adolescents—sports, bicycling, rock celebrities, TV and movie idols, electronic games, break dancing—all add to their art repertoire. In the illustration above notice how the rider fills the space, how the wheel motif is repeated to create unity, and how a feeling of motion is created by the bent back of cyclist and the flowing scarf. Campus School, University of Wisconsin, Oshkosh.

bicycles and motorcycles; and old hats, shoes and gloves. Vintage automobiles can be sketched in school parking lots.

Artifacts from other cultures and countries: masks, wood carvings, costumes, textiles, ceramics, toys, dolls, puppets, kites, armor, fans, and paper umbrellas.

Examples of children's art in varied media from worldwide sources.

Demonstrations of art techniques by teacher and students.

Introduction of a new art material or tool or a new use for commonly employed art materials.

Planned exhibits and bulletin-board displays that relate to the art project in process.

Assorted devices and equipment to help expand the students' awareness and visual horizons: microscopes, prisms, kaleidoscopes, *touch-me* kinetics, magnifiers, color machines, liquid light lamps, telescopes, microscopic projectors, computers, mirrors, and black light.

Strategic timing is of utmost importance in successful motivations. The teacher must be able to sense when youngsters have reached a fatigue point and need richer incentives to ensure progress in their work. The beginning of the class period is usually the best time to introduce new motivations, materials, and techniques, because the students are generally most receptive then. Teachers should not interrupt a class busily engaged in its project to point out something that could have been handled at the outset of the lesson. Time allotments for motivational sessions should be budgeted so that the children will not feel cheated out of their studio or activity period. The perceptive teacher learns through experience to gauge the listening alertness and interest span of the students and plan the entire strategic sequence of motivation, discussion, demonstration, studio, and evaluation purposefully, economically, and imaginatively.

Teachers of both elementary and middle schools will find many occasions during the school year to use the following resources and thereby enrich their art programs:

Birds, animals, fish, insects
Ant farms or bee colonies
Tropical fish in an aquarium
Colorful birds in cages
Acetate, celluloid, or plexiglass sheets in assorted colors
New day-glo color paint and papers
Bells from Oriental countries
Colorful paper umbrellas from Japan
Kites and fans from the Orient
Duck decoys
Eskimo sculpture in soapstone or whalebone
Fish netting and glass buoys
Indian corn, hedge apples
Gourds, squash, dried flowers
Indian kachina and Japanese kokeshi dolls
Window-display mannequins
Styrofoam wig holders
Masks: African, Indian, Malaysian, Indonesian, Mexican, Chinese opera, Mardi Gras, clown, Japanese Noh or Bugaku, Greek drama.
Mexican, Columbian, Indian pottery
Musical instruments
Model cars and airplanes
Navaho Indian rugs
San Blas Indian molas
Old fashioned hats, shoes, purses
Theater costumes and makeup
Texture table, felt board
Puppets, toys, and dolls from worldwide countries
Santos wood carvings from Mexico, South America, and the Philippines
Tissue paper in assorted colors
Spotlights
Full-length mirror, face mirrors
Bicycles, motorcycles, helmets
Sports equipment
Stained glass examples
Cloth remnants
Wallpaper sample books
Contemporary posters, travel posters
Magnifying glasses or lenses
Prisms, color modulators

This delightful watercolor painting is by a youngster from Yung Fu Elementary School, Tainan, Taiwan; it captures an experience of daily life charmingly. The child is fortunate to have an art teacher who appreciates what children can accomplish when they strive for design excellence and are provided with creative guidance.

7

EVALUATING CHILDREN'S ART

Among the many questions that teachers of art seek to answer, the one most commonly repeated is: How can I help those students who rush through their projects, who so often exclaim, "I'm finished!" when they have barely begun to tap their expressive potential? There is no doubt that the quality and promise of the school art program depend in great measure on how the teachers meet this particular challenge.

Unfortunately, there is no miracle formula, no sure-fire panacea, for dealing with youngsters who have a short interest span, whose early school preparation in art is deficient, and whose self-motivation is minimal. Every teaching strategy, every stimulative approach by the instructor, will vary, depending on the students' backgrounds, personalities, and readiness. Some youngsters simply need personal encouragement, some demand specific help, and others require only a clue, but all children at all age levels are entitled to more than vague, capsule generalizations. The best evaluative criticism provides the students with the kind of design and compositional guideposts they can understand, store, and then use over and over in succeeding art projects.

Recommended evaluating suggestions that many teachers have found helpful are listed below. They are most applicable to children in grades four to eight. Refer to the clues provided in Appendix B, "How Children Grow in Art," and keep them in mind as you evaluate the art of the different age groups. The following questions may be asked in an evaluation of line drawings and preliminary linear sketches:

Are the lines varied from thick to thin to create interesting linear movement and subtle space-in-depth?
Is the line on opposite sides of a shape or object (body, tree, vase, fruit, and so on) drawn heavier on one side and lighter on the other side to create tension and space?
Do the lines drawn complete a shape instead of floating in space?

These questions may be asked in an evaluation of composition and design:

Are the sizes and shapes of objects (people, buildings, cars, trees, and so on) varied? Do they produce interesting negative spaces?
Is informal balance employed (as opposed to formal balance) to create a varied, more flexible composition?

49

Are the shapes or objects drawn at different levels to create varied space breakup in foreground and background?

Do objects or shapes overlap each other to create unity and subtle space-in-depth?

Do some lines converge to create space-in-depth?

Do some lines or shapes touch or intersect the borders of the picture plane to create avenues into the composition?

Is contrast achieved by juxtaposing light areas next to dark ones, patterned or detailed areas next to plain ones?

These questions may be asked in an evaluation of color usage:

Is the color employed based on one of the color-wheel schemes: complementary, split-complementary, analogous, or triad?

Is the color scheme limited (monochromatic) to achieve a chromatic unity?

Are the neutralized colors in the palette (umber, ochre, sienna, and so on) employed for their special subtle effects?

Are colors or hues repeated throughout the composition to achieve movement and unity?

Are the values of the colors (tint and shade) varied for compositional interest and contrast?

Are the intensities of the colors varied for compositional diversity and subtle effects?

Are bright, high-intensity colors employed for emphasis wherever such emphasis is needed?

Has pressure been used in coloring with wax crayons or oil pastels to achieve rich, glowing colors?

Does the painting lack excitement because of too rigid a dependence on use of local color?

Are colors employed to achieve a feeling or mood: warm and cool colors, psychological-impact colors?

If there exists one fundamental element or key to the predictable success of composition in school art, it must cer-

What concentration the young girl on this page displays as she colors her sunflowers! She is using oil pastel on black construction paper. Her preliminary sketch was made in silver. Grade 5, Glencoe, Illinois.

tainly be the employment of *variety*, whether in line, shape, value, color, pattern, or texture. A study of the masterpieces of art reveals and attests again and again the artist's concern with visual variety in some aspect or form.

It is during the studio phase and the final stages of a project that evaluative strategies are most vital. A critique session wherein the teacher can sit down with a student and discuss the youngster's work at various stages is a most productive procedure. Students take turns for this evaluation. The use of a framing mat will add considerably to the success of the critique.

Concentration is exceedingly important in achieving qualitative results in art, which suggests that teachers must use whatever means they can command to establish a classroom or studio atmosphere in which the youngsters can become seriously and totally involved in their art without the interference of debilitating distractions.

The subtle strategies of high-caliber teaching lie in the words, action, sincerity, and confidence that teachers exhibit when they help their students evaluate their art efforts. What instructors say, how they say it, how much they say, and what they leave unsaid are vitally important to the success of a critique and consequently to the artwork itself. Evaluative clues are seldom emphasized in art-teacher preparation courses today, and as a result youngsters engaged in school art are cheated out of a critical learning experience. They rush from instant drawing to instant coloring without a single challenge by their teachers to examine their work in progress in terms of design and composition.

One of the most difficult evaluative tasks the teacher of art must perform is the periodic grading of students. In a content field that is so subjective, colored by expressive diversity, and in which many varied interpretations of an assignment are acceptable, the problem is compounded. Re-porting of student progress in art varies from school to school, from primary and intermediate through upper elementary grades to the middle school. Some institutions employ separate evaluations for behavior and subject mastery; some simply indicate that the student has performed satisfactorily or unsatisfactorily. The majority of report cards in the middle school use the letter-grade system. In some elementary schools the teachers write a report in the form of letter to the parents or guardians describing the child's growth in art, taking into account improvement in design-construction abilities as well as behavioral factors.

When letter or numerical grades for art are given, teachers often take into account the students' classroom deportment and working habits as a factor in their evaluation. This procedure has sometimes been questioned, but if youngsters have been forewarned that their behavior and conduct will affect their grades, such action is defensible. In almost every instance prudent and economic use of class time by the students results in a more qualitative product.

As far as the evaluation or grading of disparate art projects is concerned, this task should not prove difficult if the youngsters are advised in advance what the specific expectations include. In the project approach recommended in this book for best results, the teacher and students discuss the many possible objectives or criteria of the selected project. For greater emphasis the teacher writes these guidelines on the chalkboard or on a specially prepared chart or may even ask the students to take notes. These suggestions or expected outcomes may deal with subject matter, technique, composition, line, color employment, and the fullest exploitation of the media.

If the students are engaged in a crayon-engraving project, for example, the following self-evaluative questions will provide a working criteria:

Did I use enough pressure in applying the crayon so that the paper (white drawing or construction) is completely and solidly covered?

Did I use sufficient newspaper padding under my paper so that the crayon application—smooth and even—was a success?

Did I vary the sizes and shapes of the many crayoned areas?

Did I employ many hues and values of crayon (except black) for interest and contrast?

Did I mix the black tempera to the required (thin cream) consistency?

Did I brush off the flecks of crayon before applying the black tempera paint?

Did I add liquid soap to the tempera paint (approximately a teaspoon of soap to a pint of paint) so that it would adhere to the crayoned surface?

Did I paint the tempera evenly over the crayoned surface of the paper with a soft bristle brush, using random overlapping strokes and brushing carefully to eliminate any paint bubbles?

Did I wait for the tempera coat to dry thoroughly before attempting the engraving process?

Does my preliminary line-drawing composition for my engraving fill the space effectively?

Have I employed a variety of lines, shapes, and sizes?

Have I emphasized detail, pattern, and textures that are especially effective in the engraving process?

Did I engrave the basic outlines of the shapes in my composition first? Did I use the various engraving tools (nail, compass point, nut pick, nail file, Sloyd or Hyde knife) to create varied lines?

Did I take time to engrave details, varied patterns, and textural effects as contrasts against plain black areas?

Did I create some bold contrasts by scratching away solid areas of black to reveal the crayoned surface underneath?

Have I created exciting light and dark compositions balancing all three possibilities: engraved line only, detailed and patterned areas, and scraped-out, solid crayon shapes—all of them contrasting against the black areas?

Did I enrich the composition further by applying oil pastel colors over some of the remaining black areas?

Did I repeat the oil pastel colors in different parts of my composition to achieve unity?

Did I engrave lines, details, or patterns through the oil pastelled areas for even more subtle embellishment?

This kind of evaluative questioning can be effectively employed in every art project undertaken to give purpose, direction, and continuity to every youngster's efforts. Although the specific objectives associated with a technique or process will vary with different projects, the important, recurring criteria dealing with the fundamental art elements and principles found in all good design, structure, and composition will be echoed in project after project throughout the school year.

The most positive critiques and evaluations always take into consideration the personalities of the children themselves, their individual styles, and their natural abilities in art expression at their various age levels as well as their diverse imaginative and inventive capacities.

A handsomely designed watercolor interpretation of boats in a harbor by a middle grade student, Japan. Japanese school children from kindergarten up are provided with a large assortment of colors in tubes. They learn very early how to mix a variety of tints, shades, and neutralized hues.

These paintings by Japanese schoolchildren illustrate the differences in what primary grade and upper grade youngsters can accomplish in art when given the same theme as their subject matter. **Top:** Messenger boys in winter snow. **Middle:** A bicycle drawn in class where students view the object from several vantage points. **Bottom:** The famous French entomologist, Jean Fabre, envisioned as a boy pursuing his hobby.

8

CONTINUITY IN ART LEARNINGS

In no other subject area in the elementary and middle schools is continuity of learning so misunderstood, so neglected, and so poorly implemented as it is in art. Most classroom teachers are aware of sequential growth patterns in other school subjects such as math, science, and language. They are familiar with the specific content and skills to be mastered at each succeeding grade level and can help the students build with confidence on previous years' learnings. In elementary and middle school art classes, however, it is a different story. Teachers in the upper elementary grades are, in most instances, unfamiliar with the content of the primary-grade art program, if in fact such a program exists. Instructors of art in the middle school are often sadly uninformed about the elementary school art curriculum, seldom aware of the art skills and techniques emphasized and mastered there. In too many elementary schools, art projects are a hodge-podge of one-shot, spur-of-the-moment activities unrelated to one another or to the children's earlier art experiences. Often these token art lessons are hastily concocted to fit into, but not exceed, the 30- or 45-minute period allotted to art once a week or sometimes once every two weeks and very often squeezed in on a late Friday afternoon when the children are exhausted by the long day's activities and certainly not at their creative, physical, and mental best.

Due to a paucity in the planning and programming of sequential art learnings, children from grades one through eight are often provided with a monotonous diet of endless crayon lessons, usually seat work assignments, supposedly designed to illustrate some aspect of social studies, literature, and science. It is only natural for youngsters to become disinterested and bored when they realize they are not growing in the fundamental art skills and techniques they expected to learn but are cheated from acquiring.

Invite any parent or elementary or middle school principal to observe a class where *art is taught purposefully, seriously, imaginatively, and knowledgeably with an emphasis on the continuity of art learnings,* and the observer will see education at its finest, a total education of the whole child. He or she will witness youngsters absorbed in making hundreds of decisions: sharing, evaluating, comparing, revising, growing in language skills, and adding to their development as perceptive, discriminative, and aesthetically aware human beings. Teachers and administrators long ago discovered and will testify that all subjects in the school benefit when art is taught dynamically and qualitatively. Children, in art's charged and spirit-enhancing climate, grow year to year in confident self-expression and self-worth, as well as in verbal and visual literacy.

The implementation of a sequential, qualitative art-learnings and art-skills program in the education of all children is of vital importance today. Art in the elementary and middle schools of our nation is unfortunately becoming an endangered species, because too much time in art classes is spent on the insignificant, the peripheral, the frivolous, and the instant activity. "All right, children," says the classroom teacher at the close of the art lesson, "put away your crayons now and let's get down to something serious" (such as math, science, or language, perhaps?). Is it any wonder that principals, superintendents, and parents are questioning the validity and the worth of the art program in the elementary or middle school; yet they are as much to blame as anyone, when they settle for the unqualified and poorly prepared teacher of art and the unplanned, unstructured, nonsequential art program.

There are those in the art-education profession who believe that the present smorgasbord of studio activities should be replaced by art-appreciation classes. They insist that a program of studies dealing with art criticism would salvage art in our elementary and middle schools. I have yet to see such a proposal in operation for any length of time that has proven successful. Instead I have discovered through a half-century of teaching art to youngsters that art appreciation can be best implemented by a purposeful involvement in selective, qualitative studio experiences in which art originals, reproductions, and color slides are used to supplement and enrich studio practice. One fact escapes the protagonists of the "art-appreciation-to-the-rescue" theory. Youngsters want and need to create, manipulate, construct, and invent. In the majority of their classes they sit and read, listen and recite, learning by rote. They are entitled to an alternative morale-boosting break in the long school day. How many times have

teachers heard the children exclaim in joyful anticipation as they hurry into the art class, "What are we going to *do* in art today?" We must be ready for them with imaginative, meaningful, and dynamic studio-oriented challenges.

The solution is not to change the *doing* to *talking* and *listening* but to change the present quantitative, stereotyped, instant activities to more purposeful, substantive, and qualitative art-studio experiences, bolstered and enhanced by a use of art fundamentals, art principles, and art criticism. That is precisely what this chapter is about; indeed, what this whole book is about.

The following outline of a sequential, developmental quality art program is the rich harvest of a half-century of teaching, researching, and documenting art at the elementary and middle school levels and of countless classes, seminars, conferences, and workshops involving thousands of college and university students, classroom teachers, special art teachers, art consultants, and professional art educators. It should prove of significant value to present and future classroom teachers, who are required to teach their own art, as well as to those elementary and middle school special teachers of art who need practical, specific help in the planning and implementation of their art courses as well as in the critical areas of art-product evaluation. As readers assimilate the information provided in this chapter, they can augment their grasp and understanding of it by referring to Appendix B, "How Children Grow in Art."

When references are made to primary, intermediate, or upper grades, the following elementary school grade categories have been used: primary, grades 1 and 2; intermediate, grades 3 and 4; upper, grades 5 and 6. Middle schools, a fairly recent development, generally incorporate grade 6 of the elementary school, and, in some cases, grades 5 and 6.

AGES FIVE, SIX, AND SEVEN: GRADES ONE AND TWO

Drawing, designing, and painting

Introduce the children to line drawing, variety of shapes, value (dark and light), color, and pattern. Encourage drawing based on personal experiences and observations but welcome and praise imaginative expression as well. Provide many opportunities to draw from real objects: plants in and around the school, pets brought to class, flower arrangements, toys and dolls, classmates as figure-drawing models, self-portraits, depictions of the family in various settings, community helpers, and subject matter observed on field trips. Suggest drawing in large scale so details considered important can be incorporated. In figure drawing the size of the drawn head often determines the size of the body. Encourage the children to fill the page. In most instances the more images, shapes, or ideas the youngsters incorporate in their compositions, the more unified their drawings become. Discourage rushing just to finish and haphazard scribbling. The following rhymed stanza provides clues young children can use to add interest to their compositions:

> Something big, something small,
> Something short, something tall,
> Something dark, something light,
> Helps to make your drawing right.

Introduce your students to the various tools that produce lines and linear images: pencil, ballpoint and felt-nib pens, crayon, oil and chalk pastel, small brushes, school chalk, a nail for crayon-engraving projects, a stick in sand, or the fingers as in a finger painting. Promote discovery and use of various line patterns: stripes, plaids, circles, stars, spirals, controlled scribbles, radiating lines, and zigzag designs.

Encourage observation of pattern in clothing, school and home furnishings, and especially in the wonders of nature, such as bark, fish scales, and plumage.

Color awareness

Begin teaching color awareness with emphasis on the child's everyday surroundings from the very first day of school. Call the youngsters' attention to the myriad colors in their immediate environment: classroom, clothes, books, art materials, and paintings and posters on display in the school. Help them to identify the primary and secondary colors and the warm, sunny colors such as yellow, orange, pink, and red, with the events associated with them—the circus, county fairs, parades, Mardi Gras, autumn harvest, and shopping malls. Call attention, too, to the deep cool colors: green, turquoise, blue, and blue-violet, with the images they evoke—the mysterious night, the fathomless ocean, the rain jungle, and the deep, dark forest.

Imaginary animal in oil pastel, grade 4.

Build color knowledge with every project that uses crayon, pastel, tempera, fingerpaint, watercolors, or colored papers and yarns. Reinforce the identification of the primaries—red, yellow, and blue—and the secondaries—orange, green, and purple (violet). Check records and files on the children for evidences of color blindness so you can adapt your assignments to their needs.

Take advantage of the many stimulating games, toys, and devices commercially produced to develop color awareness: the prism, paint chips, the color wheel, and the kaleidoscope. Encourage color matching, using found materials such as scraps of art paper, wallpaper, magazine illustrations, cloth, and yarn. Use shoe boxes to store the color collection, one box for each of the various colors. Encourage the children to create new colors by mingling watercolors or poster paint (tempera) on wet or moist paper.

Second grade children in the University Elementary School, Iowa City, created these birds in a cage with colored construction paper. The cage was cut out and mounted on a complementary colored sheet of paper. They were displayed in the school's entrance hall.

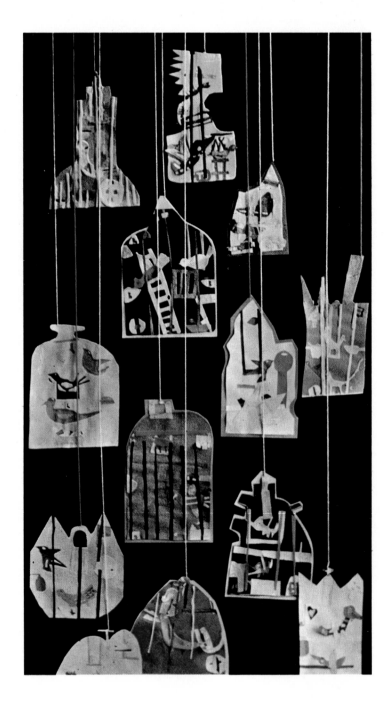

Collage (cut and paste)

Encourage youngsters in scissors-cutting skills. Invite them to create simple, basically geometric shapes out of construction paper. Do you have scissors for children who are left-handed? Provide opportunities involving pasting little shapes on big shapes. Point out how contrast is achieved by pasting a light-colored shape over a dark-colored shape and vice versa. Offer suggestions on using paste economically and effectively. School paste and wheat paste are recommended at this age level; they are economical and the easiest to control. Primary-age children often have difficulties with the liquid glues. Rubber cement is a little too costly for the elementary-art budget in most schools. In some instances the felt board can be employed to introduce children to the countless possibilities of cut-out shapes and the many ways they can be juxtaposed and overlapped to create interesting compositions. Cooperative murals employing the "cut-and-paste" technique in which each child contributes one or more parts to the whole are very satisfying projects at this age level. See the section "Mural Making" in this book. Almost any subject matter or theme lends itself beautifully to collage making at this stage: flowers in a garden, animals in the jungle, fish in the sea, birds in a tree, and butterflies in flight.

Printmaking

Simple repeat prints resulting in colorful allover patterns can be made at this age level, using vegetables, found objects, clay pieces, erasers, cellulose scraps, and hands and fingers.

In most instances colored construction paper is recommended for the background printing surface. Other possibilities are colored tissue paper, newsprint, wallpaper samples, brown wrapping paper, and fabric remnants. Printmaking activities at this age level are somewhat limited, because young children do not possess the necessary skills for complicated techniques. Certainly worth trying are styrofoam meat-tray prints with incised relief created by pencil pressure. More advanced experiences include glue line prints and collographs in these grades. Both techniques are described in detail in Chapter 11.

Ceramics

Provide exploratory experiences with clay. It is important that sufficient clay be available (a ball of clay about the size of a grapefruit is recommended for every child) and that it be of the proper plasticity—malleable, clean, not too moist, and not too dry. Check the working condition of the clay a day or two before a ceramic project is undertaken, unless commercially prepared moist clay is used. Allow the children to discover the potential of the clay: Encourage squeezing, pinching, poking, and stretching the clay. Introduce coil making and forming of the clay into small balls or pellets.

Guide the children in the creation of simple and familiar forms. Suggest that they hold the ball or lump of clay in their hands as they manipulate it into the desired shape. This procedure discourages the tendency of some children to pound the clay flat on their desks. Primary-grade children enjoy creating animals and birds in clay. They find that they can control the relatively simple sculptural forms of an elephant, hippo, cow, horse, rabbit, turtle, pig, dog, cat, whale, or resting bird, manipulating the clay in either an additive or subtractive technique.

Children at this stage can also construct simple pinch pots. With a lump of clay the size of an orange they can manage a fairly successful container, which may be bisque-fired if a kiln is available. Ask them to hold the clay ball in the palm of one hand and insert the thumb of the other hand in the middle of the clay about half-way down. As they rotate the clay they should push and pinch thumb and fingers along the inside and outside of the ball in overlapping pinches. Caution them not to make the wall or bottom of the pinch pot too thin. The marks of their fingers and thumb often add an effective natural texture. Remind them to avoid excessive use of water in moistening and smoothing their clay. Pots should be fired if possible.

A growing art vocabulary

Youngsters who grow in the language and vocabulary of art usually reap more rewards in their art endeavors. Teachers should exploit all means at their disposal, including the chalkboard and bulletin board, to call the young child's attention to the following project-related art words: balance, black, blue, bright, brown, brush, cardboard, chalk, circle, clay, coil, color, construction paper, crayon, dark, design, dot, drawing, easel, eraser, fingerpaint, glue, green, gray, hammer, ink, kiln, light, line, manila paper, mural, nail, newsprint paper, orange, oval, overlap, paste, pastel, pattern, pen, pencil, pink, pinch pot, purple (violet), rectangle, red, repeat, ruler, saw, screwdriver, scribble, shape, square, stripe, tempera paint, texture, tissue paper, triangle, watercolor, weaving, white, yellow.

Suggested subjects or themes for children's art projects

These project suggestions are suitable for children of ages five, six, and seven (grades one and two):

Playground games	Skipping rope
Fun in the snow	Our community helpers
Fun on the ice	Butterflies in a garden
A flower garden	Farm animals
My pet and me	Noah's ark
Animals in the zoo	Fish in the sea
Animals of the jungle	Land of make-believe
Playing ball	My favorite toy

AGES SEVEN, EIGHT, AND NINE: GRADES THREE AND FOUR

Drawing, designing, and painting

Continue to call attention to the immediate and visually stimulating subject or image for drawing. On sketching excursions, scout for the unusual site, the pictorially exciting vista. Choose landscapes and cityscapes with multifaceted structures and interesting towers and spires with varied foreground and background breakup. Suggest new avenues and directions in compositional design such as overlapping shapes that create unity and subtle space, achieving distance through diminishing sizes and placement of objects higher on the page, creating pattern and textural effects as contrast to quiet or plain areas, and drawing the line in a more sensitive, varied way to achieve motion and emphasis.

Children at this stage, by the fourth grade certainly, can be introduced to basic contour-drawing techniques. For an immediate visual stimulus begin with simple, easily recognizable, everyday objects: a fruit, vegetable, shoe, glove, helmet, cap, cowboy hat, baseball mitt, football, hockey puck, cup, teapot, light bulb, or water pitcher. When the youngsters' skill and confidence in contour delineation increases, introduce a combined arrangement of several objects in which the items overlap. It is of utmost importance that children are guided to look carefully and intently at the object they are drawing and that they draw very slowly and deliberately. Explain about inner contour lines, for example, in the case of a flower. Suggest that they begin in the middle with the core, adding a petal at a time, rather than with a hasty general outline of the entire flower. In other instances, for example with a banana or okra, begin with the outer contour line and then add inner contour lines to clarify the form.

A soft lead pencil is best for contour drawing. Kindergarten pencils are recommended. Erasures should be discouraged; a second corrective line more carefully observed is suggested. The youngsters may stop at critical junctures, reposition the drawing tool, and then continue drawing. The term *blind contour* refers to the kind of drawing in which the students look at the object but not at their paper as they draw. Blind-contour drawing is generally recommended for the upper-elementary-grade and middle school youngsters.

Continue to direct the children's attention to the environment, to nature, and to the variety of line, shape, texture, color, pattern, rhythm, contrasts, radiation, emphasis, and unity found there. Ask them to bring to class various examples of nature's abundant store of leaves, twigs, roots, seeds, weeds, rocks and stones, fossils, honeycombs, bird nests, nuts, pods, pine cones, seashells, and coral. Encourage the use of these natural treasures as inspirational subject matter for drawings, paintings, and prints.

The drawings on this page illustrate the progress in drawing horses made by the same girl at ages seven, nine, and ten. From the book Heidi's Horse, *by Sylvia Fein, Exelrod Press, Pleasant Hill, Calif. By permission of the author and publisher.*

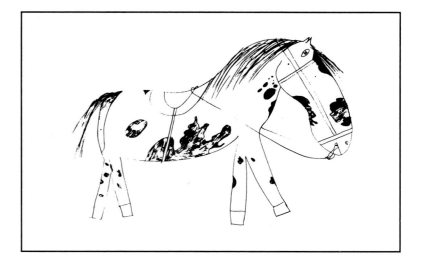

Color awareness

Review color knowledge gained in grades one and two. Introduce the children to art projects that demand multiple color choices such as a collage using colored construction paper, colored tissue paper, wallpaper samples, paint chips, and assorted color fabrics and felts; printing with found objects on colored paper; weaving with colored papers; coloring with crayon or oil pastel on colored construction paper; making mosaics with colored tesserae on colored or black background; and creating a color environment or happening in class, foyer, or corridor combining crepe paper, balloons, beach towels, hula hoops, fans, colored cellophane, ribbons, scarves, umbrellas, posters, and fabrics.

Encourage youngsters to mix and experiment with an expanded range of colors including the tints and shades. Discuss the mood and effects of warm and cool colors within a painting and in the environment. Call attention to the possibilities of related colors, those adjacent to one another on the color wheel. Youngsters at this stage are now often ready to tackle the intricacies of color neutralization (dulling a color) obtained by mixing a color with its complementary hue (opposites on the color wheel) and to appreciate the subtle yet effective contrast of subdued colors next to bright, intense colors.

Collage

Build on knowledge and technique gained in the primary grades. Introduce cut, tear, and paste projects that require the creation of texture and low-relief effects achieved by folding, crimping, pleating, fringing, weaving, braiding, and curling the paper. Direct more attention now to positive and negative shapes. Suggest how the positive shape, obtained by cutting a motif (star, leaf, heart, cross, diamond) out of a piece of paper, and the negative shape, the paper that remains after the shape is cut out, can be effectively juxtaposed in a collage design. Introduce colored tissue paper, either cut or torn, as a collage medium. Suggest that children use light-colored tissues first and build up to the darker colors, which should be used sparingly as accent and contrast. Encourage color discovery by suggesting that youngsters build several tissue layers using white construction or tagboard as the background surface and liquid laundry starch as the adhesive.

Collage projects in tissue lend themselves beautifully to nonobjective designs, to dream and mood pictures, and to visual interpretations inspired by sounds: whisper, shout, swish, rattle, squeak, titter, roar, and thunderclap.

Printmaking

The vegetable, clay stamp, and found-object prints introduced in the primary grades can now be augmented with oil pastel as a final, rich embellishment. At this stage the youngsters can now successfully manage the collograph or cardboard relief print. The collograph technique is explained in detail in Chapter 11.

A variety of printmaking processes is manageable at this age level. Recommended techniques include the glue line print (explained fully in Chapter 11); the string or cord print in which string is glued to a cardboard plate, inked, and printed; the polystyrene (meat-market tray) print in which lines are indented into the polystyrene with a pencil and the plate is inked and printed (lines will appear white in the completed black- or colored-ink print, excellent for greeting-card designs); the monoprint (single print) in which a sheet of formica or of glass (its edges taped) is inked with a brayer. Oil ink in black or dark colors is recommended. The composition is created by scratching through the paint with a stick, Q-tip, edge of cardboard piece, eraser end of pencil, or wood chopstick. A sheet of newsprint or color-tinted shelf paper is placed over the inked surface, pressed down with palm or brayer, and pulled off carefully. Use turpentine to clean inking surfaces and ink roller. It is recommended that a table be set aside for monoprinting and other printing processes that require oil ink. The number of students at the inking table should be limited. Be sure to cover the table with newspapers. Children should wear smocks or old shirts to protect their clothes. Monitor inking processes closely.

Ceramics

At this stage review the knowledge children have gained in earlier school years about clay: its source, plasticity, possibilities, and limitations. If you have the necessary resource visuals, show and describe the importance of ceramics in the everyday life of bygone and contemporary cultures. An exploratory session in clay manipulation is again recommended. Previous learnings about the properties of clay should be recapitulated as the youngsters work. They will probably remember that hardening clay is difficult to model; that clay too moist sags if the supports are not sturdy enough; that appendages unfortunately break off when the clay piece dries unless they are securely joined to the main structure; that textures, patterns, and details can be made in clay with fingers, pencils, and assorted found objects; and that a very large, solid clay piece may explode in the firing kiln unless provisions are made for the air inside to escape. In making large clay animals such as dinosaurs and elephants, the post and lintel clay structure is recommended (described in detail in Chapter 11). The basic form can then be modeled, added to, condensed, or stretched until the youngsters achieve the characteristic quality they desire. The introduction of the "fifth leg," a supporting clay piece under the stomach of any animal being modeled, will prove helpful in preventing a collapse of the form.

Children at this stage can explore more complex techniques in pottery making. The basic, simple pinch pot can become a larger container by joining two pinch pots of the same size. Use clay slip to seal the junction. Cut out openings and add feet and spouts for more complex pots. Instruct the youngsters in clay-scoring and slip-cementing processes.

A growing art vocabulary

The following words should become part of the children's growing art vocabulary in addition to those recommended for acquisition in the primary grades: asterisk, background, balsawood, batik, brayer, carbon paper, cellophane, ceramics, collage, collograph, color wheel, complementary colors, composition, cone, contrast, contour line, crafts, cube, cylinder, enamel, engraving, foreground, form, found material, gum eraser, hue, India ink, inking slab, intensity, landscape, linoleum, linoprint, masking tape, Masonite, monoprint, mosaic, negative shape, papier maché, pellet, plaster, plywood, positive shape, poster, pyramid, radiation, rasp, rubber cement, scoring (clay, paper), shade, shellac, sketch, slab (clay), slip (clay), spiral, staple, still life, stitchery, tie and dye, tint, turpentine, unity (in design or composition), value, wedging (clay).

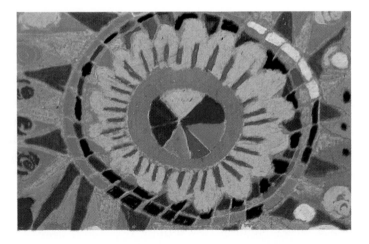

Suggested subjects or themes for children's art projects

These project suggestions are suitable for children of ages seven, eight, and nine, grades three and four:

Inside me (imaginative X ray)	Totem poles
Fun on the jungle gym	Soapbox derby
The circus parade	A tree house
The merry-go-round	Tree of life
The house where I live	Imaginary animals
The toy shop	Prehistoric animals
Animals and their young	The insect world
Autumn leaves and trees	Playing a musical instrument
The pet show	Still life (things on a table)
A magic forest	Flower market
Santa's workshop	The wedding
Here come the clowns!	The circus in action
Washing the family car	Space voyage
Boarding the school bus	Sunken treasure
Rare birds	Design in nature: radiation
Kite festival	

If I were a balloon seller, a juggler, a tightrope walker, a ballerina, a scarecrow, a skydiver, an astronaut, a clown, an aquanaut

AGES NINE, TEN, AND ELEVEN: GRADES FIVE AND SIX

Drawing, designing, and painting

Whenever possible take the youngsters on sketching field trips. Scout and select challenging sites to draw: building constructions, building demolitions, shopping malls, harbors, bridges, gas stations, boat marinas, natural museums, zoos, fire stations, botanical gardens, farm buildings, Victorian-style homes, fairgrounds, airports, national shrines,

One art project enthusiastically undertaken by schoolchildren around the world is the radiation design illustrated on this page. Inspired by radial wonders in nature—star, sun, flower, and snowflake—youngsters create their own radiating compositions. No two designs will be alike.

churches, synagogues, cathedrals, temples, aquariums and amusements parks. At this stage youngsters can be guided to create variety, space, and movement in their compositions by discriminative placement of images, objects, or motifs within the picture plane. For example, figures or buildings might rest on different foreground levels and terminate at varying heights in the background. Shapes can be juxtaposed or over-lapped to create unity and space-in-depth. Challenge the students to see the design potential of positive and negative shapes in their composition. Usually, the more varied the objects or positive elements are in size and shape, the more exciting and satisfying the background design becomes.

Continue practice in contour drawing and introduce new approaches to line design and composition such as fantasy and nonobjective- and optical-art themes. Challenge the youngsters to discover the many different ways they can use line as pattern to enrich surfaces and vitalize backgrounds.

Color awareness

Review color theories and color discoveries made in preceding grades. Recapitulate data concerning primary, secondary, and intermediate colors and reinforce learnings about complementary and analogous (related) and monochromatic color harmonies; color values, the tints, and shades; the directions for neutralizing or dulling colors; and the color spectrum and the color wheel.

Use mood music as a background for free, expressive painting. Continue to build color awareness by calling the children's attention to exploitation of color in their everyday world—billboards, new urban murals, magazines and album covers, packaging, athletic uniforms, interior decoration, foods, book jackets, store fronts, and automobiles.

The felt-nib pen X-ray drawing shown here is an excellent example of art's expanding a child's horizons. White construction paper, 12 × 18 inches, was divided into three sections with a very light pencil line, the top for the tree itself, the center for its roots underground, and the bottom for the deep soil, rock, and water strata. Upper-elementary-grade youngsters drew the tree from life and then did research in science books for help with the subsoil formations.

Augment the youngsters' color knowledge and appreciation by scheduling films on color in art and life and by exposing them to fine reproductions (originals, when available) of paintings by Henri Matisse, Hans Hoffman, Pierre Bonnard, Paul Gauguin, Claude Monet, Piet Mondrian, and J. M. W. Turner. Include contemporary colorists such as Helen Frankenthaler, Sam Francis, Paul Jenkins, Karel Appel, Clifford Still, Jackson Pollock, Stuart Davis, Arshile Gorky, Morris Louis, Frank Stella, and Wassily Kandinsky.

Collage

Recapitulate previous learnings and discoveries in the collage technique, including the exploitation of positive and negative shapes. Suggest employment of partially three-dimensional effects through paper folding, fringing, pleating, spiraling, and curling. Introduce paper scoring to students who are ready for more skillful challenges. Demonstrate the scoring technique: Place paper to be scored on a thick pad of newspapers. Use blunt point of scissors, pointed end of wood popsickle stick, or similar tool to indent the curved line into the paper; then carefully fold along indented line. Be careful not to cut the paper when indenting.

Challenge the students to scout for found objects to use in their collages: wallpaper and rug samples, fabric and ribbon remnants, yarn, discarded building materials, and old greeting cards.

Printmaking

Although the various printmaking processes introduced in previous grades (vegetable and found-object print, collograph, glue line-relief print, polystyrene print, and monoprint) can be repeated successfully at this age level, the maturing youngsters will respond now to more complex, more challenging print techniques. Linoleum printing is a favorite, especially with boys, because of the opportunity to use a variety of cutting gouges. More tools, materials, equipment, and time are required for advanced printmaking. Organization of inking, printing, and cleanup stations is a very important factor. See the guidelines for linoleum prints in Chapter 11.

Ceramics

Review previously assimilated learnings and discoveries about clay and clay manipulation. Provide for sessions of clay exploration with class discussion of clay's potential, possibilities, and limitations. More complex ceramic modeling may now be attempted. Popular subject-matter themes for this age level include animals and their young, animals in combat, portraits and self-portraits, clowns, acrobats, and mother-child depictions. Youngsters now place a strong emphasis on realistic portrayals and on the achievement of correct proportions and characteristic detail. The teacher must be prepared to offer sympathetic and supportive guidance when called upon. In most instances direct the students to the original, inspirational source of the subject matter—the figure or animal itself. If this is not possible, refer them to vicarious resources such as films, color slides, and photographs. Neither overpraise the purely realistic approach admired by youngsters nor harshly criticize it; instead, introduce students to those styles and interpretations that are aesthetically more expressive, restrained, and universal. Build a library of photographs and color slides dealing with the best in ceramic art through the centuries.

A growing art vocabulary

Build on the art vocabulary recommended and hopefully acquired in preceding grades. Augment it with the following new words: charcoal, color harmony, dowel, firebrick, glaze, gouge, greenware, grog, horizon line, lacquer, leather-hard clay, linear, mat, mat knife, mixed media, mold, monochromatic, motif, neutralization of color, opaque, palette, perspective, poster board, proportion, raffia, reed, Sloyd knife, shading, spectrum, stabile, symbol, symmetry, technique, terra cotta, tessera, translucent, transparent, vanishing point, vermiculite, wedging board, X-acto knife.

Suggested subjects or themes for children's art projects

These project suggestions are suitable for children of ages nine, ten, and eleven, grades five and six.

At the airport
At the gas station
On the subway
At the train depot
A view from a plane
Bicycle race
At the barbershop
The picnic
At the dentist's
Undersea marine life station
Fun at the swimming pool
Boarding a helicopter
Disneyland
Frontierland
Marine world
Six flags
Traffic jam
Winter carnival

Cities in outer space
Self-portraits
Portraits of classmates
Thanksgiving celebration
Landscape, cityscape, seascape
Nature study
Horse show
The marching band
Track meet
Amusement park
The shopping mall
Still life of musical instruments
Dancers of the world
Warriors in armor
Motorcycles
County, 4-H, and state fairs
Renowned sports figures
A pirate ship

Two collages by sixth grade students. Preliminary drawings were made in black ink with felt nib markers. The youngsters then applied pieces of colored construction paper and patterned sections from wallpaper samples and magazines to complete their composi-tions. The original sketches were drawn on colored construction paper. Some of the black outlines were reinforced when the pasting was completed.

Self-portraits and portraits of classmates are popular as themes for linoleum prints in upper elementary grades and middle school. It is recommended that the preliminary sketch be made with a blunt-felt-nib pen, black crayon, or small brush and ink that approximates more closely the bold effect of the gouged line.

AGES TWELVE, THIRTEEN, AND FOURTEEN: GRADES SEVEN AND EIGHT

Drawing, designing, and painting

Recapitulate and reinforce drawing and painting media and techniques introduced in the elementary grades. Continue implementation of expressive drawing processes encompassing both contour and gesture styles. Youngsters now should attempt to achieve value contrast through shading, stippling, hatching, crosshatching, and washes. They will need guidance and reassurance in the handling of color values and employment of cast shadows and reflections.

At this stage the maturing youngster will begin to realize the importance of creating strategic avenues into the composition by the introduction of lines and shapes that terminate at the boundaries or borders of the paper. These devices lead the viewer into the picture. A corollary design bonus results because the more avenues created, the more opportunities the student has to employ a variety of colors, values, and pattern in the resulting foreground and background shapes.

Unless the student specifically requests the teacher's help, it is wiser not to introduce regimented perspective rules or foreshortening techniques at this stage. However, some youngsters will want their drawings to "look right" and will likely need specific assistance in making their toppling and meandering fences stand straight, their sidewalks lie flat, and their roads disappear believably over a distant rise or hill. To help them achieve these effects the teacher must remember that fence posts are drawn parallel to the sides of the page, division lines in sidewalks are drawn at angles directed to a distant vanishing point, and roads or highways diminish in width as they move away from the viewer toward the horizon. Some students are enchanted by the mechanical, mathematical aspects of perspective drawing; their enthusiasm should not be dampened, but the teacher should enlighten them regarding the compositional limitations of rigid perspective reliance. Although the youngsters strive for "right" proportions in their figures, the instructor must help them realize that drawing something "realistically right" does not always make it "artistically right." They should be reminded that many noted artists have often ignored the rules of perspective, proportion, and color harmony to produce art of great impact and beauty.

To expand the middle school youngsters' knowledge and appreciation of master drawings and paintings, the teacher should introduce them to the art of Leonardo da Vinci, Albrecht Durer, Rembrandt Van Rijn, Paul Klee, Vincent Van Gogh, Henri Matisse, Pablo Picasso, Ben Shahn, Ando Hiroshige, Katsushika Hokusai, William Hogarth, Edgar Degas, Peter Breughel, Francisco Goya, and Andrew Wyeth. Call their attention also to the cave drawings at Altamira and Font du Gaume, to the strong and attenuated tribal-huntsmen renditions of African and Australian primitives, to the sumi-e ink drawings of China and Japan, and to the expressive graphics of the Eskimo and American Indian.

Color awareness

Youngsters in the middle school are mature enough to respond to the many subtleties and complexities of color fabrication and harmonization. Recapitulate and reinforce color knowledge mastered in earlier grades. Assign color-design projects that will challenge the students to create personal,

Top: Collograph, Japan. Bottom: Linoleum print, Iowa City.

individual color schemes and exciting color juxtapositions such as album covers, monograms, posters, logos, billboard ads, book jackets, store-window displays, stage designs, and home decor. Review the processes for making tints and shades and the neutralization of colors. Discuss the psychological effect of colors on people; the colors emphasized in packaging and advertising; the colors of ceremonies, celebrations, rituals, and rites of passage; and the symbolic meaning of colors in different countries and cultures.

Whenever possible, take the youngsters to exhibits featuring contemporary color and light shows. Encourage the students to construct a color "environment" or "happening" using found materials such as ribbons, yarn, wrapping paper, kites, cellophane, balloons, hula hoops, confetti, crepe and tissue paper in assorted colors, giant paper flowers, fabric samples, and beach towels. Other exciting projects to stimulate color awareness are construction of toothpick, stick, or box sculptures painted in bold tempera or fluorescent colors; miniature-sized, stained-glass windows, using scrap colored glass, colored tissue paper, or stage gels; optical paintings inspired by the works of Victor Vasarely and Bridget Riley; and splendid kites and masks of many colors.

Collage

The collage (from the French word *coller:* "to paste") process with its related family of montage, frottage, mosaic, collograph, and assemblage provides middle-school students with a host of opportunities to employ the important elements and

---

Collages on this page by intermediate-elementary-grade children employed the positive-negative avenue to compositional design. Students chose one color of 12 × 18-inch construction paper for the background surface with several smaller scraps of construction paper approximately 4 × 6 inches, 5 × 7 inches, and so on in colors other than the background sheet. They drew motifs with pencil in the center of the small sheets and cut them out. They then pasted both positive shapes and negative shapes on their large background paper, placing them some distance from each other. They continued this process, overlapping some shapes, until the composition filled the page.

principles of art—variety in shapes, contrast in values and color, overlapping to create unity—in design and composition-building stages.

Review fundamentals of the collage process assimilated in elementary grades: the identification and exploitation of positive and negative shapes, the creation of subtle space through overlapping, and the achievement of three-dimensional effects through paper folding, scoring, pleating, fringing, and curling.

Preliminary drawings or sketches are generally recommended for collages whose subject matter deals with landscapes, figure studies, or still lifes. In themes from fantasy, the imagination, or purely nonobjective interpretation, the direct cutting, tearing, and application of the shapes to the background may be encouraged, but in both approaches the pasting or permanent adhering of materials should be delayed until the students, with the teacher's guidance, have the opportunity to evaluate their work and make those compositional changes—additions, subtractions, and revisions—that may be necessary to enhance their creations.

The collage is an excellent first project of the year for middle school art classes. It does not put as much pressure on the youngsters as a first school-day assignment in drawing or painting would. It is not as frustrating to draw and cut out single elements as parts of a whole design. Every student in class can succeed in collage making.

New materials and found materials have expanded the range of collage creation immensely. Explore the possibilities of colored tissue on white or colored tag or on railroad board, colored sections from magazine ads, wallpaper samples, fabric remnants, and nature's store of colored and textured wonders: bark, leaves, seaweed, sand, feathers, butterfly wings, dried flowers, seeds, and snake skins.

Printmaking

Simple prints—the vegetable and found-object print, the glue line-relief print, the collograph, the monoprint, and the advanced lino print—that the children enjoyed in earlier grades can be augmented with satisfaction and success in the middle school. More complex subject matter and themes can now be employed in a variety of printmaking processes. Again, the organization and monitoring of inking, printing, and cleanup areas is of special importance. Lots of protective newspapers must be on hand.

At this grade level some sophisticated printmaking techniques can be undertaken if special heavy-duty inking presses are available and teachers are experienced in supervising advanced printmaking techniques. These processes include engravings using discarded X-ray plates (use laundry bleach to clear plate), and woodblock prints, which require the use of oil-based ink and a solvent such as turpentine. Cleanup stations and their management have a high priority in these cases.

Ceramics

Recapitulate and review earlier assimilated learnings about clay and clay manipulation. Since students may come from different elementary schools with varying backgrounds in clay experimentation and creation, provide for several sessions in clay exploration with discussions of its historical importance in the lives of people of other eras and other cultures. Obtain and exhibit reproductions either in color or black and white; also show slides of ceramic pottery and sculpture from ancient as well as contemporary cultures: Greek vases of the Hellenic period; Chinese Tang figurines as well as the outstanding life-size ceramic warriors and horses recently unearthed at Xian; Japanese Jomon and Haniwa creations; and clay vessels in the form of human figures from Mexico and Peru, especially the expressive output of the Tarascans.

Youngsters can now engage in more complex and challenging clay construction and modeling. Check out copies of *Ceramics Monthly* from the library to bring the students up to date on the newest developments in the field of ceramic pottery and sculpture. Put up a "Potter-of-the-Week" display on the art-room bulletin board with the hope that the students will become familiar with the pioneers and innovators in this art category such as Shoji Hamada and Peter Voulkos.

At this stage, if adequate kiln facilities are budgeted, students can experiment with ceramic glazes to give their pottery and sculpture glowing, colorful dimensions. Remember, however, *less* is usually *more* when it comes to decoration and embellishment in ceramic design. Guide students to be restrained and discriminative in their color choices. Always hold before them the best exemplars of ceramic craftsmanship.

A growing art vocabulary

Youngsters in middle school, coming as they often do from different elementary schools, may have varied backgrounds and skills in art-vocabulary building. It is suggested that the teacher review the words that should have been suggested for assimilation in previous grades. Write or print these words or phrases on the chalkboard or on a chart on the bulletin board and add the new words recommended for this age level as they are introduced in class projects: armature, assemblage, bas relief, bat (plaster), bench hook, burnish, caricature, cartoon, chisel, conté crayon, converging lines, crosshatch,

distortion, encaustic, etching, fixative, foreshortening, gesture drawing, hatching, incised relief, kneaded eraser, mass, montage, ochre, patina, printing press, repoussé, sandcore, sepia, sienna, solder, spectrum, stabile, stipple, turquoise, umber, wash (watercolor), woodblock.

Suggested subjects or themes for middle-school art projects

These project suggestions are suitable for children of ages twelve, thirteen, and fourteen, grades six, seven, and eight. If additional subject matter is needed, refer to themes recommended earlier for grades five and six, which can be adapted easily for expressive purposes to the middle school.

Great moments in ballet
Great moments in science
Great moments in sports
Great moments in music
Great moments in the theater and opera
Great moments in literature
Festivals of the world
Customs of the world
Costumes of the world
Historical costumes
Air show
World cup yachting races
Air balloon races
Helicopters
Dune buggies
The rodeo
Block party
Dream cars, motorcycles, and boats
Garage sale
Flying trapeze act
At the electronic game arcade
String quartet

Fashion show
Wrestling match
Log rolling
Legendary heroes and heroines

Some themes such as a "Bouquet of Flowers" and "Self-Portraits and Animal Pets" are universal and can be recommended without reservation for all grades, one through eight. If you don't find a suitable theme at one age level, check back to find it in another grade level and adapt it accordingly.

Although little has been included about projects in construction and certain crafts such as weaving, stitchery, papier maché, puppetry, and simple jewelry, all of these hands-on activities should be included in a qualitative, progressive, all-encompassing elementary and middle school art program. For example, weaving can progress from simple paper weaving in the primary grades to sophisticated, hanging woven panels in the middle school. The choice of the project depends on the youngster's readiness and ability to master the special tools and the technique needed. Mask construction, simple puppets, and stitchery can be offered at all levels. Papier maché, paper sculpture, leather and metal tooling, marionettes, and jewelry are best reserved for upper elementary grades and middle school, where many students are also ready for challenging subtractive sculpture projects in soap, balsa wood, sandcore, leather-hard clay molds, plaster-of-paris blocks, and soft firebrick, as well as additive sculpture employing toothpicks, wood scraps, wire, metal, driftwood, and found objects.

Color projects. **Top:** *Simulated stained glass. Leaded effects painted with black enamel on a pane of glass.* **Middle:** *Simulated tree trunk and insects. Construction paper.* **Bottom:** *Black construction paper with colored tissue paper pasted over cut-out areas.*

Metal repoussé. *Metal embossing or tooling is an art craft that upper-elementary and middle school youngsters will enjoy. The teacher should provide a number of visually stimulating motivational resources so that the students can create their own designs. Discourage the use of ready-made stereotyped patterns. Recommended subject themes are "Animals and Their Young," "Tropical Fish," "Butterflies," "Birds of Fancy Plumage," and "Denizens of the Jungle or Zoo." All of these ideas provide excellent opportunities for the use of detail and texture. Preliminary drawings for this project may be made on newsprint, manila paper, or notebook paper. The size should be limited for best results, for example 6 × 9, 9 × 9, or 12 × 12 inches. The copper repoussé examples illustrated on these pages are 9 × 12 inches. Heavy-duty aluminum foil or commercially available sheeting (36-gauge) is generally recommended for this project. Mask tape the preliminary drawing to the metal sheet as a guide to the initial embossing. To make the relief indentations use a blunt-pointed pencil (kindergarten variety is suggested), the end of a round watercolor brush, or a commercially produced embossing tool. After the basic preliminary outline is completely indented (student can lift the paper to check), remove the paper and work directly on the metal. Emphasize detail, designs, veins, and textures such as hair, mane, feathers, scales, grass, bark, and leaves. When the piece is completely embossed, it may be embellished further by applying black shoe polish and then wiping it off the raised or relief surfaces. If the budget allows obtain copper sheeting, emboss it, and give it a beautiful patina employing liver of sulphate coating.*

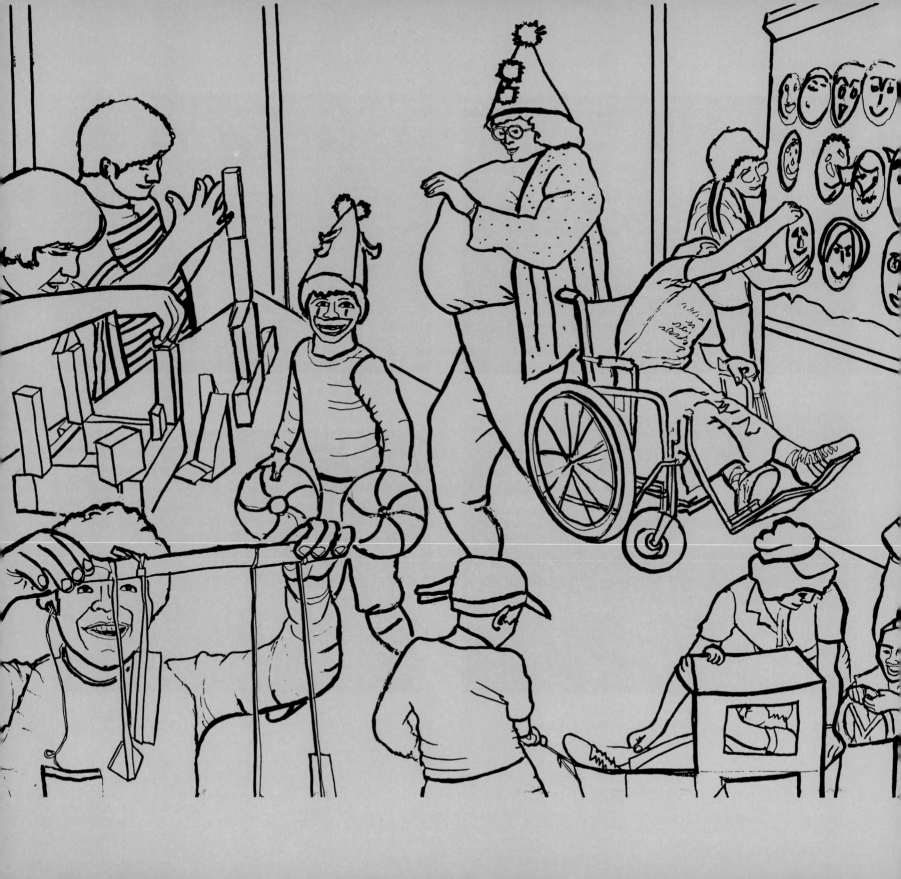

9

ART FOR CHILDREN WITH SPECIAL NEEDS

A new challenge faces classroom teachers and art teachers in elementary and middle schools today with the passage of federal legislation establishing Public Law 94-142. No longer is the education of abnormal and atypical children the sole responsibility of those specially segregated institutions charged with their care. The law now provides for the mainstreaming of children with special needs—the retarded, the physically handicapped, the extremely maladjusted, the deaf, the learning disabled, the blind, the partially sighted, and the emotionally disturbed—into integrated classrooms with children possessing normal capabilities. Children are considered handicapped or exceptional when they are impaired physically, intellectually, emotionally, or socially to such an extent that they cannot function educationally in a mode similar to that of normal children not so handicapped but may, in time, with the aid of special instruction and programming, learn to cope and even to achieve. Not all handicapped youngsters will be mainstreamed, but whenever it is possible

and feasible, the procedure is being implemented according to federal mandate. It is probable that every public school classroom teacher and art teacher will have to prepare for this contingency in the foreseeable future.

For the majority of children in elementary and middle schools the guidelines for teaching art and the program of studio projects proposed in this book should prove adaptable and effective, but for children with special needs, new teaching strategies are called for. The intent of this chapter is to provide some practical approaches to help teachers meet the challenge. First, the good news is that the art class or studio atmosphere is the best of all possible environments in which to work with disadvantaged or retarded children. There they find no threatening standard of uniform skills or tests. Each child is accepted; his or her potential is respected. Each child can excel in some way, modest though it may be. Every child can be an achiever.

The importance of the teacher and the teacher's role has

Facing page: Illustrations from Art and Mainstreaming, *a textbook dealing with art instruction for exceptional children in regular classrooms by Claire B. Clements and Robert D. Clements, University of Georgia, Athens. Courtesy of Charles C Thomas, Publishers, Springfield, Illinois. Drawings depict children in a variety of self-worth-building art activities.* **Left to right, top:** *Construction with wood scraps from lumber yard; costumes and hats designed for a parade; paper masks.* **Left to right, bottom:** *Simple cardboard and string mobile; train engines and trucks constructed from discarded grocery cartons.*

been emphasized in every edition of this book, but it cannot be stressed enough in the context of teaching and supervising children with special needs. All attributes of the dedicated teacher that we have spelled out before—sympathy, knowledge, tact, confidence, resourcefulness, understanding, equanimity, and patience—are doubly important in the successful management of a mainstreamed classroom or studio. Precedence, if any, must be given to the qualities of *understanding* and *patience*.

Here are some recommended strategies for teachers who are experiencing mainstreaming for the first time:

1. Accept the children as they are.
2. Familiarize yourself with the handicaps of the special children assigned to your class. Also acquaint yourself with the more detailed, more analytical descriptions of specific handicaps in the recommended readings (Appendix C) to help you in your new role.
3. Ascertain if a progress chart has been recorded on the children in question by a previous teacher. Note the art experiences and projects with which they have been involved.
4. Find out if teacher aides are assigned to help you expedite individual or organizational problems incurred by the special students in your class.
5. Be aware of the many specialized devices, tools, and materials now employed or being developed for use by handicapped children in art classes. See the partial list at the close of this chapter.
6. Keep your own progress report on every handicapped or retarded child in your class. In a few school systems the art teacher is required to write and implement individualized instruction plans for each special student.
7. Consider carefully the teaching procedures you will employ in the instruction of your special charges: Will you use free-choice projects in which children choose their own subject matter, materials, and time limits, or will you employ the unit or project method in which the same art activity is planned for both normal and special students? The latter format usually calls for individual adjustments and reduced expectations from the mainstreamed student. Above

all, do not permit the children in any category to participate in copying or tracing artwork. Help them create their own imagery, impoverished though it sometimes may be.
8. Consider enlisting the aid of normal students in class, especially those with proven abilities and stable, pleasant personalities, to help their handicapped classmates with manipulative problems.
9. Ascertain if there is a chapter of the Association for Children with Learning Disabilities in your community. Check out its services.

Specifically, here are some teaching strategies and tactics to follow in working with the atypical, handicapped, or retarded child:

At all times proceed *deliberately, methodically,* and *calmly.* Give directions or instructions slowly and clearly, using simple language at a rate the children can assimilate. Make sure, if possible, that you have the child's attention when explaining something.

Demonstrate more and talk less. Employ visual symbols and models. Speak in a modulated tone of voice. Dress attractively. Avoid wearing flashy or dangling jewelry.

Repeat instructions and procedures over and over again. In a word, *overteach!*

Sit on chair or stool so that your face will be at a level easier for children to see and to make eye contact when you talk to them.

Do not talk to a class while facing the chalkboard, standing in the window glare, or from too far a distance.

Plan projects that may be broken down into sequential, manageable, and explainable segments or tasks, for example, in creating a collage: the drawing stage, cutting or tearing stage, pasting stage, and framing or matting stage. Allow sufficient time for completion of a task. Do not begin a second project until the first one is completed.

Emphasize experiences that deal with kinesthetic manipulation and multisensory stimulation.

Prepare lessons to meet specific needs (for examples, hand-eye coordination, fine or gross motor-skills improvement) and to meet identifiable objectives such as color or shape naming. For partially sighted children, employ media that help them achieve success, such as large, contrasting (black and white) sheets of paper and contrasting color crayons rather than subdued values.

Reinforce all learnings and skills with visual, tactile, concrete, and sensory motivations, techniques, and evaluations.

Emphasize the fundamentals of art and the elements and principles of design as critical guideposts in visual expression; for example, identify basic shapes and colors. Emphasize, also, the awareness of environment and space.

Avoid pressuring children for explanations, reasons, or interpretations of their artwork. "Why?" often has negative connotations.

Be sure that enough materials and tools necessary for the lesson are on hand. Don't risk bottlenecks and the disorder that often result from insufficient project supplies.

Be cognizant, too, that these youngsters often resist change; that they are easily distracted, have short attention spans; plan brief, one-session projects that demand minimum memory recall. *They need constant praise and support*. Children generally respond more enthusiastically when their art experiences are successful.

Display the children's work attractively to show your approval and to elicit supporting response from their peers. Don't forget that the children's projects, though not always of a qualitative nature, can bring pride to the school, delight to parents and visitors, and an enhanced self-worth to the participating youngsters.

Many of the teaching strategies recommended above are already part of the instructional repertoire of successful classroom teachers and, if followed discriminatively, will ensure positive learning results for all children involved.

Experiences that appeal to retarded and handicapped children

Painting	Beach balls
Cutting	Opening packages
Pasting	Toys
Printmaking (with vegetables and found objects)	Kinetic games
Construction (wood, boxes, found objects)	Big cardboard cartons to hide and play in and also to transform into automobiles or trucks
Styrofoam meat-tray boats	
Weaving	Balloons

*Projects that may be undertaken successfully with retarded or handicapped children. **Top:** Puppet people constructed of characteristic body parts. Wallpaper samples and colored construction paper were provided already cut into arms, legs, body, and head. Children, with the aid of the teacher, pasted them down. **Middle:** Three-dimensional animals constructed of folded and cut tagboard. **Bottom:** Stabile constructed out of found materials.*

Fingerpainting

"Keep-a-secret" progressive
    figure drawing

Pets and animals

Flowers and trees

Dressing up, costumes, uniforms

Face makeup

Decorating the classroom

Use of mirrors

Marching, parading

Singing

Puppets

Pinatas

Television

Drums

Pantomime

Painting to music

Simple sports

Fanciful hats

Masks

Noisemakers, horns, rattles (nuts
    in a sealed pantyhose
    container)

Mobiles

Kaleidoscopes

Clowns

Bright colors in paper, cloth,
    yarn, cellophane, ribbons

Making music with assorted
    concocted instruments

Kites

Fish in aquariums

Modeling mixtures

Here are some special teaching tools and devices for use in projects with handicapped children:

Four-holed scissors that both student and teacher can manipulate at the same time

Fat-handled brushes or brushes with handles wrapped with masking or surgical tape so that students can get a better grip when painting; utility brushes ½ or 1 inch wide

Giant color crayons, felt-nib markers (water-base)

Kindergarten-size pencils (soft lead)

Painting stretchers assembled together and placed on table or desk around perimeter of project in process so that students can judge outside edges or boundaries of their work; other possibilities: cafeteria trays, styrofoam meat trays

Posters and instructional signs with giant-size letters and numerals

Touch table, touch box

Flannel boards

Building blocks in assorted shapes and sizes

Magnifying glasses

Wood or plastic colored beads and sticks in assorted sizes

Colored gelatins

Peg boards

For additional found or recycled materials useful in your art classes, see Appendix E.

For additional detailed information on the classification of handicapped and retarded children, with expectations of behavior and abilities, refer to the books listed in Appendix C under "Books for Teachers of Children with Special Needs."

TEACHING ART-GIFTED CHILDREN

Teachers also need guidelines to counsel those students who reveal special creative talents or gifts. All teachers have been approached by proud parents who claim that their children are artistically talented and offer, as examples of this talent, sketchbooks and notebooks of drawings copied from the comics or photographs. In some instances, fortunately, the drawings are truly original, creative, and imaginative. But the artistically gifted or talented child in school can pose some delicate challenges for the teacher beleaguered with a classroom full of youngsters of varying potentials. The first priority is to identify those children who exhibit artistic giftedness, which is no easy matter, since few reliable measures exist to judge creative art production.

The following characteristics attributed to the gifted or talented in art by authorities in the field should be noted by the teacher. Gifted-talented children:

First reveal their giftedness through their very early drawings.

Possess a richer store of images and ideas to draw from, the subject matter heightened by their acute observation.

Use a greater amount of detail, pattern, and texture in their drawings and compositions than most children—some of this elaboration observed, some imagined.

Have greater persistence and are able to work longer and with greater concentration on a project or problem.

*A superb pen and ink drawing of lush foliage by a gifted Japanese
girl. Grade six, elementary school.*

Often possess a photographic mind, with vivid recall of events engaged in or observed that distinguishes their efforts, characterized by a richness of details.

Are oblivious to distractions when engaged in their art and often resent interference by classmates or teacher.

Tend to minimize their other studies in favor of art experiences.

Master certain technical aspects of drawing—perspective, foreshortening, volume, shading, overlapping, spatial handling, and movement—much sooner than their classmates.

Tend to choose subjects of fantasy, usually of complex themes involving intricate structures and a host of participants for their art compositions.

May develop a personal style of drawing or painting early in their school years.

Are generally receptive to the use of new media, techniques, and tools.

Show great interest in the art world and in the lives of contemporary artists and craftspeople. They often visit art museums on a regular basis. They sometimes carry a sketchbook to record their impressions.

Learn quickly to employ the vocabulary and language of art effectively and confidently and to critique and evaluate their art production in terms of composition and design fundamentals.

Usually prefer drawing, painting, printmaking, and collage to step-by-step craftwork.

Use color imaginatively, making up their own palette of colors by combining the hues usually provided in class.

Prefer to work by themselves rather than in groups. They often use art activity as a retreat.

Appear to derive a deep, personal satisfaction from their involvement in art.

Are generally highly self-motivated and engage in art on their own—after school, at home, and sometimes, surreptitiously, during other class periods.

What can teachers do to help the gifted or talented child, to nurture and preserve the gift? They can provide a supportive environment, but overpraise is to be avoided, since it can lead to peer resentment. They can provide more challenges through multimedia techniques and subject-matter assignments that demand imaginative solutions and interpretations, for example, the depiction of a famous historical figure as a child or adolescent experiencing the first intimations of her or his future role in life.

A consensus regarding the teaching of the gifted child suggests that the best approach is the minimal one of letting the youngster alone to do his or her thing. In effect, *underteaching* is recommended, but this strategy poses problems for the teacher who uses the project method in which all students in class are engaged in the same subject-matter assignment and the same technique. To allow so-called gifted children the special privilege of working on their own subject choice at their own pace while their classmates are required to stay with the assigned project is an example of discrimination not recommended. A wiser procedure is to challenge gifted children to stretch the possibilities of the assigned project or theme to the fullest, to employ their giftedness to go beyond the expected, to outrun their classmates but on the same course. Remind the gifted that there are many moments outside the art class when they can soar creatively and imaginatively in subject themes of their choosing.

Teachers who discover gifted or talented children in their classes are fortunate, because they become witnesses to what children can do in art when they extend themselves to their fullest potential. Often instructors derive clues from the creative solutions and inventions gifted children employ in their compositions or projects that help them in the motivation of other youngsters in class. In other words, what teachers discern and learn from the characteristics and working habits of the gifted or talented child is what they emphasize in a qualitative art program: keen, sensitive observation; rich imagination; persistence; patience, concentration; and above all, art that is engaged in seriously and purposefully.

A colorful simulated mosaic employing cut and torn colored paper for the tesserae. The subject is Sakurajima Park, with a view of an erupting volcano on a nearby island. Middle school student, Kagoshima, Japan.

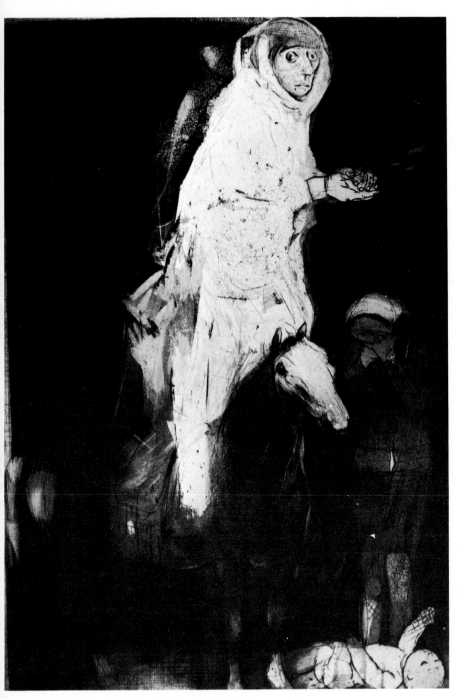

Espana, *color intaglio, Mauricio Lasansky, 1956, 32 × 21 inches, collection of the author.*

10

AVENUES TO ART APPRECIATION

Children today have infinitely more opportunities to see and appreciate art than ever before. Our burgeoning museums and art centers open their doors to all; mobile art exhibits tour many cities and states, and colorful murals now enliven countless urban walls. Municipal buildings, subways, and airports display a variety of commissioned art. Magazines consistently feature articles on art. Colorfully illustrated books on art are published in greater numbers today than ever before, and reproductions of art are available at fairly reasonable prices.

School textbooks in music, social studies, and literature are often filled with colorful, correlative art visuals. Art councils in almost all of the 50 states promote art festivals, exhibits, and "artists-in-the-schools" programs.

Despite all of these opportunities to experience and appreciate art, many schoolchildren have minimal exposure to the fine arts. What can the classroom teachers or special teachers of art do to remedy this situation, to enrich the lives of their students through art? They can invite artists and craftspeople to visit their classes and demonstrate their skills when feasible. They can plan visits to art centers, galleries, and museums. The most practicable resource is to bring the art to the children: original art, if possible; if not, then colorful reproductions, color slides, and book illustrations.

A survey of art appreciation literature reveals that there are numerous approaches to the understanding of art and almost as many categories of art criticism as there are critics. The following appreciatory guidelines may provide answers to the many troubling questions that inquiring teachers of elementary and middle school art ask.

Preferably, all teachers of child art should have a general knowledge of the history of art (as presented in a university or college basic fine-arts course) and a basic understanding of the fundamentals of art. (See Chapter 2.) They should be familiar, too, with the technical aspects of the projects they introduce to their students so that they will be ready with answers to the many questions the children may ask.

A survey of art education literature reveals that the following categories of criticism are generally employed when looking at, talking about, and appreciating or evaluating art. (One must remember that paintings and prints are by far the most common examples of fine art used in school art-appreciation sessions even though the "ideal" curriculum would include a variety of artifacts ranging from Persian rugs to Pre-Columbian ceramics.)

Category I, "Identifying the Content or Subject Matter of the Art" sets the stage for understanding a work of art. What does the viewer see: man, woman, dog, house, tree, vase of flowers? What event is being depicted: wedding, riot, sports event, fair, family reunion, rite of passage? Enthusiastic student participation usually develops when the subject matter is real or recognizable. On the other hand, troubling questions arise when the product is nonrepresentational or nonobjective as one finds depicted in many contemporary paintings and sculptures. In that case content may only be perceived and described as various kinds of lines, colors, shapes (circle, square, ovoid), and forms or as a series of abstract symbols: cross, diamond, logo, or mandala.

Category II, "Recognizing the Technique or Art Medium," often proves challenging and intriguing to inquisitive, game-minded youngsters. There are so many new directions in contemporary visual expression other than painting per se, such as collage, montage, frottage, assemblage, aquatint, engraving, etching, lithograph, collograph, mobile, stabile, light sculpture, earthwork, and combine. Actual studio involvement by the children with the media, the techniques, and the artist's materials helps them to appreciate the artist's problems and solutions.

Category III, "Identifying the Compositional or Design Factors in the Art and Recognizing Their Importance," is probably the most enlightening and satisfying task in the whole appreciatory cycle. Discovering the basic line structure; the main thrusts; the avenues into the composition; the dominating and subordinating themes; and the rhythms, balances, and contrasts of line, shape, value, color, pattern, and texture, with the pinpointing of unifying elements, all can develop into a fascinating game of search and self-discovery, an art adventure wherein both students and teacher learn that the whole is indeed greater than the sum of its parts.

Category IV, "Recognizing the Unique, Individual Style of the Artist," is another intriguing and rewarding aspect of learning through art appreciation. When youngsters, guided by a knowledgeable and imaginative teacher, achieve the critical and perceptive skills to identify the work of Michelangelo, Rembrandt van Rijn, Pablo Picasso, and Andrew Wyeth by recognizing their individual, painterly style, they are on their way to a richer understanding and enjoyment of art's world of treasures.

Category V, that most ephemeral and elusive of art-appreciation classifications, "The Search for the Meaning of the

  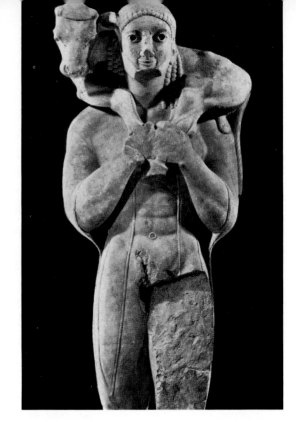

*Although these examples of the sculptor's art are continents, oceans, and even centuries apart, they are imbued with a universality of spirit to which we can respond. **Left:** Olmec, Mexico, 1000 B.C. serpentine, The Museum of Primitive Art, New York City.*

*Center: Ashura, Buddhist deity, eighth century, dry lacquer, Kofukuji Temple, Nara, Japan. **Right:** The Calfbearer, Greek, circa 560 B.C., stone.*

Art and (Hopefully) the Discovery of the Artist's Intent," is no doubt the most subjective and sensitive phase of the appreciatory cycle, fraught with hidden pitfalls. There are many opportunities to influence and/or convince the students with the teacher's own judgments and prejudices about a work of art. Tread carefully here! Avoid telling the youngsters what *you* see in the art, what *you* feel about it, until they have had a chance to tell you what *they* see, what *they* feel. You may not always agree with their analysis and judgment. But *don't force your opinions on them*. Allow the artists, the craftspeople, the architects, to speak for themselves through their art and their journals.

In looking at and discussing art, ask the students to search and study related sources: For example, in a critique of the work of Vincent Van Gogh, introduce to them the letters the artist wrote to his brother Theo. Reading them will help the older children gain a deeper understanding of Van Gogh's painting—his creative highs and his frustrating, disappointing lows. Most teachers are aware that the majority of children enjoy talking avidly about their experiences and their reactions to things and events. There will be no difficulty getting them to express themselves vocally about the art you show them or take them to see. The main problem will be to keep them on the subject, "on the track" so to speak.

Certain children will want to monopolize the discussion. Lure in the quiet, the timid, the shy youngster. Through planned, as well as extemporaneous, questioning, you can make the art-appreciation lesson a truly productive and rewarding experience for every child in your class.

In choosing reproductions or color slides for study and appreciation, consider the natural preferences of the children. Works that abound in color and contrast are generally more appealing to primary-grade children. Paintings with realistic subject matter that youngsters can relate to are usually more popular with the upper elementary-age group. The maturing middle school youngster will be able to respond to more sophisticated, more complex art themes; to moody, muted colors; and to abstract, nonobjective compositions. A variety of examples will usually bring a wider, more effective response from middle school students, since this multiple approach provides for learning through examining and analyzing contrasting styles and imagery.

The environment, the climate for viewing the artwork, is also critical. Rearrange the seating, if possible, to provide each child with an up-front advantage. Circle seating on chairs or on the floor is often recommended. Invite the children to come up to the displayed art object to point out the area or detail under discussion. Avoid reproductions that are too small for class-viewing purposes and black and white reproductions of those paintings that are noted for their exciting color exploitation, for example, works by Vincent Van Gogh, Hans Hoffman, Robert Delaunay, Claude Monet, Marc Chagall, Pierre Bonnard, and Wassily Kandinsky.

Another strategic avenue to understanding the arts is the creative correlation of art appreciation with the making of art. To ensure success in this venture the teacher should have access to a library of color reproductions, color filmstrips, and color slides of paintings, prints, sculpture, crafts, and architecture. Many school districts provide a central distribution point for visual aids. Check with the art consultant. Some schools have their own resource centers. Commercial firms that offer visual aids in art are listed in Appendix D. Many resourceful teachers have collected and organized extensive picture and color-slide files of their own. The following list of studio projects and correlative art study, employing reproductions or color slides, will provide the teacher with a variety of stimulating possibilities for art-appreciation lessons.

Suggested art project	*Correlative art appreciation*
Drawing-painting: Helping at home or school	Genre paintings of Jan Vermeer, Pieter de Hooch, Andrew Wyeth, Jean Chardin, Grandma Moses, Grant Wood, Thomas Hart Benton, Norman Rockwell, Jacob Lawrence, Robert Gwathmey
Drawing-painting: Portraits and self-portraits	Portraits by Hans Holbein, Thomas Gainsborough, Domenico Ghirlandaio, Leonardo da Vinci, Anthony Van Dyck; self-portraits by Vincent Van Gogh, Rembrandt van Rijn, Pablo Picasso, Paul Gauguin, Albrecht Dürer, Max Beckman, Andrew Wyeth
Drawing-painting: Objects on a table, chair, or bench	Still lifes by Paul Cezanne, Odilon Redon, Georges Braque, Pablo Picasso, Jean Chardin, Juan Gris, William Harnett, Bernard Buffet.
Drawing-painting: The landscape or cityscape	Maurice Utrillo, Maurice Vlaminck, J. M. W. Turner, John Constable, Paul Gauguin, Vincent Van Gogh, Raoul Dufy, Stuart Davis, Dong Kingman, Edward Hopper, Grant Wood,

Suggested art project	Correlative art appreciation
	George Inness, Paul Cezanne, Marsden Hartley, John Marin
Drawing-painting: The animal and bird world	Cave paintings at Lascaux and Altamira; Leonardo da Vinci, Jean Louis Gericault, Rembrandt van Rijn, Albrecht Dürer, Henri Rousseau, John James Audubon; Indian Moghul, American Indian, Chinese, and Japanese animal drawings
Drawing-painting: Figure composition	Pieter Brueghel, Edgar Degas, Käthe Kollwitz, Paul Gauguin, Henri Matisse, Mary Cassatt, Marie Laurencin, Pablo Picasso, Francisco Goya, Diego Velasquez, Rembrandt van Rijn, Ben Shahn, Robert Gwathmey, Joseph Hirsch, George Bellows, Alice Neal, Richard Lindner, Willem de Kooning
Drawing-painting: The abstract, the nonobjective, the surreal, op and pop, and fantasy	Piet Mondrian, Salvador Dali, Joan Miró, Joseph Albers, Victor Vasarely, Paul Jenkins, Mark Rothko, Georgia O'Keeffe, Ad Reinhart, Wassily Kandinsky, Mark Tobey, Arthur G. Dove, Bridget Riley, Jackson Pollock, Frank Stella, Helen Frankenthaler
Printmaking: Collograph, styrofoam print, linoleum block, glue line-relief print, monoprint	Albrecht Dürer, Rembrandt van Rijn, Leonard Baskin, Mauricio Lasansky, Warren Colescott, William Hayter, Gabor Peterdi;

Top: Self-Portrait, *Vincent Van Gogh, 1888, Rijkmuseum, Amsterdam.* Bottom: Self-Portrait, *Paul Gauguin, 1891, Metropolitan Museum of Art, New York City.*

	Japanese ukiyo-e artists Ando Hiroshige, Katsushika Hokusai, Kitagawa Utamaro
Mask design and construction	African ritual masks; masks of North Pacific Indians; masks from Melanesia, Malaysia, Mexico, Indonesia; Japanese Noh play and Bugaku masks; Chinese opera, Greek drama, and Mardi Gras masks
Three-dimensional construction (use of found materials)	Alexander Calder, David Smith, Lee Bontecou, Louise Nevelson, Richard Stankiewicz, Pablo Picasso, Marisol Escobar, Ernest Trova, Seymour Lipton, Edward Kienholz
Sculpture in plaster block, soapstone, firebrick, balsa wood	Jean Arp, Henry Moore, Barbara Hepworth, Isamu Noguchi; Easter Island sculpture, North Pacific Indian totem poles
Collage: Varied subject matter	Georges Braque, Kurt Schwitters, Henri Matisse, Romare Bearden, Joseph Cornell
Clay pots and containers	Korean Koryo period, ancient Greek vases and jars, Chinese Ming and pre-Columbian pottery, Japanese Jomon ceramics; Thai Sukothai period; Indian pueblo pottery; Peter Voulkos; Shoji Hamada
Clay figure modeling	Clay figures of Greek Tanagra style; Japanese Haniwa period; Mexican, Peruvian, and Guatemalan pre-Columbian ceramic sculpture

Top: White Vase with Flowers, *Odilon Redon, 1916, Museum of Modern Art, New York City.* **Bottom:** Sunflowers, *Vincent Van Gogh, Rijkmuseum, Amsterdam.*

The acrylic polymer painting illustrated above is by Professor David Hodge, art department, University of Wisconsin, Oshkosh. Seated Figure: Margaret Mary, 48″ × 48″, 1964. Professor Hodge is the coauthor of Art in Depth, a Qualitative Program of Art for the Adolescent. Note how effectively the figure fills the picture plane and note the successful employment of contrasting colors and shapes.

For additional workable strategies that involve children in art-appreciatory experiences, read about the "Gallery Game," "Description Game," "Visual Treasure Hunt," "Role Playing," "Art Auction," and "Find a Line Game" in *The Joyous Vision*, by Al Hurwitz and Stanley Madeja (Prentice-Hall, Englewood Cliffs, N.J.).

Talking about art results in another bonus for the children. They grow not only in visual language but in verbal sophistication. New words and phrases become part of their expanding vocabulary. Here are a few that come to mind:

Art nouveau	Genre
Foreshortening	Encaustic
Action painting	Armature
Critic	Caricature
Bauhaus	Atelier
Critique	Cubism
Gallery installation	Dadaism
Painterly	Impressionism
Painter's style	Magic realism
Light machine	Minimal art
Assemblage	Nonobjective art
Happening	Surrealism
Op art	Abstract expressionism
Pop art	Futurism
Funk art	Trompe l'oeil
Primitive art	Classicism
Patron	Minimalism
Naive art	Cubism
Folk art	Stabile
Earth works	Light modulator
Combine art	Neoclassicism
Mobile	

Catalogs of color slides and color reproductions are available from commercial distributors listed in Appendix D.

The illustration above shows artist James Herbert, a professor of painting at the University of Georgia, employing rubber-glove-encased hands to apply oil paint to his mural-sized canvas. Artists throughout the centuries have utilized varying techniques to express their thoughts and ideas visually. Among the multimedia employed are earth colors, casein, eggtempera, gouache, enamel, oil paint, watercolors, tempera, and mosaic tesserae. Some artists have even used egg shells, bird feathers, butterfly wings, seeds, sand, and assorted found materials.

skates, tennis racket, football, helmet, hockey mask, or baseball mitt.

The best art teachers gradually acquire an assortment of objects that are ideal as subject matter for line drawings: bones, antlers, lanterns, bottles, potted plants, assorted colorful fabrics to use as drapery, and nature's gifts of stones, feathers, seeds, cones, nuts, twigs, leaves, dried flowers, seashells, coral, and bark.

Drawing tools should be selected for their potential in producing a variety of lines. Drawing pencils (kindergarten variety with soft lead), crayons, felt-nib and nylon-tipped pens and markers, brushes, Q-tips, eye droppers filled with ink, and dowel rods or twigs, sharpened to a point as ink applicators, are some elementary school possibilities. In addition, charcoal and conté crayon are often recommended for middle school students. The ordinary steel-point pen with India ink has its merits, but these merits are often eclipsed by frustrations caused by dripped or spattered ink. The teacher should identify, discuss, and demonstrate the various drawing tools available. Care and storage of drawing tools should be emphasized.

The time and attention allotted to preliminary drawings and line compositions is most crucial. The youngsters should never have cause to feel that they are being rushed through this important drawing phase. This is the stage where teachers of art face their most critical challenge, because it is what they note here, what they approve, what changes they suggest during these drawing sessions, that can make the difference between results that are merely adequate or average and those that are qualitatively outstanding.

For mature upper-elementary grade children and for middle school youngsters, the contour method of drawing, where mind, hand, and eye must be in unison when the draw-

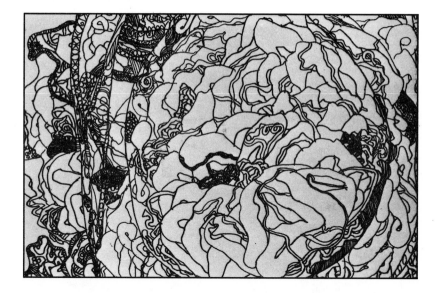

The drawings above are by intermediate-grade elementary school students in Japan. They depict the insides of the human brain and stomach and reveal the imaginative capacities of the youngsters. Felt or nylon nib pens were used on white construction or drawing paper. Saga Prefecture.

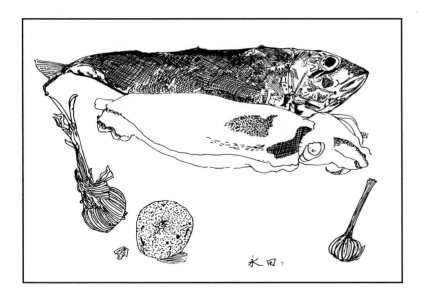

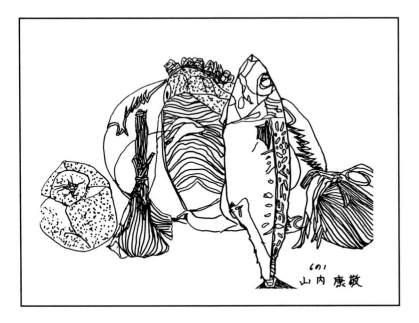

ing takes place, holds both fascination and frustration. Although the technique demands total involvement and intensity of concentration, its rewards are observable more often in the process than in the results.

For many youngsters the contour-drawing method can be a discouraging and somewhat exhausting exercise unless it is presented in sequential and understandable stages. Results are often disappointing at first, since the drawn statement does not always resemble the familiar, realistic image the youngster is accustomed to perceiving. To free students from their concern over their initial efforts, it is necessary to explain to them that realistic delineation is not of prime importance in this drawing technique. In the first contour session the teacher might suggest that students pretend their forefinger is the drawing tool and to indicate the outline of the object on their paper without actually making a mark. Continued practice is necessary to decelerate the tendency of youngsters merely to scan and draw quickly.

For initial contour lessons and exercises it is recommended that all students draw from simple subject matter such as a fruit, vegetable, cup, or bottle. After several simple studies, assign more complex arrangements that will stimulate growth in handling inner contour lines, overlapping of shapes and shallow space.

Everyday objects and selected antiques provide the best material for contour-drawing subject matter: bicycles, motorcycles, farm machinery, trucks, car motors, clocks, typewriters, electric fans, teapots, old sewing machines, coffee grinders, lanterns, steam irons, eggbeaters, corn shellers, animal traps, grocery carts, kerosene cans, kettles, old tele-

These detailed and skillfully composed still-life drawings of fish and vegetables were created by talented upper elementary grade children in Japan.

phones, old shoes and hats, lawn mowers, scooters, musical instruments, sports equipment, bird cages, and nature's bounty of seashells, driftwood, feathers, antlers, gourds, and plants.

In *blind contour drawing* the students must look intently at the object and draw its contours or edges without looking at their papers. They should be reminded not to let their eyes move faster than their drawing tools. When drawing complex subject matter they may depart from the blind approach at critical junctures, look at the object, and reposition their drawing tools on the paper. In their first attempts at contour delineation, the students should be instructed to press forcefully with their pencils and to draw very slowly. Erasure lines should be discouraged; instead, a second or third line may be attempted to correct an unsatisfactory first effort.

Drawing tools suggested for the contour technique include soft- or medium-lead pencils (the large kindergarten pencil is ideal), felt-nib or nylon-tipped pens, eye droppers filled with ink, and sharpened sticks, twigs, or dowels, which if dipped in ink produce a varied, sensitive line when allowed to run dry in their course on the paper.

The contour-line technique is perhaps the most viable and successful drawing method for upper-elementary-grade and middle-school youngsters. Suggest that the students draw in a soft-lead pencil slowly and deliberately, looking intently at the object they are drawing. The figure above is by a middle school student.

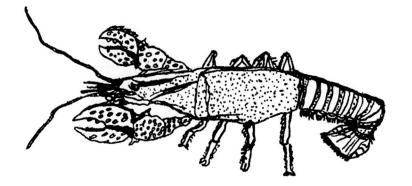

A middle school, life drawing class in action. Notice that the tables were arranged to make one unified drawing area where the model can be viewed easily by all the students. Paper size for sketching was 18 × 24 inches. Tools for drawing included sharpened dowel sticks and twigs dipped in India ink containers. If several drawings are planned, it is recommended that the class model, as well as the position of the model, be changed so that students sketching are afforded a variety of views.

DRAWING THE FIGURE, PORTRAIT, AND SELF-PORTRAIT

What skills and techniques in figure drawing should be introduced and developed in elementary and middle school art programs? What should teachers say to the child regarding the delineation of the figure or the portrait? When, if ever, should the relative proportions of the human figure be identified and emphasized? These are a few of the critical questions regarding life drawing that confront the concerned teacher. The strategy most often proposed, unfortunately, is a laissez-faire placebo. "Let the children alone. They will find their own solutions." This injunction admittedly provides the teacher with a face-saving excuse if the results are less than satisfactory but is hardly the kind of advice given to teachers regarding basic subject areas such as math, reading, and language.

If teachers want the youngsters to grow in their representation of the figure, they must provide learning experiences and practice sessions for such growth. Fortunately, there are some avenues a teacher can pursue to help children develop confidence in life drawing. They can encourage and ensure more intense awareness of the human figure and its characteristics by employing the posed model in art class at every grade level. The delineation of the figure in even the youngest child's drawings does not spring forth from a vacuum. It is the result of the varied encounters the youngster has had in perceiving the human figure both in real life and in its illustrated embodiments in books, magazines, comics, movies, and television. What is wrong, then, with the close attention, the intense perception, and the immediate identification with the figure that the class model offers?

Right: The vibrant colors of oil pastel were skillfully employed to enhance the composition. A real motorcycle was brought to the art room to make the drawing more true to life. Middle school student, Danielsville, Georgia.

Illustrations on this and the facing page reveal the directness and lucidity of portrayal and the attention paid to detail when youngsters draw from the posed class model. The models stood or sat on a table, providing an unobstructed view for all students.

Before the students actually begin the drawing, a warm-up session is generally recommended. Motivating, leading questions should be proposed: What action is the model performing? What is the model wearing? What portion of the model do you see from your drawing station? How large is the model's head in comparison to the body? How big are the hands? Ask students to place one hand over their own faces to realize its size. How large are the feet? They must be big enough to keep the model balanced. Where is the model's arm the biggest—at the shoulders, elbows, or wrists? Where is the model's leg the biggest—at the ankle, knee, or hips? Where does the body, neck, leg, and arm bend? How wide can the feet stretch apart? How high can the arms reach above the head? How far can the body turn around while standing in one position? How far does the arm reach when held at the side?

As the youngsters draw, encourage them to look at the model constantly, carefully, intently—tell them to get their eyes full! Caution them against rushing through their drawing, scribbling, or making hasty, random, meaningless lines. Remind them always to look first and then draw. Encourage making the figure large, filling the page with it, so that they can enrich it with many details, many individual characteristics. See, for example, the illustrated full-figure self-portraits. Sometimes it proves helpful if the children begin their drawing of a figure with the head at the top of the page (unless the model is holding something over his or her head).

In drawing the figure, the size of the head generally determines the size of the figure. If the students draw the head too small, the body won't fill the page; if they draw the head too large, they will not be able to fit the whole body on the page. But there are exceptions to this generalization. Children in the primary grades often draw the heads very large but somehow manage to minimize the rest of the body to fit it on the page (see illustrations), and some youngsters who draw tiny heads will stretch the legs to reach the bottom of the page. In both cases the results can be most charming and naively childlike.

When children draw their classmates, be prepared for the occasional self-conscious titter or embarrassed laughter. Be understanding when a student does not want to model for the class. There are always volunteers. The students' first struggling efforts in figure drawing should not discourage them or their teachers.

Figure drawing, like all drawing from life, teaches the child to be observant in many ways. It is amazing how quickly the growing, discerning youngsters notice embellishing details such as belts, ribbons, shoelaces, buckles, buttons, necklaces, earrings, bracelets, wristwatches, pockets, insignia, collars, cuffs, wrinkles, zippers, pleats, eyeglasses, teeth braces, hair combs, or the patterns on clothes such as stripes, checks, florals, diamonds, herringbone weave, and plaids, employing them to enrich their drawings.

Figure drawing from the model, especially in upper-elementary grades and middle school, can often lead to the use of the figure or group of figures in a painting, collage, print, or mural. The line drawings themselves, either in pen, pencil, brush, or crayon, have a validity, presence, and charm of their own. Subject-matter themes such as "I am playing ball, I am riding my bike, I am flying a kite, I am brushing my teeth, I am holding my pet, I am playing a musical instrument, I am holding a bouquet of flowers, I am cheerleading, I am skipping rope, I am a ballet dancer, I am a football or basketball player, I am watering the garden or lawn, I am on my swing, I am playing tennis, I am setting the table, I am exploring space, I am twirling a hoola hoop, and I am lifting

Illustrated on the next two pages are self-portraits by schoolchildren from grades one through eight. The medium is black crayon or felt nib marker on 9- by 18-inch manila paper. Activities portrayed range from flying a kite to playing the piano. Approximate drawing time was 90 minutes.

GRADE ONE   GRADE TWO   GRADE THREE   GRADE FOUR

GRADE FIVE

GRADE SIX

GRADE SEVEN

GRADE EIGHT

This direct yet sensitively drawn model of a seated adolescent was created by a middle school youngster in a U.S. Defense Department school in Manila, Philippines.

barbells" lend themselves effectively to space-filling compositions.

Because many teachers believe they lack the expertise to guide children in figure-drawing techniques, they settle for what the youngsters can accomplish on their own. The children should get help, but the wrong kind of direction is not the answer either. Formulas such as stick or sausage figures and face proportions measured by rulers can create a stereotype dependence. The best instruction emphasizes heightened observation and repeated simple-to-complex drawings.

Figure-drawing strategies to employ with primary- and middle-grade children in elementary school have already been described. Successful approaches in figure delineation to whet and hold the interest of upper-elementary grade and middle school students follow:

Pose a student in a colorful costume (clown, cowboy, dancer) or sports uniform so that everyone in class has a clear view of the model. The elevation needed may involve the use of a table or counter top.

Pose the model in the center of a circle of sketching classmates affording each child a different view. Change the action and direction of the model chosen on subsequent poses. This approach results in an interesting overlapping, multifigure composition.

Introduce new drawing and sketching tools such as free-flowing felt-nib markers, small watercolor brushes, Q-tips, eye droppers, twigs, and balsa woodsticks sharpened at one end as ink applicators, as well as charcoal and conté crayon.

Pose the student model against a sheet of cardboard, hardboard, or Masonite, approximately 4 × 8 feet—in any case, slightly larger than the model chosen. This will help the youngsters relate the posed figure to the boundaries of their paper. For additional interest you may decorate the board with drapery, burlap, fish net, or colorful posters.

Demonstrate new techniques and directions in drawing the figure: contour, gesture, scribble, and mass methods. Suggest cutting the figure out of construction paper without a preliminary drawing.

Suggest a pose with more than one student taking part. Stage the model in conjunction with a background still-life arrangement.

Challenge the students to use their imagination in drawing. Let the action or stance of the model trigger a fantastic or legendary figure they can capture in line.

Assign different class members to take 5- or 10-minute turns in posing in various sports actions. Suggest that the students overlap the figures as they draw.

Vary the size of the paper the youngsters use for drawing or sketching. Try a 9 × 18-inch or 12 × 24-inch sheet for a standing figure. Challenge them to fill the page.

If you have sufficient space in your classroom or art room, give the youngsters the opportunity to express themselves on large 24 × 36-inch paper with wide felt-nib markers, giant chunk crayons, syringes filled with ink, or big watercolor brushes.

Introduce a variety of papers on which to draw: plain newsprint, cream or gray manila, white drawing paper, assorted-colors construction paper, wallpaper samples, white or brown wrapping paper, and classified ad sheets from the daily newspaper.

Older youngsters might benefit from the exploitation of varied resource material such as a real skeleton, a department-store mannequin, or a life-size medical chart of the body muscle structure.

Inexpensive, lightweight drawing boards can be constructed out of heavyweight chipboard, hardboard, or Masonite. The edges of these boards (recommended size 18 × 24 inches) can be protected with edge-overlapping masking tape. During the drawing sessions these boards can be tilted against table or desk, giving the student a better working position from which to view the model. These boards are excellent for drawing field trips.

Fifth- and sixth-grade youngsters created these sophisticated self-portraits employing oil pastels on black construction paper. Preliminary drawing was in white chalk or crayon. Notice the perceptive and sensitive handling of the eyes, eyelids, hair, and face planes. The birds add an effective counterpoint to the figures. Iowa City, Iowa.

For action or gesture drawing that requires a loose and free approach, the youngsters should to hold the crayon, pen, pencil, charcoal, or chalk horizontally as they sketch rather than in the tight, upright manner used in writing.

One of the most effective and immediate subjects for expressive drawings in all grades is the children themselves. The self-portrait or portrait of a classmate should be on the agenda of every school art program.

Motivations for portrait drawing should include among other things a visual presentation of color slides, films, and reproductions revealing different styles and media of portraiture as expressed by noted artists, past and present. Widen the student's horizons by showing portrait studies by Leonardo da Vinci, Albrecht Dürer, Hans Holbein, Rembrandt van Rijn, Jan Vermeer, Diego Velasquez, Edgar Degas, Henri Matisse, Vincent Van Gogh, Amadeo Modigliani, Thomas Gainsborough, Pablo Picasso, George Bellows, Grant Wood, Ben Shahn, Mary Cassatt, and Andrew Wyeth.

Teachers should, if possible, divert the students from their reliance on the typical portrait stereotype: the symmetrical frontal pose with arms stiffly at the side. Instead, suggest using the arms and hands as contrasting counterpoints in the total composition. Assorted objects to hold or manipulate, uniforms, costumes, and a variety of headware add interest to portrait depiction. Here are some suggested poses: holding or playing a musical instrument, holding sports equipment, putting on a hat, combing or brushing hair, applying makeup using a hand mirror, holding an open umbrella, holding a bouquet of flowers, with arms folded above the head or

It is extremely important that students have rich visual stimulation to create quality artwork. Many teachers build an ever-changing still-life environment in their classrooms or art rooms as a challenging and continuing motivational resource. Here a young adolescent, interestingly attired, models against a panoply of intriguing antique Americana artifacts. The resulting contour drawing on the facing page by a middle school youngster is testimony to the success of this teaching strategy.

akimbo, straddling a chair with head resting on folded arms, holding a small pet. The use of the three-quarter or full-profile view should also be considered. Often the background against which the classmate poses can add immeasurably to the composition: a foliage arrangement, a multipaned window, a giant travel poster, and a folding screen are examples.

Stereotyped portraiture is usually the result of hasty, superficial observation. If the teacher can bring the students to look intently at the model, whether it be their own image in a mirror or classmates posing for them, to pay close attention to their unique characteristics, a giant step toward qualitative portrait drawing results. Discuss different shapes of the head, how it changes from brow to cheek, from cheek to chin. Call attention to the hairline, how the hair follows the contour of the head. No scribbles allowed! Discuss the shape of the ears (tell them to feel their ears) and their junction to the head, the possibilities of delineating the nose (show drawings by Henri Matisse, Pablo Picasso, and Ben Shahn), the delineation of the lips as two subtly differing forms, and the eyelids so important as complementary features to the eyes. In a motivating discussion bring out the astonishing fact that no two people, no two faces, are alike and, furthermore, that even the two sides of the same person's face are not alike.

If the youngsters are sometimes concerned that their drawing does not look like the posed model, tell them that the aim of expressive portraiture is not the achievement of a photographic likeness but one that captures the spirit or character of the subject, that the same model drawn by various artists would look different in each rendition.

Although many of the suggestions on portraiture offered here will be more applicable to the upper-elementary grade or middle school youngsters, wise teachers will be able to adapt the recommendations to benefit the younger children as well.

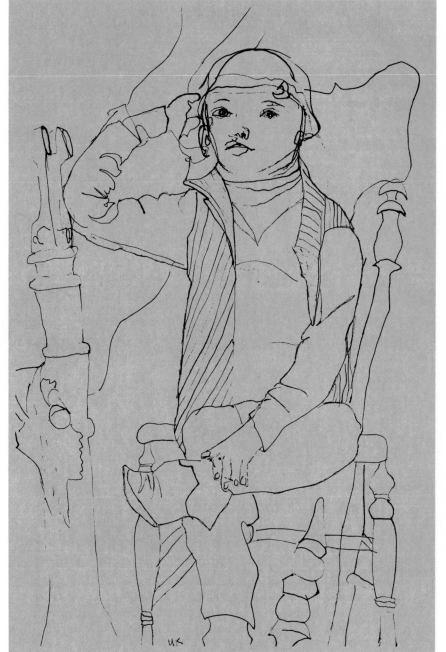

How sensitively observed, drawn, and delineated is this charmingly complex neighborhood scene viewed from a school window. Notice how the free-form preliminary washes tie the composition together and how the overlapping trees create a subtle depth in space. Notice, too, the variety employed in the lines, shapes, and positions of the buildings, the windows, and the roofs, and finally, observe how the houses and trees terminating at the paper's edge create avenues leading the viewer into the composition. Medium is brush, ink, and watercolors on white drawing paper. Actual size. Grade 9, Dubuque, Iowa.

DRAWING THE LANDSCAPE OR CITYSCAPE

Although very young children in the elementary school primary grades enjoy drawing simple themes and single objects such as a butterfly, bird, pet, themselves, a classmate, or a house, maturing youngsters respond to the challenge of the complex composition: the still life, the landscape, and the cityscape. In the upper-elementary grades and middle school they are interested in outdoor sketching and the excitement of field trips. The busy and infinitely varied world beckons and unfolds at their doorsteps.

The building construction down the street
The challenging perspective down an alleyway
The colorful and crowded street of shops
The giant city skyscrapers
The county fair
The cluster of farm buildings on a country road
The city park bandstand
The church, cathedral, synagogue, shrine, and temple
The boat marina
The harbor with its ships
Cape Canaveral at launch time
The view from a bedroom or classroom window
The factories and foundries
The amusement parks
The bus, train, and airport terminals
The gas station
Special places such as Six Flags, Watts Towers, Frontier Land, and Disneyland

These sites, as well as imagined cities of the future, can become the inspiration for their sketches, compositions, paintings, prints, and collages. A variety of media can be used for field-trip sketching: pencil, chalk (school chalk is recommended for sketches and preliminary drawings on colored construction-paper backgrounds), charcoal, crayon, felt-nib or nylon-tip marker, conté crayon, a stick dipped in ink, depending on the maturity of the youngsters.

A majority of children on a field trip draw with enthusiasm and confidence, but a number of them will besiege the teacher with perplexing questions such as: "What should I draw first?" "Where should I start on the paper?" "Must I put everything in my picture?" Sometimes the complex view overwhelms them. Often the spatial and perspective problems confuse them. Fortunately, there are proven avenues to successful landscape and cityscape drawing that teachers have found helpful in guiding their students. In one approach the instructor recommends that the youngster begin with a light pencil or chalk sketch to establish the basic shapes and general outline. Values and details can be added later.

Another strategy that is successful (and also recommended in the section "Drawing the Still Life"), especially when the view is complex, is to have the students begin by drawing the shape in the center of the site—a doorway, window, telephone pole, tree—and draw it as completely as they can and then proceed to draw the shape to the right and left of it, above and below it, and so on, until they fill their paper to the border. They will find and discover that incomplete shapes touching the paper's edge will create line avenues into their compositions. Encourage them to enrich their drawings, adding details, patterns, and textural effects. There will be instances of students who draw on a very small scale whose composition will not fill the space. Every composition should be accepted on its own merits, although its design potential should always be encouraged.

Problems youngsters have with defining distance in space can often be clarified by an understanding and employ-

Drawing landscapes or cityscapes directly at the site is recommended for upper elementary grades and middle school, but sometimes conditions make it inadvisable. The illustrations center and bottom on the facing page as well as the oil pastel composition above show what can be accomplished when youngsters draw from a series of selected color slides projected on a screen. First the instructor projected slides of towers, steeples, and chimneys, which were drawn high on the page; then facades and store fronts with

ment of the following guidelines: Objects or shapes in the foreground plane, those closer to the observer, are usually drawn larger, lower on the page, and in more detail. Objects farther away from the viewer, in the background plane, are usually drawn smaller, higher on the page, and with less observable detail. Effective space is subtly created by overlapping shapes and elements in the composition, such as a fence, tree, or telephone pole against a building.

Simple perspective principles based on the employment of the horizon line, vanishing points, and converging lines should be introduced only when the youngster indicates a need for them. Youngsters in grades seven and eight in the middle school will probably be ready for this challenge. Simple exercises in perspective may appeal to them, but remind them that mastery of perspective rules does not ensure compositional success.

Sketching field trips should be undertaken only with adequate planning and preparation on the part of both teacher and students. Permission to be away from school must be cleared with the principal's office, and, when necessary, signed permission slips should be obtained from the parents. Arrangements for use of the school bus or alternate transportation should be made well in advance. If possible, exciting subject matter should be scouted by the teacher beforehand. Avoid the barren view or monotonous vista that provides little opportunity for a varied breakup of compositional space.

A class discussion before the field trip is a means of emphasizing specific challenges in advance. Things to look

their characteristic signs were projected for the middle plane; and finally, street furniture, lamps, telephone poles, hydrants, mailboxes, traffic lights and signs, parked cars, motorcycles, and trucks were projected to complete the foreground composition.

for include the architecturally significant character of the buildings; value contrasts of windows in daylight; foreground space to be allowed for steps and porches; and suggestions on making roads, sidewalks, and fences recede.

On the day of the field trip the teacher should review rules of behavior for such excursions and remember to caution students about respecting private property in the sketching vicinity. Directions for proceeding to and returning from the sketching site should be made clear, especially if it is within walking distance from the school. Keep the class in a line or group, bringing up stragglers when necessary. Appoint responsible monitors. If roads or highways are to be crossed, stop signs to be held by teacher or monitors to warn and halt traffic are recommended.

In most instances materials or supplies for drawing or sketching should be distributed to the class before leaving the classroom. In some cases the teacher may want to carry the drawing tools until the site is reached and gather them up again at the close of the field trip. Students can carry their own drawing boards if they walk to the site. A recommended drawing board for field trips is an 18 × 24-inch piece of Masonite or hardboard with its edges protected by masking tape. Drawing paper can easily be stapled or tacked to this board. If a bus is used, class monitors can be responsible for bringing the materials, drawing tools, sketchboards, extra paper, and thumbtacks, which can be distributed on arrival. It is the teacher's responsibility to check beforehand that there are enough boards and supplies.

At the sketching site the teacher should discourage students from sitting too close together. Teachers have learned from experience that many a field trip can end up as a time-wasting social hour.

The teacher should remind the students that in drawing the landscape or cityscape they may use the artist's prerogatives of changing, adding, deleting, or simplifying what they see at the sketch site and that the criterion is not necessarily photographic reality or rigidly measured perspective. If the students desire they may add more trees, fences, telephone poles, fire escapes, air vents, chimneys, or windows; they may change a roof line or the cast of a shadow; they may delete a parked car, a trash dumpster, a billboard, or graffiti on a wall. Each decision they make, however, should be qualified by design considerations, so that the final composition embodies the dynamic rules of art: variety, unity, balance, emphasis, contrast, and repetition.

The most important responsibility of the teacher at the sketching site is to guide the students in a self-evaluation of their drawings, employing the perennial principles of composition and design; but in the final essence, if all the teachers did was to bring the youngsters to *see* something they had not really seen before, to *notice* something they had never noticed until then—perhaps the molding or cornice on a door or window frame, the shadow of a tree against a wall, the tilt of a telephone, the overlapping pattern of shingles, the color of a terra cotta tile, the intricacy and beauty of stained glass, the variety in tree bark, or the texture of a brick wall—they have succeeded in enriching the lives of their students a thousandfold, because they may have started them on an exciting quest for shapes, patterns, textures, and color—on an endless journey of discovery.

Facing page: A Shinto shrine comes to life in this sensitive and highly detailed drawing by a sixth grade youngster from Osaka, *Japan. Note how the tiles on the roof, the shoji window panes, and the pebbles on the ground are painstakingly delineated.*

Youngsters look at everyday objects with a new understanding and appreciation when they are challenged to draw them seriously and perceptively. Widen their horizons by introducing them to a host of exciting artifacts and antiques as subject matter for their art expression. An old coffee grinder, a railroad lantern, a kerosene lamp, a mantle clock, an antique sewing machine, a steam iron, and assorted musical instruments take on new dimensions when captured in sensitive drawings. Discover your own early Americana treasures and then share them with your students through art.

DRAWING THE STILL LIFE

The still-life arrangement, whether as inspiration for drawing, painting, print, or collage, is an especially effective means of encouraging awareness and keen observation; of developing a sensitive perception of shapes, contours, and proportions; and of appreciating the subtle, shallow space achieved through overlapping of arranged objects. It also provides the added bonus of initiating a growing interest in, and appreciation of, commonly observed everyday things. The creatively planned still-life arrangement offers the most immediate and commonly available motivational resource that teachers of art have at their command.

From the third grade on children can be guided to see the limitless design possibilities in still-life compositions. The best still-life arrangements are similar in many respects to complex cityscapes; observe for example, how a tableau of buildings and a group of bottles on a table present the same compositional challenge.

In selecting objects for a still-life arrangement, teachers and students should be avid scavengers and scouts, continually searching for a variety of objects, both old and new. Antique shops, secondhand stores, garage sales, army-surplus warehouses, flea markets, attics, basements, and garage sales can provide rich sources for unusual and visually stimulating objects that can contribute to exciting still lifes. Eschew the trite, miniature figurine or bud vase.

The still life in various forms is constantly a part of our everyday environments. We live in a world of still-life arrangements: the piled-up desk; the cluttered kitchen sink; the open garage, car trunk, tool shed, cupboard, or closet; the box of playground equipment; and the table set for dinner.

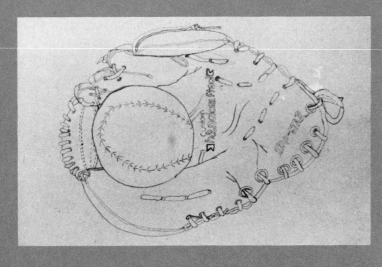

The placement of the various objects in the creation of a still life is critical to the ultimate success of the composition or design. Sometimes it is possible to make the construction of the still life a motivating, adventurous part of the art lesson with the students as participators. Arrange the objects, for example, on an antique table, old sewing machine, ancient rocker, stepladder, window ledge, desk top, or table in the middle of the room where the children can be seated in a circle as they draw. Employ a variety of heights and levels (use cardboard cartons as well as plastic or wooden crates or storage units as supports); create space through placing some objects behind others; work for an informal rather than formal balance in the arrangement. Use assorted fabrics, colorful beach towels, flags, banners, fish net, bedspreads, quilts, afghans, or tablecloths as drapery to unify the separate elements or to suggest movement from one area to another.

In most cases the more objects used in the still-life grouping, the more opportunities the youngsters have for selection and rejection. Indeed, the more objects the students include in their compositions, the more effectively and richly they achieve a successful pictorial design. As in all creative undertakings, no two still-life interpretations will be alike, even though the youngsters work from the same arrangement.

There are several ways to begin drawing the still life, as veteran teachers have discovered. One recommended strategy that children respond to, and have success with, is to begin by drawing the central object in the still life seen from their point of view and placing it in the middle of their paper. They then continue drawing the objects next to it, left and right, above and below, until they have either filled the page or completed the still-life arrangement. This suggests that the more varied, complex, and abundant the still life is, the more space filling the composition will be.

The most common everyday object is a likely subject for drawing, but artists have often found that items which specifically relate to or fit the human body possess unique lifelike qualities and natural contours that lend themselves most beautifully to dynamic, effective drawing. Among them are gloves, sandals, shoes, boots, caps, hats, jackets, masks, and sports gear such as baseball mitts.

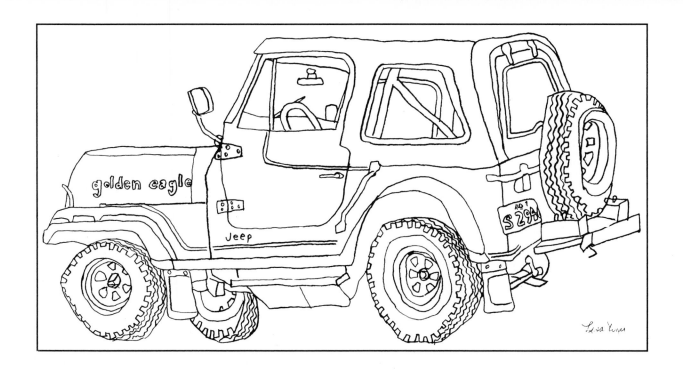

Vehicles such as Jeeps, campers, and station wagons afford excellent possibilities for contour-line drawing, as shown in these two illustrations from the American Military Dependents School in Seoul, Korea.

In most instances the teacher, with the assistance of the students, arranges the still life employing varied levels, objects of contrasting sizes and shapes, and unifying elements such as fabrics and plants.

Another tactic is to have students select items from a general store of still-life material, choosing one object at a time to sketch at their desks or tables, building their compositions gradually, employing the principles of variety in size and shape of objects, overlapping, repetition, avenues into the composition, and informal balance.

Some teachers suggest to their students that they make a light, tentative sketch in pencil, charcoal, or chalk to obtain a general, allover rendering of the arrangement. This preliminary drawing is then developed, stage by stage, employing value (light and dark) and texture effects, pattern, shading, detail, and linear emphasis.

Still life in contour line by middle grade student, Iowa City, Iowa, exemplifies successful manipulation of the picture plane. Notice how quiet areas complement detailed sections and how the eye is led into the picture by lines that intersect with the borders.

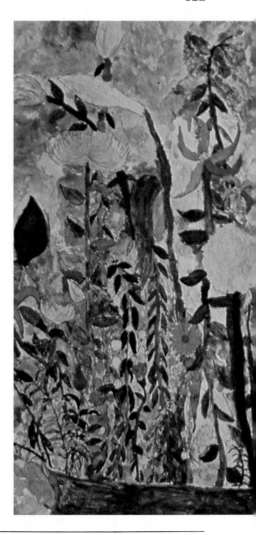

The still-life interpretations on this and the facing page are a visible testament to the variety of art techniques youngsters can choose to make their graphic statements. **Left to right:** *Crayon, grade 1; tissue-paper collage, grade 3; watercolor, grade 6; found-materials collage, grade 5; oil pastel on colored construction paper, grade 6. The common denominator in all of them is an effective use of the picture plane.*

Pencils, sticks cut to a point and dipped in ink, and felt-nib or nylon-tipped pens are recommended for small, intimate sketches. Charcoal, conté crayon, chalk, crayon, oil pastel, Q-tips, eye-droppers filled with ink, and large-size blunt or square-tipped ink markers can be used effectively on large-sized compositions. Drawing surfaces suggested include newsprint, cream or gray manila paper, colored construction paper, brown and white kraft or butcher paper, and wallpaper remnants or samples. A simple yet inexpensive drawing board can be salvaged from a giant cardboard carton. A more sturdy board—called hardboard—is commercially available. Cut it into rectangles approximately 18 × 24 inches and edge it with masking tape. These boards can also be used as drawing surfaces on classroom desks.

An animal drawing project or lesson might begin with a trip to the zoo. Before the excursion the teacher and children might discuss the special characteristics of selected zoo denizens, including the unique features of the various species—their stance, action, and individual physical attributes. Attention might be called to the textural pattern of the rhino's skin; to the wrinkled, leathery face of the orangutan; to the repeated yet ever varied spots of the leopard; to the rhythmic rings of the armadillo; to the subtle op-art variations of the zebra's stripes; and to the gracefully curved horns of the antelope.

When the youngsters draw, they should be encouraged to take advantage of the paper's proportions to fill the page. The larger the drawing, the more opportunities the child will have to define and delineate characteristic detail, pattern, and texture.

These on-the-site drawings might be limited to capturing significant form, to an expressive line sketch that might de-

Top: Drawing by Dutch artist Rembrandt von Rijn. Center: Drawing inspired by a visit to the zoo. Primary grade, Ann Arbor, Michigan. Bottom: Woodblock by Kiyoshi Saito, contemporary Japanese printmaker. Note how the grain of the wood is exploited to add to the allover design.

scribe the spirit of the animal, rather than to attempting a completed, detailed study. The refinements and textural nuances can be added later when the students return to class.

It is recommended that upper-elementary-grade and middle-school students on sketching excursions limit their drawing activity to a single animal, developing the study in depth. This practice is more beneficial than cursory attempts to draw several different animals in the limited time usually allowed to field trips. If scheduling permits, the teacher may plan subsequent visits so that the youngsters will have ample opportunity to sketch a number of animals. Students might also be encouraged to draw detailed studies of an animal's eye, ear, snout, or horns.

Suggest that the youngsters draw the animals in some characteristic action such as resting, grazing, running, bathing, or grooming and nursing their young. Older students can be challenged to note the peculiar stance of the animal: the swinging rhythm of the chimpanzee, the arching stretch of the giraffe, the sway of the elephant's trunk, or the nervous tension of a horse's legs—all serving as keys to successful animal drawing.

Careful, deliberate observation and sensitive handling of line, both contour and gesture, are fundamental requirements in the drawing of animals. For inspiration let the youngsters look at celebrated animal drawings: Rembrandt van Rijn's lion and elephant; Eugene Delacroix's horses and those by Chinese Han- and Sung-period artists; Albrecht Dürer's hare, squirrel, and rhinoceros; and Andrew Wyeth's birds.

Drawing or sketching from the animal itself is the pri-

Center: A mounted owl served as the immediate inspiration for this sensitively drawn composition by an upper-elementary-grade youngster. Notice the expressive delineation of the fine feather pattern. The leafy background drawn from a potted plant complements the bird's mass. **Bottom:** *Notice how the seaweed performs the same unifying function for the fish. Grade 5.*

mary recommendation, but when this prospect is out of the question, supplemental motivation—color slides, films, filmstrips, opaque projections of magazines, and book illustrations, including photos provided by the zoos and government agencies—can provide the necessary vicarious enrichment. In the primary grades the visual material might be examined and discussed and then posted on the bulletin board for further reference. Photographs and color slides fulfill a definite need, but it should be made clear to the student that they serve for inspirational and informational reference only and are not to be traced or rigidly copied.

The students need to be reminded also to consider the entire composition in their drawings of animals. In too many instances the animal is isolated in the middle of the paper, floating in space without a hint of complementary foreground or background atmosphere. To aid the students in this respect the teacher might hold a discussion on the exploitation or handling of the surrounding space, including the introduction of enriching compositional elements such as trees, shrubs, grasses, rocks, bushes, vines, hills, cliffs, clouds, and companion animals in foreground or background.

Unusual and interesting plants, dried foliage, roots, stones, and flowers can serve as visual reference motifs for the animals' habitat. Rocks and twigs from the immediate school vicinity might be drawn in giant size to become escarpments, mountains, and jungle trees.

Both in the classroom and on field excursions youngsters should be provided with continuing opportunities to draw directly from nature's bounty, to become aware of nature as an endless source of design.

---

*The animal world has always proven fascinating to child artists. It is fortunate that the variety of species in the animal kingdom (encompassing birds, fish, and insects) is virtually limitless. **Top:** A third-grade child captures the essence of a leopard by emphasizing its spots. **Center and bottom:** Sixth-grade youngsters sketched these animals at a natural museum. Medium is oil pastel.*

The boldly direct and colorful painting of a watercolor box in use is by a talented teenager and was exhibited at the School Art Symposium, sponsored by the art department of the University of Georgia, Athens.

PAINTING WITH WATERCOLORS

Tempera is probably the most common and most popular painting medium in elementary and middle school art programs, but in many instances teachers schedule painting experiences employing transparent watercolors. These watercolors are commercially produced paints in semimoist cakes, packaged in metal or plastic containers, available in primary and secondary colors plus black.

Transparent watercolor painting, as teachers and youngsters soon learn, demands special technical skills. Mature art students and professional painters devote countless hours to its mastery, employing a wide range of watercolors available in tube form as well as costly sablehair brushes. School projects in watercolor, limited too often by the time allotted to art, succeed if they manage to introduce the children to simple, basic techniques in this medium.

The watercolor paintings illustrated in this section are by Japanese elementary school children who are provided with a spectrum of watercolors in tubes and painting palettes from the first grade on. The majority of their watercolor paintings begin with a preliminary sketch in pencil or pen. In some cases the children moisten the paper before beginning the coloring. As these paintings reveal, they persevered and produced rich, space-filled compositions that exhibit the characteristic spontaneity of transparent watercolors.

Employing the possibilities of this mercurial medium, teachers worldwide have introduced their students to free-flowing watercolor painting on wet paper to discover new

This delightfully entrancing watercolor titled My Friend and Me *is the work of a first grade child in Japan.*

color transparencies, often resulting in expressively abstract and sometimes nonobjective compositions in the manner of Wassily Kandinsky, Arthur Dove, Paul Jenkins, and John Marin. Others have successfully employed watercolors in "Painting-to-Music" projects.

Teachers in upper-elementary grades and middle schools often employ the semimoist watercolors to instruct their students in the study and mastery of color properties: hue, value, and intensity. They introduce the mixing of primary colors to obtain secondary colors and secondary colors to obtain tertiary colors; they suggest the mixing or dilution of a color with water in gradual stages to produce a color-value chart; and they help their students become aware of color neutralization through the mixing of complementary hues. Teachers also encourage the youngsters in creating watercolor washes on moist paper to achieve dark-to-light sky and water effects.

A primer for watercolor projects

White watercolor or construction paper is generally recommended for watercolor paintings. For studies and practice washes, manila paper is often employed.

Newspapers placed under paintings in progress help expedite cleanup chores. They often provide a surface to practice on.

Round, pointed, soft-bristle, camel-hair brushes are recommended for painting. They should always be rinsed clean at the end of the art period and stored bristle-side up or flat in a container.

Watercolor boxes containing the semimoist cakes of paint should be rinsed and wiped clean at the close of the art period and then allowed to dry open.

Watercolor paintings such as those illustrated on this page display the spontaneous quality associated with this medium. **Bottom and top:** *Japanese elementary school children.* **Center:** *Intermediate grade child. Iowa City, Iowa.*

Water containers should be changed when the water in them becomes muddy. Paper towels are a handy asset for spills and for blotting or soaking up excess paint on work in progress.

Preliminary sketches in pencil, felt-nib or nylon-tipped pen, or light watercolor applied with a small brush are generally recommended for pictorial compositions.

Areas or sections in the painting that should appear white or light in the final result can be masked with rubber cement or masking tape cut to the shape desired. This should be done before the paper is moistened or the painting begun. When the painting is completed and dry, the masking elements may be removed by rubbing or peeling. A final touch-up may then be made.

Watercolor washes of the same color in the same value applied over one another will tend to darken the color. It is generally recommended that students begin a painting with light colors or values of colors and build to darker colors for detail.

When painting on a wet surface, the paper may have to be remoistened from time to time for best results. This may be done by lightly sprinkling the surface with water.

Paintings created by employing semimoist colors appear vibrant and contrasting when moist but unfortunately lose their brilliance when dry. A second application of watercolor paint over a dried color may help

Watercolor paintings while wet or moist should not be stored on top of one another. If no drying rack is available, store them on the floor around the perimeters of the room.

Many teachers have discovered through experience that some of the most successful projects employing watercolor as a painting medium are those in which it is combined with colored crayons as in the technique described fully in the section "Crayon Resist."

The watercolor painting on this page of a still life Bouquet of Flowers *was created by an art-gifted Japanese girl. Grade 6.*

An exuberantly expressive use of tempera in a wide range of hues marks this delightful painting The Bunnies' Easter Egg Hunt Party, *12 × 18 inches, by a primary-grade school child. Colored construction paper served as the background.*

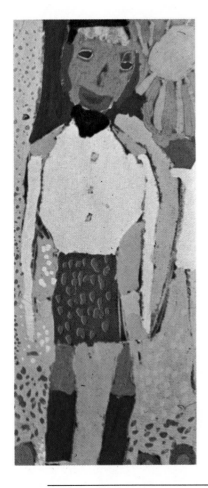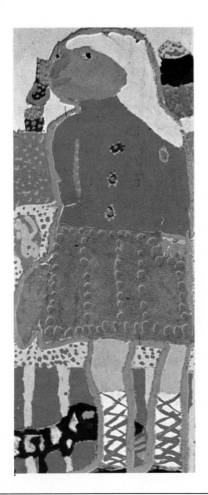

These large, 12 × 24-inch, colorful tempera paintings prove once more how distinctly individual youngsters can be in their art expression, even though the medium employed and the theme, in this case "A Self-Portrait," is the same. Here again, qualitative, in-depth art-teaching strategies are the key: the preparation and pa-tience involved in mixing a varied range of tempera hues, the time devoted to making preliminary sketches, as well as the many deliberate, personal choices in selecting and applying the colors. Grade 3, Oshkosh, Wisconsin.

Caution children about painting next to a wet paint area so that colors will not run together.

When making a color change, suggest that the children wait until a color is completely dry before painting over it.

If brushes must be cleaned during the painting session, tell students to squeeze out the excess water thoroughly before using them to paint again. If not, the paint in the individual containers will become water diluted and less intense.

Supervise storage of paintings so that wet paintings are not placed on top of one another. They may be placed to dry on the floor in the classroom or hallway or left on desks and tables if a recess or lunch period follows the painting session.

An upper-elementary-grade youngster completes the painting of a rhinoceros he contributed to a group mural of a jungle theme by retouching the black contour lines. The preliminary drawings were first made with school chalk on large cardboard sheets salvaged from mattress boxes and then reinforced with brush and black tempera, which ensured a variety of line. The children then colored the composition painting up to but not over the black outlines. The murals are presently enlivening the children's ward of a hospital.

In the upper-elementary grades and middle school, youngsters can handle the varied and complex applications of tempera paint because of their developing ability to control the paint and brush. They may design with paint on moist, colored construction paper; use the dry brush or pointillistic approach to achieve texture; and explore the mixed media techniques of combining tempera and crayon, tempera and pastel, and tempera and India ink in a semibatik process.

Older youngsters can be encouraged to mix a greater variety of tints, shades, and neutralized hues to achieve a more individual and personal style. They can use discarded pie tins, TV dinner trays, and plastic cafeteria trays for their palettes. They should be cautioned, however, to be economical and not mix more paint than they need. Paint tins should always be rinsed out at the end of painting class.

It is important to remember that concerned youngsters cannot rush through a tempera-painting project any more than they can hurry through any qualitative creative endeavor; therefore, sufficient time must be allotted for all phases of the undertaking: motivational resource period; preliminary sketching session; the studio activity involving color choices; achievement of contrast, pattern, and detail; evaluation of the work in its several stages; and finally, the exhibition of the completed paintings.

Tempera painting should by all means be included in every elementary and middle school art program, because it enriches and expands the youngster's world of color and color relationships.

Top: Record cover design. Tempera paint. Middle school, Athens, Georgia. Bottom: Two middle school students engaged in painting their designs for a record cover in tempera paint.

 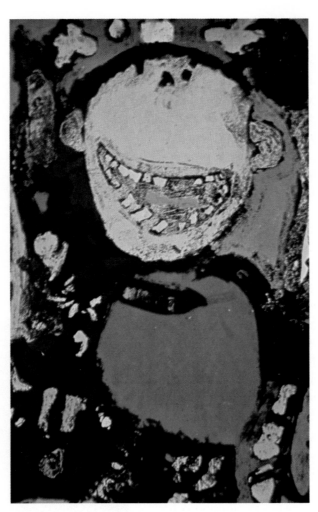 

TEMPERA RESIST

For middle-school youngsters who have had many elementary-school experiences painting with tempera per se, the tempera resist that employs both a liquid-tempera underpainting and a final coating of India ink is a challenging technique replete with hidden surprises. Although highly recommended as an exciting project in painting, it presents a number of materials problems, among them the high cost of India ink, that must be resolved before successful results are achieved.

The tempera paint employed should be a good quality liquid tempera. Powdered tempera is not recommended, although some art teachers claim that, mixed with a small amount of liquid glue, the powdered tempera works. Liquid or powder, the paint must be of a creamy consistency. Watery paint will absorb the final ink coating rather than resist it. Bright, intense hues of tempera should be employed for the highest contrast of black ink against color. Dark blue, dark purple, and brown tempera do not provide such contrast. Subtle grayed hues such as sienna, ochre, light umber, and light gray are effective. White may be employed with discrimination but generally should be repeated, since a solitary white area often detracts from the rest of the composition.

The second important consideration concerns the type of paper best adapted to this process. Successful tempera resists made by the author years ago employed a sturdy paper called

*Steps in creating a tempera-India ink resist. The preliminary drawing is made in school chalk on white or light-colored construction paper. Paint is applied up to the chalk outline but not covering it. Allow the paint to dry completely. India ink undiluted is applied generously over the tempera surface, allowed to dry thoroughly, and then rinsed off at sink. **Facing page:** Tempera resist, grade 1.*

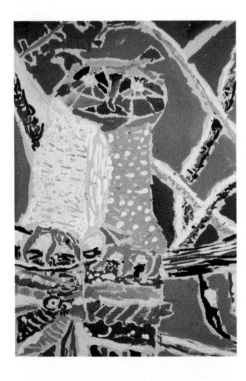

"Muraltex board," but this textured cardboard, unfortunately, is no longer on the market, so teachers have turned to substitutes: construction paper in white or light colors (orange, pink, light purple, and blue are suggested), cardboard scraps from store cartons, oatmeal paper (if available), and cream manila (because of its fragility, special care must be employed during the rinsing phase).

The third factor concerns the amount of time needed for the various steps in the process: the preliminary drawing, the tempera painting, the inking, the rinsing, and the coating with clear shellac or polymer gloss (optional).

The sketch or preliminary drawing should be made in school chalk. Encourage the students to vary the pressure of the chalk lines so that they will vary from thick to thin. This will be an important consideration in the second phase when the ink is applied and soaks into the chalked lines. As students paint with the tempera, suggest that they paint up to, but not over, the chalked lines. The more varied the chalk lines or the paper surface remaining between painted areas is, the more successfully contrasting the composition will be. Remind the youngsters not to paint those shapes, areas, and details they want to appear black in the completed painting.

Pressure must be applied when painting so that there is a strong bond of paint to paper. Caution the students that a tempera color painted over another dry tempera area will wash off in the final rinse, so they must plan their color scheme carefully in advance. However, tempera-paint patterns or designs over wet tempera areas can be effective.

Illustrated on this page are before *and* after *results in a tempera and India ink resist project by a middle school youngster. For successful results be sure the tempera paint is a quality brand liquid type. The India ink is used undiluted.*

Flower gardens, birds, insects, butterfly, and clown themes lend themselves most effectively to the tempera-India-ink-resist tech- *nique. Grade 6, Oshkosh, Wisconsin.*

Illustrations above and on facing page are tempera resist paintings by middle school students. Note how beautifully they fill the picture plane. The one on page 147 is drawn from a studio still-life arrangement of found objects, including an animal skull.

Encourage youngsters to be expressive in their color usage, to employ many kinds of green for grass and trees, many values and intensities of blue for skies. After all of the desired colored areas are painted, the work should be stored to dry completely.

For the inking phase cover a working surface with protective newspapers. Wipe off the chalk remaining in the lines with a cloth, paper towel, or facial tissue. Place the painting on newspapers and coat it with India ink using a watercolor or other soft-bristle brush. Apply ink in random, circular strokes. Cover the painting completely and store it to dry completely. The length of the drying time may vary from one to several hours. Do not rinse too soon.

For the final rinsing put the painting on a sheet of Masonite or sturdy plastic and wash or rinse it off using cold water from faucet or spray. As the painting gets wet, it will adhere nicely to the Masonite board. In mild weather the paintings may be taken out of doors and rinsed off with a water hose. Be sure the paintings are always on the board during the washing, because if handled when wet, they will tear very easily.

It is best to begin the rinsing in the center of the work and move outward. Do not direct the water to the same area too long. Too much of the paint will wash off, or, even worse, the paper may disintegrate. Sometimes a moist sponge or finger rub can bring out the color in a section where the ink sticks stubbornly. When the washing is completed, a final clean rinse is important. Lift the painting very carefully, put it on a desk or counter, and blot it with flat, open paper towels; allow it to dry thoroughly.

When the tempera-resist painting is completely dry, it may be given a protective and enhancing coat of clear shellac, liquid wax, or glossy polymer medium.

147

Group mural by primary-grade children employing a reverse stencil method. Each child drew and cut one animal out of tagboard (oaktag), pinned it securely to a 24 × 36-inch or a 36 × 48-inch corrugated cardboard or wallboard, and then applied paint with a spray can. Youngsters who finished first contributed additional birds, trees, bushes, flowers, and butterflies. Animal cutouts were reversed for more variety. Overlapping of animal shapes created unusual special effects. Protective newspapers were pinned around the background cardboard as well as placed on the floor underneath. Spraying of paint should be done in a well-ventilated area.

MURAL MAKING

If the planning and making of a group-project mural is to be a rewarding and worthwhile art experience for the youngsters, the compositional requirements of mural art should be considered as carefully as possible. The students and teacher must decide whether the subject matter and technique are adaptable to a mural undertaking. Certain themes are more appropriate and more justifiable for mural endeavors because of their universality, complexity, and appeal to varied age groups. For very young children the following mural subjects are suggested: A Butterfly Dance, Land of Make Believe, Fish in the Sea, Noah's Ark, and A Flower Garden. Intermediate-elementary-grade children respond to On the Farm, Birds in a Tree, Animals at the Zoo or Animals in the Jungle, Fun on the Playground, When Dragons Roamed the World, and Fun at the Beach. Upper-elementary-grade and middle-school youngsters react positively to Astronauts in Space, A Kite Flying Contest, Aquanauts Exploring the Sea, The Rodeo, Rock Festival, Block Party, State Fair, Three Ring Circus, Winter Carnival, and World of the Future.

Before the class begins a mural, the teacher might ask the following questions: What is a "mural" (from Latin *muras*, meaning "a wall")? What is the purpose of a mural? Who painted the first murals? Show cave paintings from Altamira and Fonte de Gaume. Are there any murals in our city, county, or state? More specifically, the teacher might ask: What theme should we select for our mural? What medium or technique should be employed? How large should our mural

be? Where can we work on it? Where will it be displayed when completed? How shall each student's contribution to the mural be decided?

If, for example, a collage-type, pinup mural is agreed upon, the following procedure is recommended: When all youngsters have completed their individual contributions to the total mural, the teacher and students should devote at least one art session to composing the mural, discussing the merits of the placement and design. Here the teacher's tact and gentle persuasion play an important role. It should be brought to the children's attention that a mural in one sense is like a giant painting and consequently demands much the same compositional treatment. Ask the youngsters to strive for varied sizes of objects or figures, varied heights, varied breakup of space in foreground and background, overlapping of shapes, grouping of objects to achieve unity, quiet areas to balance busy or detailed ones, and larger shapes or figures at the bottom and smaller ones at the top to create an illusion of distance.

Inevitably there will be the delicate dilemma when for compositional reasons one child's work must overlap that of another. Here the teacher can calm troubled waters by pointing out that overlapping shapes create space, suggesting at the same time that the children take turns in overlapping on subsequent mural projects. When the separate segments are finally arranged in a composition that is unifying and pictorially satisfying, they may be more permanently pinned or stapled down. If the mural is stapled to a separate piece of hardboard, celotex, or heavy carton cardboard, it can be dis-

played in the school's entrance foyer, hallway, or lunchroom for all children to enjoy.

If, for example, "Fun on the Playground" is selected as the theme of a mural employing collage (cut and paste) as the medium, the following questions need to be resolved: How many different kinds of games (sports) should be included? List them on the chalkboard. How shall we decide which activity each student will select to portray? How many different areas of the playground will be included? What types of playground equipment will be included? Should all children be the same size? Why not? Will they all be dressed alike? Make a list on the chalkboard of the different kinds of clothing and uniforms they might wear. What patterns might be shown on their clothes? (In this context perhaps wallpaper samples or fabric remnants may be employed for pattern.) What else could be included in the mural? Make a list on the chalkboard: trees, benches, bushes, goal posts, fences, dogs, clouds, sun, birds, airplanes, kites, drinking fountains, nets, signs, lights.

Varied techniques and media may be employed in mural making. For freestyle, expressive murals that are painted directly on background surfaces such as oaktag, cardboard, poster board, and hardboard, use tempera paint, enamels, or latex paint. A preliminary outline in black paint and brush provides a point of departure. Sometimes this black contour

The world of nature constantly provides a variety of themes for exciting mural making as illustrated in these colorful giant collages of animals by first-grade children, fish by upper-elementary-grade youngsters, and birds in a tree by intermediate-elementary-grade children. Each child in class was a contributor.

Billboard mural, 10 × 25 feet, designed and created by second-grade children of Laurens, South Carolina, elementary schools. Medium is wax crayons on billboard paper. Children made small sketches of dragons from which a selection for the billboard was made. A number of youngsters worked on each dragon in tandem so that each child would have an opportunity to contribute. Two donated billboards were on display in the community during Youth Art Month. Illustration courtesy of Davis Publications, Inc., Worcester, Massachusetts. For a detailed description of this unusual project, see the February 1983 issue of School Arts magazine.

may remain to spark the composition. See the Iowa City children's fence mural in this section. For murals that are assembled after children have created the separately assigned segments, use colored construction paper, wallpaper samples, cloth remnants, colored magazine ads, felt-nib felt-tip markers, oil pastel, crayon, and assorted found materials.

Some teachers have taken advantage of the great opportunities for mural display that billboards offer. The whole community shares the wonder and delight of such effort. See what the children of Laurens, South Carolina, created as illustrated in this section.

In the pinup or staple-on type of mural, the children pin their contributions to a selected background such as celotex, hardboard, wall board, or discarded mattress-box cardboard container. Other more lightweight surfaces such as oaktag, display paper, corrugated cardboard, or 24 × 36-inch colored construction paper may be used, but these items must first be attached to a bulletin (cork) board so that the pins or staples will hold. Children who complete their assigned main segments early may volunteer to do additional parts to enhance the composition. Depending on the theme of the mural, these parts may include butterflies, planes, clouds, birds, trees, bushes, fences, benches, rocks, kites, snowflakes, rainbows, sun, moon, stars, telephone poles, signs, street furniture, cars, trucks, bicycles, motorcycles, frisbees, balls, mailboxes, rainbows, dogs, and cats.

The group mural Fun at the Park *was painted by elementary-school children, Iowa City, Iowa, on a 10 × 200-foot plywood construction barrier. The preliminary sketch on the previously paint-primed plywood was made in chalk and then reinforced with black enamel applied with ½-inch and 1-inch wide utility brushes. Parents donated leftover paints in a variety of colors for the project.*

Examples of murals and art room wall displays. **Top:** Stitchery mural by Oconee Elementary School, Georgia, primary grade children. **Bottom right:** *Mural made by pasting small pieces of yarn to* a *Masonite backing.* The Jungle, *Athens Academy, Georgia, grade 3.* **Bottom left:** *Sunflower collage project displayed in art room. Glencoe, Illinois Elementary School, grades 5 and 6.*

A cat and kittens brought to class by the teacher provided the immediate motivation for the colorful, 12 × 18-inch crayon painting illustrated above. The preliminary composition was drawn in line with a white crayon on orange-colored construction paper. Approximately three 50-minute class sessions were required to complete the picture. See the facing page for three more interpretations of the same cat and kittens employing a similar medium. Notice that each one is a highly personal, individualized depiction.

CRAYON

The wax crayon, available today in as many as sixty-four colors, has been a standard and commonly accepted art medium in elementary schools for almost a century. More recently, resourceful teachers have combined it with other media to provide variety and a renewed interest in its exciting potential. A number of these innovative techniques including crayon resist, crayon encaustic, crayon engraving, and multicrayon engraving are described in detail in this book.

Unfortunately, the varied and rich possibilities of the wax crayon with its own singular merits as an expressive coloring agent have not always been fully investigated and employed in the schools. The typical classroom projects in crayon are usually weak in color intensity, value contrast, and texture quality. Crayon is employed in most instances as a pallid, sketchy coloring agent instead of the glowing, vibrant, and excitingly expressive medium it can and should be. It is vitally important that the rich possibilities of the crayon be identified, explored, and implemented from the first grade on, if children are expected to grow in crayoning skills.

At every grade level from one through eight, a studio session of crayon manipulation and experimentation is recommended. Whenever possible, request that the youngsters or the school supply agent obtain the large forty-eight- or sixty-four-color crayon box with its beautiful range of tints and shades of color as well as its wide selection of neutralized hues. To help the children achieve the best results, the teacher may have to prompt the youngsters to apply the

*Crayon was used again most effectively in these interpretations of a tree house illustrated above. Countless motivating questions were proposed. What is a tree house? How large must the tree be? How will you climb to your tree house? What will you store in your tree house? Who will come to visit you in your tree house? Colored construction paper was employed as background for the compositions. Grades 3 and 4. **Facing page:** Insect allover pattern designs. Crayon on colored construction paper. Grade 2.*

crayon with heavier pressure to bring out the deepest, richest color. "Who can make the color sing?" "Who can make it shout?" as opposed to "Who is making it mumble?" Remind children also to use a lot of newspaper padding under the paper to be crayoned; point out the effects of contrasting colors, juxtaposing dark next to light colors, neutral next to high-intensity colors; challenge the students to create patterns of stripes, checks, plaids, diamonds, stars, spirals, and dots. Show them paintings by impressionists and pointillists.

The entire mood and essence of crayon composition changes when the crayon is applied to varicolored or varitextured surfaces. Invite the children to work on backgrounds other than the commonly used cream manila or white drawing paper. Explore the potential and effectiveness of colored construction paper as the crayon surface. Students and teacher alike will be surprised and elated by the results of crayon employed richly on pink, red, orange, purple, blue, green, and even black construction paper. If the children allow some of the background to show, especially between objects, they will eventually notice how the background paper color can unify their compositions. They will also learn how the crayon color changes on different color papers: yellow changes to dull green on black construction paper; all of the warm colors, the reds and oranges, are slightly neutralized when applied to green paper but shimmer vibrantly when applied to red, pink, and orange surfaces.

Preliminary sketches for crayon pictures on colored papers may be made with school chalk or a white, metallic, or light-colored crayon. This will rule out the frustration children experience when they try to manipulate a blunt crayon to color the minuscule details of a pencil sketch. Encourage the children to use the crayon boldly and imaginatively.

Suggest that colors be repeated in different parts of the composition to achieve an echoing unity. Completed crayon pictures may be given a glowing surface sheen by burnishing or rubbing them with a folded paper towel or facial tissue.

One of the most vexing problems the teacher of art faces is that of the children who rush through their crayoning or who quickly color in a few shapes and claim they are finished. There are no sure-fire remedies for such recurring dilemmas, but certainly one of the most successful strategies for ensuring a successful outcome in a crayon project is a teacher's well-planned, resourceful motivation that leads to a richly conceived and detailed preliminary drawing, which in turn provides the basis for the use of the expressive, multi-hued crayon.

A summer flower garden comes to life in this enchanting crayon-resist painting by a second-grade child. Sometimes youngsters call this art process "crayon magic." To be successful in this technique the children must be encouraged and guided to apply the crayons with a strong pressure so that the wax will resist the watercolor. White drawing or construction paper is recommended for the background. A preliminary drawing in a light-colored crayon rather than pencil is suggested.

CRAYON RESIST

The combination of vibrant, glowing wax crayon and translucent, flowing watercolors on white drawing or construction paper provides an exciting, creative art experience for youngsters of all ages. Subject-matter themes that are rich in pattern and allover design such as fish, birds, and reptiles are highly recommended for this technique. The insect world, too, especially butterflies, provides a wealth of inspiration for crayon-resist projects. Youngsters are genuinely excited by the variety of insects found in their environment, and the teacher can stimulate further participation by encouraging them to collect specimens to share with their classmates. Other sources such as illustrated books, periodicals featuring wildlife, color slides, and films will aid in broadening the youngsters' awareness of nature and give them a deeper understanding of its variety.

A study of the insect world especially augments the children's art study, because in the structure of almost every insect they discover various aspects and components of design: the filigree pattern in the wings of a butterfly, dragonfly, and moth; the rhythmlike segments of a grasshopper's abdomen; the contrasting motifs on a cicada's back; the symmetrical balance of a ladybug's body; and the curvilinear grace of a praying mantis's legs.

Children gathered a variety of leaves and drew them in crayon in a bold contour-line technique, emphasizing the veins but not coloring them solidly. They filled the white paper in an allover design, the leaves turning in all directions, some touching, some overlapping. Then using their watercolors and brushes, they applied the transparent colors over and between the leaves.

In the crayon-resist technique, the pattern, details, and designs of the subject to be depicted are of utmost importance, adding as they do to the sparkling effect of the finished painting. Whatever subject theme the youngsters select, the more detail they incorporate into their crayon compositions and the more they overlap the shapes, the richer and more complex the design becomes, and consequently, the negative areas evolve into varied shapes as well. Background embellishment including flowers, weeds, trees, vines, webs, rock formations, pollen, and clouds can help tie the composition together.

A successful crayon resist depends on the following requirements: The crayon must be applied with a heavy pressure so that it will resist the watercolor (or water-diluted tempera) in the final stage of the process. Some teachers demonstrate the recommended method and the watercolor application before crayoning begins so that students can see how hard they must press to achieve the best results. One way to ensure a solid application of crayon is to place several layers of newspaper padding under the sheet to be crayoned. To capitalize on the total effect of this medium, the student should plan to leave certain areas of the paper uncrayoned, for example, between two solid shapes, between two colors, and between object and background color. Negative space can be enriched with a pattern of radiating lines or rippling lines such as those formed around a pebble dropped in water, together with dots, spirals, circles, hatching, crosshatching, and scribble lines.

Encourage the youngsters to be imaginative and experimental in their employment of the crayon colors. Reliance on natural or realistic colors should be minimized. White crayon can be especially effective in this technique, providing a happy, magical surprise when the paint is applied. Black

This outstanding painting of an iguana was created by a fourth grade child in Oshkosh, Wisconsin. The space-filling is commendable, the coloring vibrant. Motivational support by a master teacher added a qualitative dimension to the class project.

crayon provides strong contrast; however, if a final black tempera wash is planned, the black crayon should not be employed in the crayoning stage.

When the crayoning is completed (and after a final evaluation by teacher and student), two techniques of resist may be employed—the wet- or dry-paper process. In the dry method students paint directly over their completed crayon compositions using watercolors or tempera. It is highly recommended that the teacher test the working viscosity of the tempera on a sample crayoned sheet before allowing the youngsters to proceed. Students may limit themselves to one color in painting the background or employ a variety of water colors as exemplified in the multileaf composition illustrated in this section. If the crayon has been applied heavily the students can paint directly over the crayoned areas, which provides a desired textural effect.

In the wet method the desks or tables where painting will take place should be covered by protective newspapers. If there is a sink the youngsters should immerse their crayoned sheet in water until it is thoroughly wet and carry it to their painting stations. It is recommended that the crayoned sheet be placed on a Masonite board or large metal tray during the soaking. When wet, it must be handled carefully or it may disintegrate or tear. Transport it to the painting station on the board and lift it off carefully.

Students should load their brushes with watercolor or diluted tempera and then drop or float the paint on the white areas of their paper. They may also direct the paint-loaded brush around the edges of the crayoned shapes and let the color flow freely. They may use one watercolor wash (blue or blue-green is a favorite) or a variety of hues for more excitement. They must be careful that the bright colors they use do not flow together to create a dull or grayed color. The wet-

Steps in a crayon-resist painting. Ordinarily, the preliminary crayoning in contour line takes one class session; the crayon patterns, background details, and selected solid crayon areas, a second class period; and the watercoloring, a final art class. Remind students to keep the watercolors transparent by adding sufficient water so that the paint does not obliterate the crayon design.

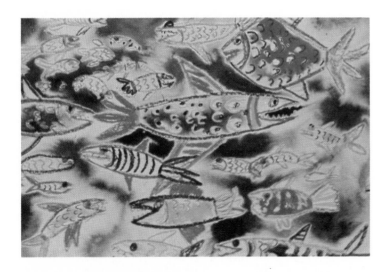

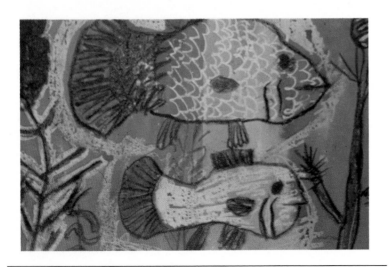

Butterflies in the blue sky and underwater themes are most effective for crayon-resist paintings. The illustration at the top is from a Rangoon, Burma, children's art class taught by the author.

resist method is especially recommended for compositions dealing with undersea, aviary, and flying-insect themes. Often white areas of the paper left unpainted can add to the charm of the picture. For a large class the teacher might prepare in advance several containers of water-diluted tempera or watercolor in assorted hues. Use the watercolors that come in tubes for this purpose. A large table or counter space near the sink could be designated as a painting area, and students could take turns applying the wash over their crayon composition while the rest of the class is still crayoning or otherwise engaged.

In addition to subject ideas mentioned earlier, the following themes are recommended for crayon-resist projects: A Flower Garden, Fireworks Display, The Circus, The Fair, Umbrellas in the Rain, Halloween Parade, Falling Autumn Leaves, Kites in the Sky, In the Swimming Pool, Underwater Explorers, Jungle Birds of Plumage, and Imaginative Designs.

Children express their ideas in direct, inimitable ways. Teachers may guide them to notice the multiple aspects of nature's designs, to help them with special art techniques and processes when the need arises, and to support them at critical stages, but what youngsters depict so honestly and naively is often colored by a mystique that defies explanation. Notice, for example, in the crayon engraving above how economically, boldly, and directly the child makes a statement about flowers and insects. In the circle on the facing page, a youngster applies a crayon undercoat for his engraving.

CRAYON ENGRAVING

Crayon engraving, sometimes referred to as "crayon etching," is a fascinating technique involving the use of sturdy, white drawing paper or tagboard, wax crayons, black tempera paint, soap, brush, and assorted engraving tools. It is considered a standard and popular project in elementary and middle schools, although its many exciting and varied possibilities have not yet been fully explored. Students are often satisfied with quick, superficial designs or with hasty scribbles and random scratches. New worlds of pattern and color overlays are yet to be discovered, and the combination of crayon engraving with other media, such as oil pastel, to enhance the process invites further investigation.

Basically, the crayon-engraving technique emphasizes a graphic, linear approach. Therefore pictorial themes and compositions that are rich in line, pattern, detail, and texture are ideal subject matter for this medium. Students can turn with confidence to the natural world for their inspiration, for example: animals such as the porcupine, anteater, armadillo, zebra, leopard, tiger, and rhino; birds, especially those of exotic plumage; reptiles such as turtles, iguanas, and horned toads; insects such as dragonflies, praying mantises, butterflies, grasshoppers, and beetles; crustaceans such as crabs and crayfish; fish, shells, and coral of many species; and all varieties of plant life.

The preliminary drawing for a crayon engraving should be made in pencil on newsprint or manila paper of the same size as the desired final composition. This will prove beneficial if students decide to retrace their drawings employing white dressmaker's transfer paper.

The first step in a crayon engraving is to apply varied colors of crayon solidly to the selected paper surface. Recom-

mended papers for this process include, in preferred order, sturdy white drawing or construction paper, white or cream tagboard, and cream manila. The crayon should be applied evenly with a strong pressure so that no part of the paper background is revealed. Sometimes coloring in two overlapping directions will ensure a rich coat of crayon. Several layers of newspaper employed as padding under the paper to be crayoned will help ensure a satisfactory coverage. The children may begin the crayoning phase by first making a scribble design in a light-colored crayon all over the paper and then filling in the resulting shapes solidly with a variety of bright colors; as alternate methods of crayoning, they may apply swatches or patches of color or relate their crayoned areas to coincide with their compositions. Either a limited or full-color range can be employed for the crayon background depending on the mood or effect desired. In any case, the most intense and most brilliant colors are recommended for the richest results. *Black crayon should not be used*. Avoid

 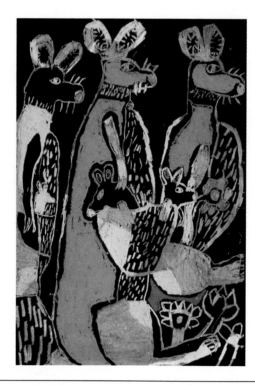 

Three stages in a crayon engraving by a third-grade child. **Left:** *The initial line engraving with a nail through the black tempera coating to the crayoned surface underneath including characteristic details and some textural effects.* **Center:** *The scraping away of black to produce some solid crayon shapes as well as the introduction of oil pastel areas.* **Right:** *The completion of the oil pastel embellishment. Some children prefer the secondary stage.*

the use, too, of gray and the metallic-color crayons such as gold, silver, and copper; in the engraving process they lose their sheen.

After the crayoning has been completed, the surface crayon flecks should be brushed off with a cloth or paper towel. *Caution:* Be sure the youngsters put their names on the backs of their crayoned sheets before the paint is applied. The black tempera paint, either the liquid brand or powder tempera mixed with water, should be about the consistency of thin cream. To make it adhere to the waxy, crayoned surface, it must, in most cases, be conditioned with liquid soap—approximately a tablespoon to a pint of tempera (or the brush filled with tempera can be rubbed over a bar of soap before applying it to the crayoned surface). In both cases the teacher should make a test swatch beforehand and, when dry, ascertain its engraving potential. In some instances when the paint is too thick, it chips during the scratching or engraving phase.

When the paint is thoroughly dry (usually it is best to wait until the next art class), the students may transfer their sketches or preliminary line drawings by coating the reverse side of them with white crayon, then paper-clipping them (crayon-surface down) to the black tempera-coated side, and with a pencil or ballpoint tip make the transfer. A white transfer paper recommended for this process is available from art supply firms.

The next step is the actual engraving or incising of the basic linear composition through the tempera coating down to the crayon surface using a nail, point of scissors, compass, or similar tool. Be sure that students place protective newspapers on the working surface, because the engraving phase can be messy.

After a linear composition is completed, the youngsters can delineate the textural, patterned, and detailed areas employing a variety of found tools including nut picks, forks, and pieces of old combs. High contrast can be achieved by scraping away some solid shapes down to the crayon surface using a plastic paring knife. One tool highly recommended for crayon engraving, if the school budget will allow it, is the Sloyd or Hyde knife, a sturdy, short-bladed knife that can engrave a fine line with its point or scrape away a whole surface with its edge. It is also a relatively safe tool.

The insect world has unlimited possibilities for creative interpretations as illustrated in the crayon engravings on this page by intermediate-elementary-grade youngsters. All of them have been enhanced in the final stage by an application of oil pastels on the background areas while allowing interstices of the black to remain and tie the composition together.

After the students have completed the engraving process, they may enrich their compositions by applying oil pastel colors over some of the black tempera surfaces. Finally, the composition may be further enhanced in many instances by engraving characteristic patterns, details, and texture through the pasteled areas.

Crayon engraving is a challenging mixed-media technique that opens up new avenues of discovery in line, color, contrast, pattern, and texture for children of all ages but especially for intermediate- and upper-elementary-grade youngsters as well as for those in middle schools.

*The illustration above is an example of a multicolor crayon engraving. The technique that requires a great deal of patience calls for the application of several layers of crayon beginning with a light hue such as yellow or pink and building layer on layer through darker colors to a final brown, dark blue, or black. Paper surface recommended is oaktag or colored railroad board in sizes 9 × 12, 12 × 12, or 12 × 18 inches. Nails, pointed scissors, nut picks, and Sloyd knives are suggested as engraving tools. Primary grades, Ann Arbor, Michigan. **Facing page, top:** Crayon engravings by middle school youngsters. **Bottom:** Grade 3.*

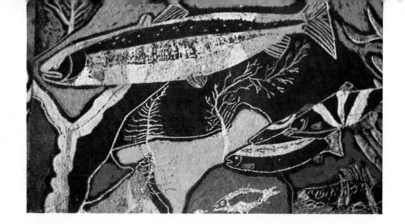

The charming paintings illustrated above were created by employing the melted crayon or encaustic method. The size of the surface cardboard is approximately 8 × 12 inches. Color reproductions of flower paintings by noted artists such as Odilon Redon, Vincent Van Gogh, Paul Cézanne, and Paul Gauguin were displayed and discussed during the project. A bouquet of freshly picked, multi-hued anemones provided the immediate motivation. Grade 3, Athens Academy, Athens, Georgia.

CRAYON ENCAUSTIC

Crayon encaustic may be too pretentious a title for the simple, though exciting, melted-crayon art technique described in this chapter; it is, nonetheless, a fascinating new word to add to the youngsters' vocabulary and a challenging new painting medium to add to the upper-elementary-grade and middle school art repertoire. The encaustic process is the kind of creative adventure reserved for those teachers and students who are brave in spirit, eager to try something new, and persevering enough to salvage a year's supply of broken crayons.

What this unique project demands more than anything else is an abundance of discarded crayons in assorted colors. Many resourceful teachers make encaustic painting an annual late-spring event, which the youngsters eagerly anticipate. One forward-looking teacher even times it with the blossoming of colorful anemones, which become the visual motivation for the project. Because the crayons are used throughout the year, this project is recommended as a school-year's-end art experience.

The steps in making a crayon encaustic are as follows: Remove paper wrappings from the accumulated crayons, break the crayons into small pieces, and put them in baby-food jars or similar containers, each holding a different color. Muffin tins also work well. They should fit into a deeper and slightly larger baking tin so that there is space for the water under the muffin tin. Because of space limitations, the number of colors employed may have to be curtailed. The primary and secondary colors plus white, black, and a selected number of tints should be made available.

The most functional working station for encaustic painting is a large, sturdy, newspaper-covered table. Place one end of the table against a wall near an electrical outlet. Place an electric hot plate in the middle of the table. If necessary, two single plates may be used or one large plate with two burners.

Put the crayon-filled containers (make sure none of the containers is made of plastic or paper) or the muffin tins in the 2 or 3-inch-deep metal baking pan. Fill the pan two-thirds full of water and place it on the hot plate. Turn on the electric current. When the crayons have melted, reduce the heat and place one or more Q-tips or watercolor brushes into each crayon container. These brushes should be old, reserved for this encaustic project only. If the hot water in the baking tin is kept at the level of the melted crayon in the containers, the crayons will maintain a flowing paint consistency.

Caution: Never crowd the working station. A limited group of four to six students, depending on the size of the table, is recommended.

White or colored cardboard approximately 9 × 12 or 12 × 12 inches is recommended for the painting surface. Scrap mat board, chipboard, gift-box covers, and grocery-carton cardboard coated with latex are some possibilities.

A preliminary sketch for a crayon-encaustic painting is generally recommended unless the theme is purely nonobjec-

---

If one layer of melted crayon color is applied over another in the encaustic process, an unusual color effect can be produced by scratching through from one layer of color to another with a nail or nut pick, resulting in an incised design.

tive in the manner of Jackson Pollock, Clifford Still, Hans Hoffman, and Paul Jenkins. Subject-matter possibilities include a flower bouquet, butterflies, an exotic bird in foliage, a fantastic fish among shells and seaweed, an imaginary monster, and a clown.

The teacher must supervise encaustic painting carefully. *The water must not be permitted to boil out in the pan.* The electric current may have to be regulated from time to time so that the melted crayon does not cool off. Additional pieces of crayon will have to be placed in the containers. Remind students that brushes or crayon applicators should not be switched from container to container. Youngsters must be patient and learn to wait their turn for a color. *Caution:* Crayon containers should not be taken out of the heated pan during the painting.

This is a project that cannot be rushed. Sometimes the beauty of an encaustic painting does not materialize until several layers of melted crayon have been applied. There will be an exciting impasto quality to the finished work if time is taken. When one color is applied over another, there is the possibility of further embellishment by incising lines with a nail through the top coat to reveal the crayon color underneath. When a large area has to be covered, some teachers have employed powered tempera mixed with melted paraffin to solve the problem. This is a project producing paintings with a color richness and glow unsurpassed.

Subject-matter themes for crayon encaustic paintings are almost limitless, but children respond enthusiastically to natural motifs such as flowers, butterflies, fish, birds, and, as the illustrations on this page prove, happy circus clowns.

Animals in the Jungle, *grade 3. Oil pastel on pink-colored construction paper. Color slides of jungle animals were projected on a screen. The children made their preliminary drawings in school chalk. When animals were drawn, slides of trees, bushes, and birds were screened to provide further motivational and compositional material. Even though the visual stimulation was the same for the whole class, no two compositions or color interpretations were alike, as evidenced by the illustrations on the facing page.*

OIL PASTEL

The introduction of oil pastels in their rich and exciting array of hues has opened a whole new world of color exploration and expression in both elementary and middle schools. Available from several art supply firms, these glowing pastels are generally within the budget range of most schools. One of their most attractive features is the ease with which children can apply them to obtain shimmering, vivid, painterly color compositions. Their only drawback is minimal: Because of the oil content they may stain clothing. Youngsters should be cautioned against this possibility.

Oil pastels work especially well on deep-colored construction paper in which the color background often serves as a unifying or complementary factor. Although oil pastels can be used impressionistically, blending color over color, young students should be encouraged in their first effort with the medium to apply the pastels boldly in solid color areas, pressing hard to achieve a glowing surface and keeping color contrasts in mind. Because the intensity of the pastel hues is affected by the paper color, it is suggested that youngsters experiment on the reverse side of their paper with small color swatches to note the effect.

The following recommendations have been found helpful in oil-pastel projects especially where colored construction is used for the background:

Make the preliminary drawing or sketch with white (or yellow) school chalk or light crayon. Chalk is excellent, because it can be erased easily (use paper towel or facial tissue) if the students want to make changes. Undesired crayon outlines can also be scraped off.

Apply the color with pressure for richest effects. One suggestion for coloring in small or complex shapes is to apply the pastel in a line close to the chalk outline and then fill in the shape. Discourage haphazard, scribbled application of color.

A collection of butterflies, as well as color photographs of butterflies in a garden, provided the motivational inspiration for the oil pastel by an upper-elementary-grade youngster illustrated above. Notice *how different sizes and shapes of butterflies were employed to achieve variety. A host of patterns were used for the background: circles, dots, and wiggly and rippling lines.*

Remind students that colors have many tints and shades including the neutralized or dulled hues, for example: basic green, light green, dark green, yellow-green, blue-green, dull green. This awareness is important when coloring leaves and grassy fields in all of their nuances of light and shadow.

Black, white, and gray pastel colors can be employed successfully with any color scheme.

It is important to remember that the colors, both tints and shades, bright and dull, including the blacks and whites, should be repeated in different parts of the composition to achieve unity. Use variety in your repetition of colors—repeat the colors in different sizes, shapes, and intensities.

A vital strategy in successful color orchestration, especially recommended for upper elementary grade and middle school students, is that a color or hue repeated for unity should be differentiated in value contrast so that the echo of the color is there without the monotony of stereotyped repetition. This admonition is especially true when the youngster is delineating a pattern such as bricks on a wall, tiles on a roof, or stones in a walk in which the repetition of the same color could become static and lifeless unless it is sensitively and expressively altered.

Remember that although colors may be different in hue, for example basic red and green, they may be alike in value. Be aware of this when you are working for sharp value contrasts.

In some instances when you want the colored-paper background to show through as a complementing factor, apply the pastel impressionistically in strokes, lines, or dots.

Students may expand the color range available by applying pastel over pastel to create new colors. *Caution:* A very light color such as yellow, pink, or light green cannot be altered effectively by the application of a dark color. To change the light-color shape to a dark one, you must scrape away the light color first. You can lighten a dark color by the application of white, but be careful! Red turns to a candy pink, which you may not want. Add a little yellow for a subtler hue. Colors can be dulled or neutralized through a discriminative application of their complements: red over green, orange over blue. To alter a color the student must apply the second color with just enough pressure to effect a change but not so much pressure that the base color is destroyed. Use controlled application or soft pressure with varidirectional strokes and then increase pressure until the desired change is accomplished.

Oil pastels can be successfully employed in multimedia projects: over tempera paint compositions, as a final stage in crayon engraving, and as a final embellishment in vegetable or found-object prints.

---

*Top and center: Astronauts in and out of their spaceships was the theme for these third-grade oil pastels. **Bottom:** A fourth-grade class turned the same theme into a group mural project.*

OIL-PASTEL RESIST

Teachers and students familiar with the crayon-resist technique will welcome oil pastel as a resist medium, because it does not require the time or the intense exertion on the part of the youngsters that the rich, solid application of crayon demands. There are, however, some limiting factors regarding the process that will be treated later.

Basically, the same steps as outlined for the crayon-resist technique are followed. A preliminary drawing in school chalk is made on a sheet of colored construction paper of the student's choice. Encourage the youngsters to vary the width of the chalk line with emphasis on thicker lines. This step will prove of strategic importance in the final resolution of the technique. The pastel is then applied with a heavy pressure so that it will resist the final coat of paint. The chalk lines should not be covered or colored. Avenues of uncolored paper (the chalk outline) should remain between objects or shapes, between objects and background, middle ground, or foreground. The surface paper between patterns such as plaids, diamonds, stripes, and dots should also be uncolored to allow the paint to flow into those spaces. The brightest most intense hues of pastel should be employed. White and gray may also be used, but do not use black, since the final resist effect will be achieved by a coating of black paint.

Facing page: Oil pastel resist. ***This page:*** *Steps in the process.* ***Top:*** *Preliminary drawing in school chalk on colored construction paper.* ***Center:*** *Oil pastel applied in solids and patterns up to but not covering the chalk lines.* ***Bottom:*** *Slightly water-diluted black tempera applied lightly with a soft-bristle brush.*

Evaluate the final pastel composition for a variety of colors, repetition of colors, and pattern. Look for a variety of patterns: dots, circles independently drawn or overlapping, wiggly lines, radiating lines in circles or rays, ripple-in-a-stream lines, hatch and crosshatch lines, stars, asterisks, diamonds, and spirals.

Before applying paint, gently brush or wipe off the chalk lines. Place the composition on a newspaper-protected surface and apply a coat of tempera paint. This phase, as hinted earlier, is the most critical stage of the whole project. The paint must be exactly the right consistency—not too thin, not too thick. Always test the paint on a sample, pastel-covered practice sheet before allowing the students to use it. The brush should have soft bristles—a large watercolor brush is recommended—and the brush should *float* over the pastel. If the paint covers the pastel areas, it is too thick. *Caution:* The resisting oil in the pastels dries out soon after it is applied to the paper, so don't wait too long to apply the black paint.

Some tempera paints on the market, both powder and liquid, now contain an adhesive additive and are not recommended for this process. Write for sample tempera products and use the brand that works.

Oil-pastel-resist compositions may be given a protective coat of polymer medium glossy or clear shellac when completely dry, which often enhances their beauty.

Imaginary creatures—part animal, part bird, part fish, part insect—inspired these fantastic oil pastel-resist paintings by fourth- and fifth-grade children. Youngsters at this age respond enthusiastically to the compositional challenges these creatures provide. Facing page: Oil pastel resist, middle school youngster.

181

A welcome feature of cut-and-paste projects is the fact that children can arrange the separate shapes in varying configurations before they finally decide where they want to paste them. Preliminary drawings for collage projects in primary grades are not required. However, the separate parts of the composition may be drawn before being cut out.

COLLAGE

One of the most popular forms of visual expression in elementary and middle schools today is the art of collage with its related family of montage, decoupage, mosaic, collograph, and assemblage. More than a half-century ago, shocking dismay greeted the initial collages of Pablo Picasso, Georges Braque, and Kurt Schwitters. Today their creations in paper, paste (the word "collage" derives from the French "to paste"), and other found materials from the wastebasket appear relatively tame. The wellsprings from which contemporary artists draw their materials is so bountiful in content and variety that it is limitless in its possibilities.

The collage technique has provided teachers of art with one of the most effective and rewarding avenues for introducing youngsters to design and space creation through overlapping of shapes, color, positive- and negative-shape identification, value contrast, pattern, and texture. In collage, youngsters have the unique opportunity of rearranging and changing their placement of separate pictorial and design segments, until, through an evaluating process, they can achieve a structurally satisfying composition.

There are many approaches to the art of collage. They range from simple cutting, tearing, and pasting of paper to

*Facing page: Motivational sources and resulting collages. **Top:** Colored magazine sections with supplemental oil pastel. **Bottom:** Cloth remnants with black tempera outline. **This page:** Cloth remnants, yarn, ric rac, buttons, and colored construction paper.*

Mixed-media collage, grade 7, Oshkosh, Wisconsin. White chalk or crayon preliminary drawing on dark-colored construction paper. Notice how areas of the background paper remain untouched, providing a unifying element through the composition. A variety of found materials were used to give the collage pattern and texture: yarn, burlap, newspapers, three-dimensional packing inserts, buttons, plaster grouting, and balsa-wood strips.

complex sewing, shearing, and gluing of fabric, plastics, plywood, and cardboard. Some recommended materials for collage creation are colored poster and construction paper, fluorescent and Day-Glo paper, cloth remnants, wallpaper and rug samples, paint chips, multicolored tissue paper, and found materials such as posters and colored pages from magazines.

A preliminary drawing or sketch is generally recommended as a guiding reference in the case of collages whose subject matter is the landscape, figure composition, or still-life arrangements. In themes from the imagination, fantasy, or purely nonobjective designs, direct cutting, tearing, and pasting is acceptable, but in both processes the permanent adherence of the separate parts should be postponed until both student and teacher critique the work for compositional strengths and weaknesses.

Teachers will find the following suggestions useful in helping youngsters with their collage projects:

Cut and arrange the large shapes or motifs of your composition first.
If you are employing a colored background include it in your design by allowing some of the background to show, which will help unify your composition.
Small details and patterns can be pasted on the large shapes before they in turn are glued to the background surface.

These middle-school girls made intricately detailed drawings of an open-doored van parked on the school's premises but were not rigidly bound by their preliminary sketches in their creations of the collage adaptations. Notice how the addition of a gas pump and commercial logo enhanced one of the compositions.

"On our Street" was the subject of this colorful colored construction-paper collage by a first-grade child. Motivation concerned kinds of houses, garages, churches, synagogues, stores, trees, bushes, hedges, fences, sidewalks, cars, trucks, telephone poles, traffic signs, billboards, mailboxes, pets, and other environs.

Wallpaper samples and colored construction paper provided the basic materials for the primary grade child who designed this colorful collage. Flowers from an early summer garden provided the motivation.

Overlapping of shapes is a major design feature of collage making and helps youngsters become aware of subtle space created through this process.

Certain eye-catching materials such as aluminum foil, synthetic silver and gold foils, shiny plastic, and cellophane have a strong fascination for children, and if not properly guided they are apt to use them in an unrestrained manner. Suggest their use as points of emphasis only and even then omit them if they destroy the unity of the total composition.

Repetition of a color, shape, value, pattern, or texture will add unity to a collage; however, instead of repeating the element, color, or shape in exactly the same size or intensity, change it slightly to achieve subtle variety.

Recommend the use of an uneven rather than even repetition of elements. For example, repeat a certain shape or color three times rather than twice. An objective reason for this procedure is difficult to find; as a suggestion from the art of the Orient, it is usually more effective.

In the same vein as the previous injunction, encourage the employment of informal (asymmetrical) rather than formal (symmetrical) balance for most collage compositions.

Avoid a lot of "sticky" problems by using discarded magazines as paste-applying surfaces. When youngsters need another clean pasting area, they can turn to another page.

See Appendix E for a list of materials suitable for collage projects.

Recycle scraps of colored construction paper into collage projects such as these examples by primary-grade children. Youngsters chose paper scraps in assorted sizes, shapes, and colors to arrange their compositions. Supplemental details, patterns, and motifs were added employing crayons, oil pastels, felt-nib or nylon-tip markers, paper punches, or brush and paint.

The beautifully composed, colored-tissue-paper collage illustrated above is by a talented middle-school student from Athens, Georgia. Photographs and color slides of matadors, toreadors, and "brave bulls" provided the visual stimulation. The preliminary drawing was made with a felt-nib pen (permanent black-ink type) on white construction paper. Before the application of the colored tissue, the student chose selected shapes—matador's trousers, jacket, and so on—for a patterned embellishment and pasted colored sections from magazines on those parts. The tissue was applied by coating an area first with liquid laundry starch, placing the tissue over it,

TISSUE PAPER COLLAGE

On the first day of a tissue-paper-collage project, the teacher can surprise the class by opening and unfolding a package of assorted-color tissue papers. The excitement grows as one color tissue overlaps another on a white paper background or against the window while the youngsters are invited to choose each overlapping color and then identify the resulting hue.

To encourage color awareness and color exploration, a free-design, nonobjective, colored-tissue collage is recommended for children from the third grade up. Using a sheet of oaktag, white drawing paper, or construction paper approximately 12 × 18 inches as a background surface, the youngsters cut or tear different sizes and shapes of tissue and adhere them to the background using undiluted liquid laundry starch as the adhesive, overlapping the various shapes as they proceed. A ½-inch utility brush or a large watercolor brush makes an excellent starch applicator. The students should begin with the lighter colored tissues first and proceed to darker values. It is most difficult to change the value of a dark tissue by overlapping. Reserve the darker colored tissue for the second phase of pasting, if desired.

It is recommended that the children first apply a coating of starch to the area they want to cover with tissue. Then the tissue should be placed down carefully over the wet area and another coat of starch applied over it. Brushes that pick up some of the color from the moistened tissue may be cleaned with water. Be sure that all loose edges of tissue are glued down carefully. Discarded half-pint milk cartons are economical and practical starch containers. Although the abstract

and then coating it again with the starch, making sure all edges were smoothly secured. Light-colored tissue was applied first, progressing to the darker colors. Caution was employed in the final stages so that dark-value tissue did not obliterate the important form-defining ink lines.

composition has an aesthetic validity of its own, it can be augmented as follows: After the students build and extend their tissue compositions to the borders of the paper, challenge them to look for unusual hidden shapes of animals, birds, insects, fish, or fantastic, imaginative creatures. Once a form or figure emerges and is identified, it can be emphasized and clarified by gluing additional torn pieces or strips of tissue in deeper colors to suggest or indicate arms, legs, wings, tails, ears, horns, tusks, beaks, claws, fins, combs, manes, and other appendages to give it a significant character and individuality. One thing to avoid is the outlining of the revealed figure so boldly that it is isolated from the rest of the composition. Employ a variety of dark-color tissues for this step rather than a single hue. Black tissue can be used but only in a most discriminating, restrained way. The same principle goes for the employment of the black felt-nib markers to outline the figures. If only one figure is so outlined it will isolate it, but if all emerging figures are outlined in black a unity will be achieved.

In addition to black felt-nib markers, students can use crayons, colored markers, and tempera paint in white, gray, or black to add exciting linear delineation to a shape where desired, such as bark on a tree, scales on a fish, feathers on a bird, and veins in a wing or leaf. As an alternative, the positive shapes could remain untouched while the background is enriched and embellished with detail, pattern, and texture. In all cases remember to wait until the tissue surface is dry, especially if you are using water-soluble markers.

Top: Colored-tissue-paper collage, grade 1. Center: Fifth grade youngster applying the colored tissue to his preliminary drawing. Bottom: Completed colored-tissue-paper collage on white construction or drawing paper, 18 × 24".

The colored tissue compositions illustrated above began as free-form collages. The youngsters cut or tore the tissue and applied it on white construction paper in overlapping stages with liquid laundry starch. When it was dry, they used black and colored felt-nib markers to search and outline recognizable shapes. Some children used crayons, others paint and brush. Suggest that the students begin pasting light values of tissue first and progress to darker values. A dark-color tissue area is difficult to change to a light value if needed. One solution is to paste a sheet of white paper over the area and start again.

The free-design approach with colored tissue described above is only one of many avenues open to youngsters who want to create with colored tissue. Another recommended technique capitalizes on a preliminary drawing made with black or dark-color crayons or a permanent-ink felt-nib marker on white drawing or construction paper or tagboard surface. After the drawing is completed, the cut or torn tissue paper is applied as suggested in the previous method, beginning as recommended with the lighter hues first. Remember to cut or tear the tissue sheet slightly larger than the shapes drawn. The drawn lines may sometimes be obscured by dark tissue overlays, but when the tissue layer is dry, the lines may be redrawn for emphasis. Colored tissue used in conjunction with patterns and lettering from magazine ads or wallpaper samples adds another dimension to the tissue collage.

Illustrations on this page are colored-tissue-paper collages by middle school youngsters.

The storage of the tissue is a critical consideration. Tissue wrinkles and crumples very easily, compounding storage problems. Provide separate storage boxes (shoe boxes are one possibility) for the various hues of tissue. At the beginning of a tissue-collage project cut the large sheets of tissue into manageable sizes that will fit into the storage boxes.

MOSAICS

The multifaceted technique of mosaic art, with its colored segments (tessera), has found its way into both elementary and middle school art programs to enrich the design experiences of the youngsters. It is a welcome, albeit challenging, addition to the repertoire of child-art expression. It requires a more generous time allotment, supplemental storage, and, above all, students with patience and persistence. Children can achieve wonders employing standard art materials such as colored construction paper, paste, and scissors.

Motivation for the project might include visits to contemporary mosaic installations in churches, synagogues, mosques, temples, civic centers, hospitals, hotels, banks, schools, airports, and post offices. Color films and slides that

Recommended background surfaces for paper mosaic projects include construction paper in assorted colors, railroad board, chipboard, oaktag, or discarded gift-box covers. Suggested adhesives include wheat paste, school paste, white glue, or rubber cement. Bird mosaic, left, employed vinyl and linoleum tesserae glued to a Masonite board with color-tinted grout as a filler. Grade 6.

illustrate mosaic art, past and present, including San Vitale in Rome, Gaudi's Cathedral in Barcelona, Rodia's Watts Towers in Los Angeles, and the mosaic-paved avenues of Rio de Janeiro should be shown when available. Subject matter for paper mosaics that is manageable yet exciting enough to interest youngsters includes Birds of Plumage, Fish in the Sea, Animals in their Habitats, A Bouquet of Flowers, Butterflies in a Garden, Flying Kites, Dragons, and Clowns.

In mosaic design, as in most two-dimensional art expression, an important initial step is the preliminary sketch made from life and nature, from visits to natural museums, or from references to photographs, color slides, and films. These sketches are then developed into a satisfactory linear composition the size of the actual mosaic desired. The background surface may be colored construction paper, oaktag, railroad board in assorted colors, chipboard, or salvaged-container cardboard and gift-box covers.

One of the most critical factors in the success of a mosaic project is the effective organization of the materials and tools. There must be an adequate supply of tesserae on hand. In the case of colored construction paper, narrow strips of paper, not necessarily the same width, can be precut with scissors or paper cutter and stored according to color in shoe boxes. These strips can then be cut as needed into individual tesserae by the students but not necessarily into perfect squares. Some can be rectangular or triangular. Suggested adhesives for paper mosaics are school paste, wheat paste, or

Underwater themes are especially effective for mosaic exploitations because of the variety of shapes, details, and patterns found in fish, shells, coral, and seaweed. These beautifully space-filled compositions are by upper-elementary-grade youngsters. Notice the variety in the sizes and shapes of the tesserae. Oshkosh, Wisconsin.

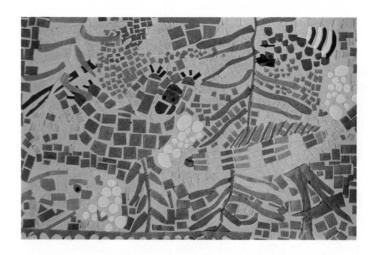

liquid glue slightly diluted. Liquid glue can also be dispensed directly from plastic, nozzle-tipped containers.

During a mosaic project students should be requested to take turns selecting the desired color strips or tesserae from the supply-table boxes. They may begin by pasting tesserae on any part of the composition they wish. The thinned-down paste or glue should be applied to the background paper and the tessera placed firmly on it. Usually, it is best to begin on the outer edge of a shape and work inward toward the center of the shape. Avoid a rigid, bricklaying technique—the minute, open spaces between tesserae should vary somewhat for best effects. Tesserae should not touch or overlap each other in order to achieve the mosaic effect. The youngsters should be reminded that in professional mosaic work a grout is mortared in between tesserae, and if they create a mosaic using vinyl or linoleum they may be required to do the same.

Youngsters may create excitement with their mosaic compositions through a contrast of tessera colors in specified areas—the wing of a bird against the body, the stamens against a flower petal, an insect against a leaf. An important strategy in achieving expressive mosaic quality is to employ several values of a color in the larger areas: For example, use two or three values of blue in the sky, two or three values of green in the grass and leaves, and several kinds of brown, ochre, umber, and sienna colors for earth and tree trunks. The brightest, most intense colors may be reserved for sharp contrast or emphasis—on the beak or claws of a bird, the horns of a bull, the eyes of a tiger, or the stamen of a lily. Mosaics may be protected with a coat of clear shellac or polymer medium glossy, but warn the students that this will darken the value of the construction paper colors.

These attractive colored-construction-paper mosaics were composed by fifth- and sixth-grade students at the Campus Elementary School, University of Iowa, Iowa City.

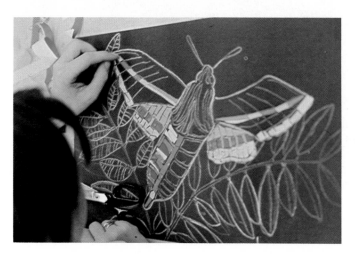

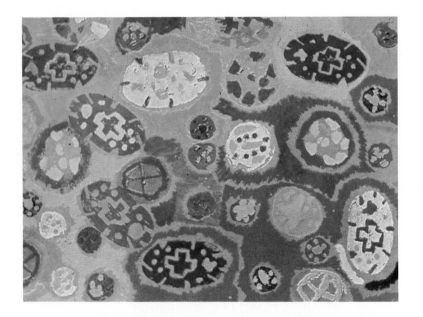

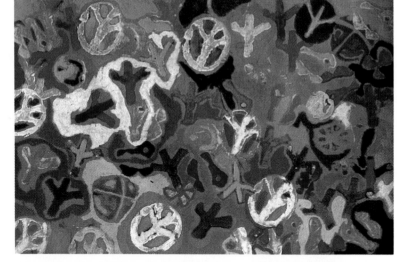

Vegetable-stamp printmaking appeals to youngsters, but caution must be exercised in cutting the designs. Use nails, plastic knives, and melon scoops for this process. In the printing phase do not insist on a measured, rigidly controlled design. Vegetable prints may be embellished by an application of oil pastels between printed motifs. Allow some background paper to show, unifying the composition.

PRINTMAKING WITH FOUND OBJECTS

Printmaking projects should be wisely programmed by the teacher so that they range from simple processes in the primary grades to complex techniques in the upper elementary grades and middle school. Some of the most colorful and successful prints can be made by very young children employing vegetables and fruit as well as found objects such as buttons, flat or round wooden clothespins, wooden spools, bottle caps, mailing tubes, corks, sponges, and erasers. Cord can be glued to the smooth metal top of a condiment container in a free design to produce a printing stamp. Assorted vegetables (okra, cabbage, mushrooms, peppers, carrots, artichokes) can be cut in half or in pieces, painted, and printed. The excitement quickens when the students discover, perhaps for the first time, the beauty of the hidden design in these natural forms. The halved or quartered vegetables are painted on the cut side with colored tempera of a creamy consistency or pressed on a tempera-coated, folded paper towel and then printed on a sheet of colored construction paper or tissue paper to form an allover or repeat design.

The most popular of the vegetable-print projects uses the common potato as a printing stamp. The potato is cut in half with a paring knife and the flat, open surface is incised to create a relief. Children must be reminded to exercise cau-

Vegetable prints may be enhanced by the application of oil pastels as illustrated here. **Top:** *A youngster applies the pastel colors between the printed motifs allowing some of the background paper to show. Notice in the bottom example how the employment of the blue-colored pastel has enriched and unified the basic print shown center.*

tion when using vegetable-cutting tools. Recommended tools include small scissors, fingernail files, nut picks, and assorted nails. Melon-ball scoops are excellent for creating circular designs. Discarded dental tools are another possibility. In the upper elementary grades and middle school, paring knives may be employed if used with extreme care. Investigate the availability of the Sloyd or Hyde knife with the short blade—an ideal tool for this project.

Youngsters should be encouraged to work for a simple, bold breakup of space in their cutout or incised designs. Suggest the use of crosscuts, wedges as in a pie, assorted-sized holes, star, asterisk, cog wheel, sunburst, and spider-web effects, always keeping in mind the positive and negative design factors. Monogram motifs are also a popular theme

with children, but remember that letters and numerals must be reversed to print correctly. Youngsters should make a preliminary drawing on paper the shape of the cut potato to guide them in their cutting. It may be possible to reverse the drawing at the window and then copy it on the potato surface with a fine felt-nib or nylon-tip pen. Large potatoes are recommended for monogram motifs.

The vegetables must be fresh, crisp, and solid for controlled carving, cutting, and printing. They should be refrigerated between printmaking sessions. Another possibility suggested for coloring the vegetables in order to print them is the employment of water-soluble printing ink available in tubes. Squeeze and roll them out on a Masonite sheet, pie or cookie tin, or a sheet of glass with edges taped for protection. Since water-soluble ink dries quickly, students may have to sprinkle water over the ink-supply slab from time to time.

Construction paper in assorted colors is perhaps the most popular and most serviceable surface for vegetable printing, although other papers, including colored tissue, colored crepe paper, cream or gray manila, and wallpaper, have been successfully employed. Assorted fabrics are also recommended. Generous newspaper padding should be placed under the paper to be printed to ensure a good impression. Students must exert a steady pressure when making the print. Sometimes a couple of wedges cut out of the opposite end of the potato provides a better grasp.

A few practice applications of the vegetable stamp on scrap sheets of paper are recommended to check the clarity of the print. In certain vegetable-print projects children might be encouraged to develop a repeat pattern. Suggest that they repeat the motif in several places on their paper (this does not have to be a measured, mathematical repeat), allowing some prints to go off the page to create an allover effect. In other instances the design can be left to the child's own inventiveness, but discourage rushing just to finish, which often results in sloppy printing. Often the imperfection of a child's effort lends a naive, spontaneous quality to the product. Children will discover that by sharing their vegetable and found-object stamps they can produce exciting variations in pattern and design.

Vegetable and found-object prints have artistic potential in their simplest, unadorned form, but they can often be embellished with other art media to add richness and variety. One of the most successful of these augmentations is the application of crayon or multicolor oil pastel to the negative spaces between the printed shapes. Unity can be achieved by allowing some of the background surface to remain uncolored between the pasteled or crayoned areas and the printed motifs. One or a variety of colors may be used for this background enrichment. Older students can carry the found-object print technique into even more complex undertakings by combining it with colored tissue overlays or colored yarn.

Vegetable and found-object prints make excellent covers for notebooks and pencil containers (glue the printed paper to a discarded box or can). Protect the surface with a coat of clear shellac, varnish, or polymer medium glossy.

Vegetable-print, allover repeat designs make excellent covers for notebooks, pencil holders (recycle a soup or coffee can), and household dispensers. To protect the surface apply a coat of clear shellac, plastic spray, or polymer medium glossy.

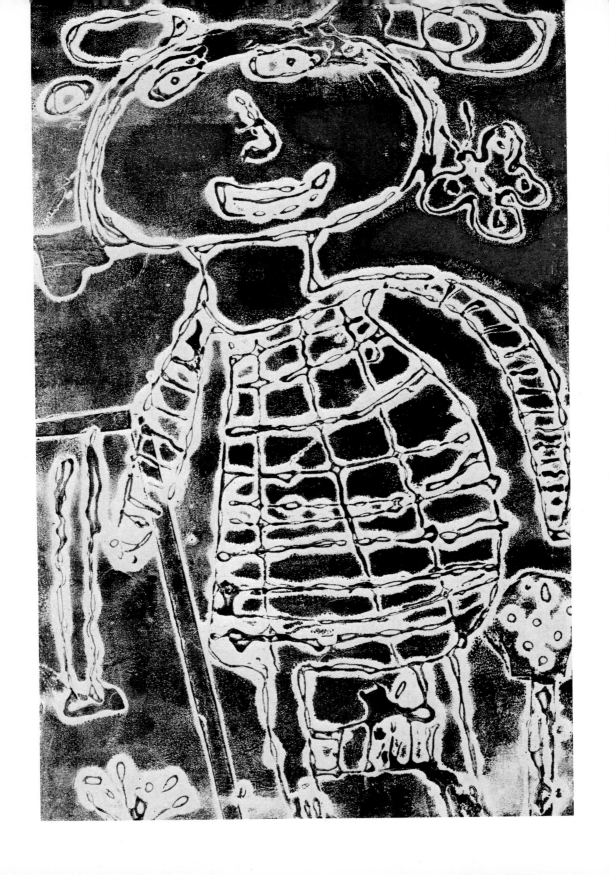

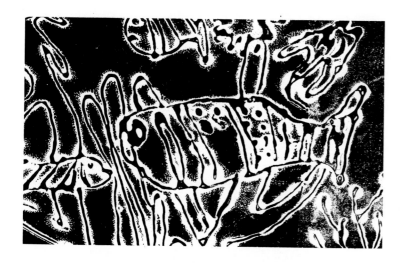

GLUE LINE-RELIEF PRINTS

A printmaking process that is remarkably successful with youngsters in all grades is the applied glue-line-on-cardboard print. It is a relatively simple technique but requires at least two class or studio sessions, because the glue must dry thoroughly before printing can take place. Youngsters will probably have to take turns during the inking and printing stages.

Materials required are pencils; a smooth-surfaced cardboard (discarded, glossy-surfaced gift-box covers are excellent) or tagboard for the printing plate (plate sizes recommended are 9 × 9, 9 × 12, 12 × 12, or 12 × 18 inches); white liquid glue in the small, plastic container with nozzle; water-soluble printing ink (black is recommended); a soft

*Facing page: Glue line-relief print, 12 × 18 inches. A self-portrait by a first-grade child, Oshkosh, Wisconsin. **This page:** Print in same technique, same size, by a sixth-grade youngster. Because of the pressure applied by the soft-rubber ink brayer, the water-based printing ink covers parts of the background as well as the glue lines.*

rubber brayer or roller for inking; and for an inking surface, either a 12-inch-square sheet of tempered Masonite, a similar-sized sheet of glass with its edges mask-taped, a discarded cafeteria tray, an aluminum cookie tin, or a commercially available, plastic-surfaced inking platen; also, newsprint, tissue paper, or classified sections of newspapers to print on. In some instances cream manila and colored construction paper may be employed as printing surfaces, but the impression will generally be limited to the line relief only. Lots of newspapers to protect working surfaces are a must.

Subject-matter choices for glue line prints are almost limitless. Young children will respond to natural motifs such as butterflies, birds, fish, flowers, and animals. Students in the upper elementary grades and middle school may choose more complex themes such as historical legends and biblical stories, space-science explorations, still life, cityscape compositions, and portraits and figure studies.

A preliminary drawing is definitely recommended. Tell the youngsters to keep the basic drawing bold and simple, if possible. They should minimize the intricate details that a pencil can produce but that, unfortunately, will blend together in the glue application and be lost in the printing. On a 9 × 9- or 12 × 12-inch printing plate (cardboard) it is more expedient for the youngsters to limit themselves to one large motif (bird, insect, fish, animal) and its complementary foliage or seaweed than to attempt several smaller motifs. In this procedure the students can clearly delineate the characteristic features of eye, beak, whiskers, antenna, claw, feather, fish scale, or horn with the flowing glue. At the close of the drawing phase teachers should evaluate the linear composition with each student emphasizing space-filling design, variety of sizes and shapes of motifs, exciting pattern, and avenues leading into the composition.

The cardboard plate with its linear composition is now ready for the glue application. Holding the nozzle of the glue container against the cardboard at the point you want to start, gently squeeze the container trailing the glue over the drawn line. With older students the teacher might point out that the flow of glue and, consequently, the thickness of the glue line can be varied as desired by controlling the pressure on the container, but in most instances a linear variety is achieved naturally, because it is difficult to manage an equally steady flow of glue. Dots of glue will produce sunburst effects in the final printing.

The glue must be allowed to dry thoroughly (store plates on counters, on the floor around the room, or on desks if it is the last period of the day) before the cardboard plate can be inked. Most teachers recommend an overnight drying period. The glue will look transparent when dry. White ridges and welts indicate that the glue has not dried there. At the close of the school day prick these welts with a pin to hasten drying.

Designate both an inking and a printing station in the room. These stations could be large tables, teachers desks, or counters protected by newspapers. Demonstrate the application of the glue, the inking, the printing, and the wet-print storage procedures for the entire class. This will save a lot of time usually spent in giving individual instructions.

At the inking station squeeze out a brayer-width ribbon of water-soluble black printing ink on the inking surface. Roll out the ink with the brayer. Keep rolling until the ink is tacky—you'll hear a snapping sound—and then apply the ink to the cardboard plate with a strong pressure. It is recommended that students stand during this procedure. Roll the ink on the plate, with the rubber brayer in several directions—up and down and across—to be sure all parts of the plate, especially the edges and corners, are inked thoroughly. Then lift the inked plate carefully and carry it to the printing station. Place a sheet of newsprint or tissue paper (cut slightly larger than the cardboard plate) over the plate and apply pressure with the palm of the hand, beginning in the center and smoothing out to the borders of the plate. This must be done carefully so that the paper does not shift during the process. Some teachers recommend that students tap the paper down all over with the palm of their hands before applying pressure and smoothing it down.

The most exciting and successful glue line prints are those in which the inked areas of the background as well as those of the raised glue lines are captured in the final print. This will require pressure with fingers in the smaller background areas as well as with the palm. In either case there will always remain uninked areas between glue lines and background to provide the necessary contrast between light and dark. For the demonstration the teacher might use white or light-colored tissue so that the youngsters can see the actual absorption of the ink by the paper and detect areas that need more pressure to be effective. Don't forget that water-soluble ink dries quickly, so don't wait too long to pull your print. Several prints may be pulled from the same glue line-relief plate.

Trim borders of prints, if necessary, and mount the print on colored construction paper for an exciting display.

The glue line plate itself can be attractively framed and displayed. Give it a coat of colored ink or stain it with commercially available patinas. It can also be enhanced with a sheet of heavy-duty aluminum foil for a stunning effect. See the section "Aluminum-Foil Reliefs."

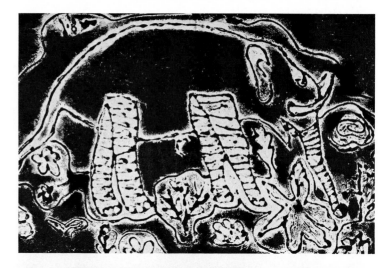

This beautifully composed collograph is by a Japanese upper elementary grade youngster. The technique of the collograph, begun in Japan many years ago, is widely popular in their art program.

COLLOGRAPHS

Youngsters in the intermediate and upper elementary grades as well as middle school are interested in and challenged by more complex, more technically demanding approaches to printmaking. Cardboard prints, sometimes referred to as "collographs" (a word combination of "collage" and "graph"), which can be created with commonly available materials and nonhazardous tools, offer this kind of variety. The final surprising results are often comparable to woodblocks and lino prints. The flexibility afforded the students of rearranging, changing, or deleting the elements in the composition before the final glueing of the separate motifs is an especially welcome feature of this print technique.

The following tools and materials are required for the printing plate: a sheet of sturdy cardboard (the lid or bottom of a stationery box or other similar-sized gift box), chipboard, discarded scraps of illustration board (tagboard is not recommended), glue, scissors, assorted-weight papers (smooth or textured), assorted-size paper punches, soft rubber brayer or roller, water-soluble printing ink (black is recommended although other dark colors may be employed), newsprint, shellac and solvent, utility brush, and lots of newspapers to protect inking areas.

Subject-matter themes for collographs are unlimited, although the animal world is a favorite. There should be the same concern for a strong, lively composition that is the requisite of all graphic-design projects. Especially important is an emphasis on the effective use of a variety of cutout shapes

A middle-grade youngster, referring to his preliminary pencil sketch as a guide, glues his shapes cut out of oaktag board to a more sturdy cardboard surface for his collograph printing plate. The completed print is shown below.

to fill the space of the cardboard size the child has selected. A preliminary drawing of the total composition is not a requisite, but it may help the student resolve design problems. Separate motifs or shapes may certainly be drawn first before cutting. A recommended printing-plate size for intermediate- and upper-elementary-grade youngsters is a sheet 9 × 9, 9 × 12, or 12 × 12 inches. Plates much larger than this can create a management problem in crowded classrooms, especially during the inking, printing, and drying phases.

Students draw and cut out the separate, individual shapes from tagboard (oaktag), cream manila, construction paper, and other assorted-weight papers and create open patterns in some of these shapes, employing paper punches and single-edge razor blades. *Caution:* The teacher should wrap every blade securely with masking tape so that only a small cutting point protrudes at one end, then number these blades with a permanent-ink felt-nib pen, and be sure that all of them are accounted for at the end of the studio period. The students then arrange these separate elements on the background plate or cardboard until a satisfactory composition is realized. Some shapes may overlap for unity, spatial effects, and interest; however, the relief must not be built up too high if a successful print is desired. When the youngsters, with the teacher's guidance, achieve a satisfying, space-filling design, they carefully glue the separate cutout on torn pieces to the plate surface beginning with the first layer. Use a discarded magazine as a glueing surface and turn to a clean page for each application. It is strategically important that all edges of the applied piece be glued down firmly and securely. The

This and facing page: Steps in making a collograph print—gluing the separate pieces, inking, and pulling a print. Caution: *If water-based printing ink is employed, the plate must be given a protective coat of shellac or varnish.*

whole composition is then given a coat of shellac to seal it, thus preventing the separate pieces from dissolving and coming loose during the printing with water-base ink or the cleaning phases. A separate table or counter protected by newspapers should be designated as a shellac-application area. Store the shellacked plates out of harm's way and allow them to dry thoroughly before the inking phase.

The inking and printing stage of this project is naturally the most exciting phase for the youngsters involved, but unless the teacher has planned this activity carefully it can develop into a chaotic bedlam. Have on hand several inking surfaces such as 12-inch-square pieces of tempered Masonite, discarded cookie tins, cafeteria trays, or commercially available plastic platens; soft rubber brayers or rollers, 3 or more inches wide (do not use the gelatine type); black water-soluble ink; and newsprint or light-colored tissue paper.

In a typical classroom or studio situation it is recommended that inking and printing tables covered with newspapers be designated where four students can stand and work comfortably. After squeezing and rolling out ink on the inking surface until it feels tacky, apply it to the plate in both directions using an even, strong pressure so that every part of the plate, especially the edges and corners, is inked. Take the inked plate to either the printing table or a desk that has been covered by newspapers and set it down, inked-side up. Carefully place a sheet of newsprint paper (slightly larger in size than the plate itself) over the inked surface and pat it down gently at first with palm of hand. Then apply more pressure and using heel of hand bear down in circular motions over the whole plate from the center toward the edges. A rubber brayer may also be employed to achieve even pressure. Using fingers, press down on edges, corners, and between pasted shapes. Where you want the print to be darker, press harder. *Caution:* Do not wait too long to remove the newsprint from

Block prints on this page are by middle school students. **Top:** *Osaka, Japan.* **Bottom:** *Lily Hill Middle School, Manila, Philippines.*

The Jungle, *18 × 36 inches. Group project collograph by intermediate-grade-school children. A paper punch was employed to create* eyes and open patterns in some of the oaktag shapes before gluing them to the printing plate. Pinking shears were also used.

the plate. Water-soluble inks dry quickly and the paper may stick to the plate. Lift it off very carefully and store it to dry. All wet prints should be placed on shelves, counters, or on the floor or spring-clipped with clothespins to a line.

The process of inking and pulling a print should be demonstrated step by step by either the teacher or a student under close supervision of the teacher for the whole class so that it does not have to be repeated each time a student is ready to print. It is recommended that the number of prints a student pulls be limited, so that all students can get in their turns at printing. Additional prints may be made after school or at a later date from a plate that has been inked and has dried thoroughly. Plates need not be washed between studio sessions, but the ones with the proper shellac coating can be.

Facing page: Collograph print, The Pied Piper. Group project, Japan, grade 6.

Finished prints can be attractively mounted for display. Youngsters may want to exchange prints. The plate itself can be painted, shellacked, mounted, and framed. It can also be covered with heavy-duty aluminum foil and further embellished. See the section "Aluminum-Foil Relief."

Students can exploit the collograph technique even further through the employment of a variety of found materials to create diverse textural qualities in the print. Suggested materials include masking and decorative tape, gummed reinforcements, textured wallpaper samples, fabric, string, yarn, confetti, liquid glue, and a variety of found objects. Remember, for best results keep the relief fairly shallow. Avoid the use of thick cord, bottle caps, buttons, and similar high-relief items.

Woodblock print, actual size. The block was painted with colored tempera and printed in several stages to achieve the color overlays.

Grade 7, Iowa City, Iowa.

LINOLEUM PRINTS

A technically demanding form of expression recommended for youngsters in the upper elementary grades and middle school is linoleum ("lino" for short) block printing. Boys especially are challenged by the possibilities of cutting designs into wood or lino blocks with diverse tools and by the ability needed sometimes to manipulate the heavy roller press. Both girls and boys look forward to the pulling of the first print. Because of these built-in attractions, teachers will have little trouble introducing lino prints into the art program.

Unmounted, gray, pliable linoleum suggested for this project may be obtained from art-supply companies. In some instances it is available from furniture, floor covering, and department stores, but the teacher must make certain it is the pliable type and not the brittle, hard-surfaced plastic kind. Cut linoleum plates large enough to give the students ample opportunity for a rich composition. A minimum size of 9 × 9, 9 × 12, or 12 × 12 inches is recommended. The basic materials and tools needed include sets of lino-cutting gouges for the students to share; rubber brayers (rollers to apply ink); inking surfaces (sheet of tempered Masonite, cookie tins, discarded cafeteria trays, commercially available plastic platens, or sheets of glass with edges taped); assorted papers to print on such as newsprint, brown wrapping or colored construction paper, colored tissue paper, wallpaper samples, fabric remnants, classified sections of newspapers, colored pages from magazines; black or multihued, water-soluble printing ink.

Subject-matter themes for lino prints are almost unlimited, but teachers and students should choose those that promise an effective light- and dark-value composition with a variety of shapes, pattern, and detail. Some possibilities are

---

Right: Woodblock prints. Upper grades, elementary school. Japan.

Sketching field trips to a natural history museum provided the subject matter for this handsomely detailed linoleum block print by a fifth-grade Iowa City, Iowa, youngster. Separate drawings were made of the mounted animals and finally combined in class with a unifying jungle background. Notice especially the effective contrast of light and dark areas.

birds, jungle animals and their young, insects, fish, shells, old houses, legendary or mythological figures, portraits and still-life arrangements composed of musical instruments, sports equipment, plants, household utensils, and antiques. A field trip to a natural history museum will provide a wealth of motivational material.

A preliminary drawing on newsprint or manila paper in a self-leaded pencil, black crayon, felt-nib pen, brush and ink, or white crayon on black paper is an important requisite for a successful lino-print project, because it usually determines the final composition, including the dark and light pattern, variety of textural exploitation, points of emphasis and lines of motion. It is important for the student to realize that the final print will be the reverse image of the drawing. Letters and numerals must be reversed in the sketch.

After preliminary drawings have been made and evaluated for design potential, the youngsters may use them as a reference for their drawing on the lino plate, or they may transfer them to the lino plate with carbon paper or dressmaker's white transfer paper. If the lino surface is dark and no white transfer paper is available, paint the block with white tempera paint first. To reverse a sketch before transferring it to the block, hold it against the window and trace lines on back of sheet. Another solution is to place the drawing pencil-side down on the block, tape it down to secure it, and rub over it with a metal spoon. A serviceable transfer will result.

Before the cutting begins, check to see that there are enough sharpened gouges in various sizes for the entire class.

Woodblock prints on this page are by Japanese children, grades 4 and 5. Notice how much was observed and recorded in these space-filled compositions. Printmaking incorporating woodblock cutting tools is introduced in the third grade in Japanese schools.

Here are two more examples of linoleum blocks printed over colored tissue collages. At left, white printing ink was employed over a dark tissue design; at right, black printing ink was used over a lighter valued tissue underlay. Be sure the tissue is glued down firmly and smoothly for best results and is thoroughly dry before pulling the print. Middle school, Iowa City, Iowa.

Students should be introduced to the potential of the many gouges through a teacher demonstration that should emphasize the correct way to hold and manipulate the gouge. Never put a supporting hand in front of a cutting tool. Use a bench hook, if available. Each lino gouge makes its own particular cut, and although it does not lend itself to the same control as a pencil or pen, it produces linear effects that are often more direct and dynamic. The many gouges from veiners to scoops and shovels should, if possible, be used to the fullest extent to achieve the richest print effects.

The veiners or V-shaped gouges #1 and #2 are suggested for making the initial outlines. Another approach is to use the scoop or shovel gouges, working from inside the shapes and thus minimizing tightly outlined compositions.

Sometimes the student can prevent mistakes in cutting by marking an "X" on those areas of the lino surface that are to be gouged out. It is recommended that the youngster employ directional gouge cuts by following the contour of the object, like ripples around a pebble tossed into a stream. The students should be instructed not to make their cuts too deep into the lino, because low ridges remaining can produce a unique textural effect. If the youngsters have difficulty with cutting because the linoleum is too hard, heat the lino on a cookie tin over an electric hot plate turned to a low setting.

Proofs of the lino print in progress may be made by placing a sheet of newsprint over the cutout block and using the side of a black crayon or oil pastel to rub over the paper with a steady and even pressure. The resulting proof can furnish the students with clues to their progress.

As in all printmaking activities, paper-protected areas for inking, printing, and print storage should be designated.

Either oil or water-soluble printing ink may be used. Oil ink is generally recommended for best results, but water-based ink is suggested for crowded elementary-school situations in which expeditious cleanup is an important factor.

Papers to print on include newsprint (which is also recommended for trial prints), brown wrapping paper, construction paper and tissue in assorted colors, wallpaper samples, and colored pages from magazines.

Squeeze out ink on a tempered Masonite sheet, cookie tin, or commercial plastic platen and roll it out with a rubber brayer until tacky. Apply it to the lino block (which has been

Linoleum prints, 12 × 12 inches, grades 4 and 5, Iowa City, Iowa.

cleaned with a moist towel and allowed to dry) with pressure in two directions so that the whole block, including borders and corners, is inked completely.

There are several ways to make or *pull* a print. After carrying the inked block to the printing station or individual desk, students place the paper (cut slightly larger than the block) carefully on the inked lino plate and tap it down gently with heel of hand. Then, exerting stronger pressure with rubber brayer, heel of hand, jar cover, spoon, or commercially available *baren*, they go over the entire surface, especially the borders and corners. Pull the paper off the block carefully. To check the impression the student can lift the paper partially off the block from various sides and if not satisfied with the results can apply more pressure. If water-soluble ink is used, the pulling of the print may have to be speeded up, because the ink dries quickly and may cause stickiness.

Some schools have invested in equipment that makes lino cutting less hazardous. One device is a wood bench hook, which is anchored against desk or table edge providing a supportive ridge for the block.

Above, right: Self-portrait by Käthe Kollwitz (1867–1945), German expressionist artist renowned for her powerful prints and drawings. Left: Upper-grade Japanese youngsters were inspired by Kollwitz to create self-portraits in woodblock prints. Note how the heads fill the space and how detailed the facial features are.

Busy upper-elementary-grade youngsters at work on a group-project reduction linoleum print. The students first cut away selected areas of the linoleum and pulled a number of prints using red printing ink. While these prints were drying, the youngsters gouged out additional sections of the block. The cleaned plate was inked again in green and printed over the first red edition. Care was taken to register or match the second printing over the first. While these two-color prints dried, the students cut away the final selected areas and then used black ink for the third and last impression. Completed print shown left. Oshkosh, Wisconsin.

The aluminum-foil relief, as illustrated on this and the facing page, is an exciting bas relief and embossing adventure that has untold possibilities for exploration in the art program, especially at the upper-elementary-grade and middle school levels. It uses everyday, household, heavy-duty foil instead of expensive metal sheeting. Other easily available materials required include cardboard, white glue, blunt-pointed pencils, and water-base printing ink. The glowing finished product makes a great gift.

CREATING WITH CLAY

All children, in both elementary and middle schools, should have the opportunity to create and express their ideas in clay. Clay is a hands-on wonder—sensuous, malleable, unpredictable, and, on occasion, messy. Some youngsters respond to clay more enthusiastically than others, but all children can benefit from the unique challenges provided by this gift from mother earth.

Very young children in the primary grades are natural clay manipulators. They need very little encouragement as they poke, squeeze, pound, stretch, and roll the moist clay. They enjoy exploring all of its possibilities.

No two primary-grade youngsters will tackle clay modeling the same way, paralleling somewhat the different schema they use in drawing the figure at this stage. Some children will pull out features from a ball or lump of clay; others will add pieces to the basic form. Some may begin a figure with the main body structure, and others may start with the appendages and head.

The teacher's main responsibility at this early stage is to provide the children with an adequate supply of workable clay. Check the plasticity of the clay at least a day or two before the project takes place. If it is too dry, moisten it; if too wet, put on plaster of Paris bats to dry it out. A ball of clay the size of a grapefruit is recommended for each child. Use newspapers or plastic sheeting to protect desk or table tops

---

*Facing page: Terra cotta clay sculpture by a middle school adolescent, London, England. Notice how the textural quality of the clay has been retained to give the work a spontaneous naturalness. Photo courtesy of London Sunday Mirror. **This page, top and center:** Clay relief portraits, Glencoe, Ill. **Bottom:** Japan.*

These Gaudi-like clay constructions, reminiscent perhaps of fantastic prehistoric dwellings, are the imaginative sea-castle expressions of young Japanese schoolchildren. In most instances these constructions are assigned as group table projects.

and introduce just enough stimulating subject-matter motivation (animals and their young) to get the class started.

A period of exploration and experimentation with the clay should precede every clay project. This is especially true in the upper elementary grades. Youngsters need to acquire the feel of the clay before they can express a particular idea. During these orientation sessions the teacher might call the students' attention to the desired plasticity of the clay, the necessity of keeping excess clay moist by rolling the crumbs into a single ball, and the mechanics of cleanup.

One method to introduce youngsters to the feel and potential of clay is by playing the "clay-in-a-paper-sack-game." Give each child a ball of clay about the size of a grapefruit or orange and a sturdy paper sack. Instruct them to put the clay in the sack and, without looking inside, manipulate the clay in the sack until they feel they have created an interesting form. Encourage them to think with their hands—to stretch the clay, squeeze it, and poke it. Above all, they must not peek to see how it is developing. When completed, the finished pieces may be displayed on desks or counters. Ask them if anyone sees a real form hidden in the clay creations: an animal, a bird, a fish? What did they learn about clay?

The animal kingdom provides a wealth of inspiration for the young clay manipulator. Four-legged mammals such as cows, horses, pigs, hippos, elephants, rhinos, and bears are especially suitable, because the child can model sturdy legs to make them stand up. Other popular animals to construct in clay are cats, dogs, rabbits, turtles, frogs, squirrels, whales, porpoises, and alligators. Group projects such as Noah's Ark, Three-Ring Circus, The Zoo, The Farm, and The Jungle are very popular with young children. Human figures are sometimes difficult for them to master unless the children are guided to provide additional supports or to model thick sturdy legs that will hold the figure in balance.

Primary-school children are especially interested in the mobility and adaptability of clay. They may describe a sequence of action with one figure such as a clown or acrobat, manipulating it to create various postures—standing on its head, bending backwards and forwards, and falling down. For very young children, clay manipulating and modeling may fulfill a therapeutic and storytelling need.

Some technical assistance may have to be given to young children who experience difficulty with their clay construction. For youngsters who have a tendency to pat and pound their clay into a flat cookie shape, suggest that they cup the ball of clay in their hands as they model the body of the animal, bird, or fish they are creating. In this way they will have more success in achieving a three-dimensional form. Once they have modeled the characteristic shape of the animal or bird they can pull out or add legs, tails, trunks, horns, tusks, beaks, and wings.

*Three stages in the construction of a clay hippopotamus are illustrated. **Top:** Basic body with legs and tail added. A tongue depressor may be used to create the open mouth. **Center and bottom:** Addition of characteristic details: ears, eyes, teeth.*

The teacher might suggest a simple procedure to make the appendages adhere strongly to the body by inserting them into holes made in the clay body with a stick or fingers. For youngsters in the upper elementary grades and middle school, the process of scoring and welding clay can be demonstrated and explained. To counteract a sagging form, supplementary clay supports such as a "fifth leg" under the animal's body can be suggested. When the clay is leather-hard, this support can be removed. At all times the teacher should emphasize the importance of a sturdy, basic form.

Although many children in the primary grades are not concerned with detailing as such, a number of them will find excitement in discovering and experimenting with textures and patterned relief on their clay creations. A collection of found objects such as popsickle sticks, bottle caps, nails, screws, plastic forks, spoons, wood clothespins, wrapping cord, toothbrushes, dowels, pieces of wood, and wire mesh will spark interest in decorative possibilities. Objects should be washed, rinsed, and dried at the close of the project.

When youngsters reach the middle grades they are more successful in mastering the complexities of advanced clay modeling, but they may ask for specific help with the problems of figures and appendages that sag or come apart, with balance and proportion, and with intricate delineation of features such as eyes, mouth, nose, and ears.

At this stage a number of effective motivations may be included in the teaching repertoire: field trips to observe and sketch animals at a farm, ranch, zoo, animal shelter, pet shop, or natural museum; family pets brought to class to serve as models; photographs and films of animals in their habitats and with their young; and reproductions of drawings, paintings, and sculptures of animals by noted artists.

As a subject for clay sculpture, the prehistoric dinosaur

fires the imagination of youngsters, especially those middle- and upper-elementary-grade students who are developing a strong interest in natural science and in the wonders of the universe. The story of these primeval monsters intrigues them, especially if they have read that the bones of some prehistoric species have been found in their own country. They may even have seen colossal, reconstructed skeletons of these mammoths in a natural history museum. The dinosaur is uniquely adapted to interpretation in clay, the characteristic mass of the creature being ponderous, monumental, armor-encrusted, with its wrinkled, scaly skin evoking the quality of the ancient earth itself.

A preliminary drawing for figurative clay projects in the upper elementary grades and middle school is optional. Often, however, it helps youngsters clarify their usual concept of the animal or human they plan to model. For a clay-dinosaur project the teacher will have to allot a larger amount of clay per student than is suggested for primary-grade clay activity. In any case, extra prepared clay should always be available for emergencies.

For those students who need assistance in creating their clay dinosaur, a fundamental body structure based on the post and lintel pattern is suggested. A lump of clay about the size of a large grapefruit is rolled out into a thick, heavy coil to form the body, tail, neck, and head of the creature, although the head could be added later. For the legs, four or more sturdy coils are attached to the body securely. Follow the advice made earlier of making a hole in the clay body and pushing the leg coil into it; then use additional clay around the junctures for reinforcement. To prevent uneven shrinkage of the clay or cracking and exploding when the clay is fired, avoid using armature supports of wood, wire, reed, or twigs inside the clay structure.

The directness of clay manipulation holds a fascination for children that is universal. The delightful clay figure illustrated here possesses a mobility only the clay medium captures so well. Youngsters can make a figure in clay perform many feats: walk, strut, sit, twist, dance, juggle, bend, and even stand on its head.

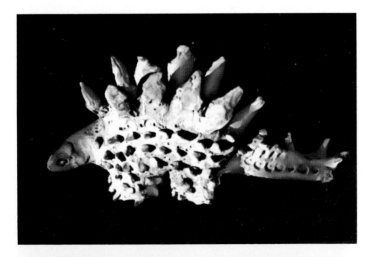

Ancient ceramic Haniwa horse from the pre-Jomon period, Japan. Hollow clay cylinders form the animal's basic shape. Notice how clay coils were flattened to add characteristic reins and saddle. **Top:** *Clay dinosaur, grade 3, Iowa City.*

Planned preliminary discussions involving students and teacher should emphasize the structural elements that can give character to their dinosaurs—the sway of the body, stance and counterstance of the legs, swing of the tail, tilt of the head, action of the jaws, flow of the mane, and flare of the wings. In some instances an imaginatively expressive dinosaur may combine the characteristics of a number of different prehistoric monsters. At all stages during the modeling the clay sculpture should be viewed from every angle so that the student can develop the form as three-dimensionally as possible. A 12 or 16-inch-square Masonite sheet as a working base will help make this possible. If the budget permits, commercially available ceramic turntables in metal or plastic are recommended. Some teachers have commandeered *lazy susans* (kitchen turn tables) for this job.

There are almost no limits to clay-relief pattern and textural exploitation as upper-elementary-grade and middle-school youngsters will testify. Whether their creation is a clay pot, a figure, an animal, or a tile, the field of decoration is wide open. The found-object collection described earlier will provide a welcome source of texture-producing stamps. To achieve the scaly, armorlike epidermis of certain dinosaurs, students might roll out balls, coils, and ribbons of clay and apply them to the body of the creature. Slip (water-diluted clay) can be used as an adhesive to secure the pellets and coils of clay to the clay body surface. Discarded broken saw blades and combs can be used to incise linear effects. Squeezing moist clay through metal screen mesh produces multitudinous strings of clay to employ as manes or tails.

If a kiln is available, and the clay sculptures are to be fired, they should be allowed to dry evenly and slowly until leather-hard. They may be stored to dry in a cabinet (a discarded refrigerator) or on a table or counter under a sheet of plastic. In the case of large animals or figures, holes or hollows should be made in their understructures while they are still leather-hard. These apertures allow the moisture to escape during the firing stage and prevent the piece from cracking and exploding. Remember that one exploded piece can destroy several others in the kiln.

Kiln-glazing of the fired clay pieces is rarely undertaken in the elementary schools because of limited budgets and lack of firing facilities. However there are other avenues to the enrichment of bisque or fired clay that are described in connection with pottery construction recommended for upper elementary grades and middle school.

In the overcrowded middle school classes of today, the beleagured teacher of art would find it difficult if not impossible to instruct every youngster in the sophisticated, highly technical and time-consuming craft of throwing pottery on a wheel. Rather than frustrate a majority of students by demanding skills that college ceramics majors work long hours to possess, the teacher might concentrate on programming hand-built techniques that every youngster from fifth through eighth grade can master.

The students must be guided in their pottery construction to avoid the trite, poorly designed bud vases and ashtrays and to aim instead for honest, natural, organic creations. Introduce them to the exciting output of contemporary potters such as Peter Voulkos, Win Ng, Paul Soldner, and Shoji Hamada and to the beautifully functional clay vessels of the Pre-Columbian craftspeople of Mexico, Gautamala, Colombia, and Peru.

Encourage the youngsters to collect an assortment of stones, pebbles, shells, seedpods, nuts, and driftwood, to learn nature's limitless sources of three-dimensional design.

Encourage children to hold the clay in their hands when modeling small sculptural pieces, especially in the beginning stages.

The handsome branch pots illustrated above started out as basic coil, slab, and pinch-pot forms, but, through the addition of complementary clay and feet and the elegant decoration of surface forms, they have emerged as distinctive, one-of-kind ceramic containers. Grade 7, Oshkosh, Wisconsin.

Decoration should always enhance rather than disguise or destroy the fundamental ceramic form. Intensity of stains can be toned down with earth rubbed over clay body. Sgraffito designs can be engraved through stained surfaces. Liquid wax can provide a subtle sheen as well as a surface protection.

Plan an exhibit of the collected treasures where they can be identified and examined at leisure. Enrich the students backgrounds by showing selected close-up photographs of natural forms with color slides and films that corroborate the variety of design in nature as well as those dealing with contemporary ceramic techniques, especially slab, pinch-pot, and wheel-throwing processes. Challenge them to express in clay the bark of a tree, the veins in a leaf, the intricacies of a gnarled root, or the modulations in a seashell. Alert them to the almost endless variety of organic forms in pods, pebbles, and nuts that could serve as the catalyst for their own clay containers or constructions.

Evaluation and critiques of clay projects in process should be standard procedure during every studio session. Students should have many opportunities to appraise their efforts with the guidance of the teacher and also to share their discoveries and successes with their classmates.

The basic shape or form in any ceramic undertaking must be the first critical concern. Whether organic (derived from a natural source), geometric, or free-form, it must stand by itself as an integral sculptural statement, a true example of three-dimensional design. No amount of additional embellishment or decoration can redeem it, if it is weak in formal concept or structure.

Variety in the basic sculptural form should be a vital consideration in the total design. Because students have been exposed to commercially made porcelains and china where the accent is on symmetrical styling, the teacher must learn to guide the youngster to see the beauty and honesty of asymmetric delineation. Variety can also be achieved through the employment of contrasting shapes and forms of the appendages, spouts, necks, feet, and bases and through the exploitation of positive and negative spaces created by openings in the vessel, by the handles and the lids, and by the delineation of incised and bas-relief areas to create dark and light pattern.

Unity is also vital to the total impact of the clay pot or sculpture. There should be a natural flow from one plane or contour to another. Appendages should grow naturally from the basic body structure, be in scale with it, and complement, not detract from, the whole. This holds true for decoration, whether incised or low relief; it should, like the final staining or glazing, enhance the sculpture or container, not camouflage or compete with it.

Suggested procedures in clay slab construction: At least one generous slab of clay for each student should be prepared in advance by the teacher with student assistance. Slabs should be approximately 12 × 18 inches and ½-inch thick. Moist clay, a rolling pin, a burlap- or linen-covered board, guiding strips of wood ½ inch thick, and plastic cloth to keep slabs moist during storage will be needed. Additional slabs can be made as the project progresses.

Fired clay pellets and relief stamps with found objects

Illustrated, right, a double pinch pot, 14 inches high, grade 5. Two pinch pots are joined together and then tapped with a cord-wrapped paddle into a more varied shape. Foot and neck are added and necessary openings made when clay has set slightly.

Youngsters can employ round objects such as buttons, clothespins, bottle caps, bark, wire mesh, shells, coral, nuts, pine cones, and acorns to add texture and pattern to their clay creations.

may be impressed on the moist slab to enrich the surface before construction of the container begins. Divide the large slab into the number of desired slabs needed for sides and bottom (and sometimes top) of the container described. It is recommended that the junctures where two slabs are to be joined be scored (roughened) and covered with water or slip before attaching the slabs. When slabs are joined, use a wood paddle to attach them more securely or to alter the shape of the container. Two or more clay slab constructions in different sizes may be joined together for a larger, more complex structure.

Suggested procedures for pinch-pot sculpture: For pinch-pot sculpture approximately 5 pounds of moist clay per student is recommended. First, a large portion of the clay is shaped into a large ball and cut in half. The students then form each half into a pinch-pot shape, keeping the walls fairly thick and each pot similar in size. They then join the two pinch pots together (scoring and moistening the junctures if necessary) and pinch the seams tightly to form a hollow ball. Holding the hollow ball of clay in one hand the student paddles it with the other hand until the pinched seams disappear. A recommended paddle for this procedure is a piece of scrap wood, $1 \times 2 \times 18$ inches, wrapped at one end generously with cord. Youngsters should keep turning the ball as they paddle it. It is important that the entire clay ball is paddled evenly as it is rotated. This action packs the clay and seals in enough air to support the walls. During the paddling process students can change the shape of the ball to resemble a pod, nut, shell, or gourd. Although the cord-wrapped paddle produces a definitive texture, additional decoration may be done employing stamped, incised, and bas-relief motifs. For unusual effects students may apply clay pellets, thin coils, and ribbons to the pot. Be sure the surface clay is moist for this application. If not, moisten it or use slip.

Feet, handles, bases, and other appendages may be

added for functional or decorative purposes, but the sealed ball should not be opened until the whole container is complete. Once it is opened, necks and spouts may be added. Many exciting developments and discoveries occur when the youngsters combine two or more pinch-pot balls of various sizes into one unified container or sculpture.

Experienced teachers soon learn that disappointing accidents can occur during the bisque firing if the clay pieces still retain air bubbles. Proper wedging of clay helps. Adding sufficient grog to the clay eliminates some explosion hazards. Solid, heavy clay sculptures, especially bulky animals, fish, and reclining figures, should be hollowed out on their undersides when leather-hard. Another suggestion applicable to the slab and pinch pots just described is to inject pin holes in them during the leather-hard stage, which will allow air to escape during firing.

Suggestions for staining and coloring the clay pieces: For those middle schools with relatively small art classes, generous art-supply budgets, and adequate ceramic facilities with especially large-sized kilns, the technique of glazing can project the ceramic process to a rich aesthetic culmination for the young adolescent. In most schools, however, the burgeoning classes and the restricted firing facilities make glazing a limited activity. It is relatively easy to fire greenware, because raw clay pieces may be stacked closely inside of or on top of one another or rest against one another in the kiln, and the baking of one class's ceramic output can be accomplished in a few firings. Even engobe-decorated pieces, in which the clay slip is applied to greenware and sometimes scratched through for graffito designs, will not burden the firing schedule too much. Students must remember not to let the clay get too dry before applying slip or engobe decoration, since peeling will result during the firing.

Glaze firing, as most teachers are aware, is another problem. The glazed ware must be stacked carefully so that

no glazed piece touches another piece or the wall of the firing chamber. In many cases special supports such as stilts or pins must be employed, and if the complex stacking process is done properly, it may take weeks of glaze-firing schedules to complete the project, especially if the students have been challenged to create clay structures of some magnitude.

Inventive teachers have discovered other avenues and directions in the enrichment and coloring of bisqueware. Staining the work is definitely one possibility. Oil and polymer stain, shoe polish, wood stain, and oil pastels all possess a unique patina that can enhance the quality and beauty of the bisque-fired clay pots and sculpture.

The various stains, especially the turpentine-diluted oils in ochre, burnt or raw umber, sienna, oxide green, and other neutralized hues can be applied to the bisqueware with a cloth or utility brush. Begin with the lighter hues and make sure the stain penetrates the recessed and incised areas of the clay. Before the applied stain dries, the bas-relief or raised surfaces may be toned down partially with a turp-moistened

Top right: Ceramic container, Middle School, Oshkosh, Wisconsin.
Left, top, and bottom: Students concentrate as they create their clay projects.

236

rag so that the darker recessed areas will create a contrasting effect.

Sometimes moist dirt or soil of another shade or value than the bisqueware itself can be rubbed on and into the incised areas. Oil pastel, Rub'n'Buff, Treasure Gold, and other commercial patinas may be blended into the ware. In almost all cases in which staining or coloring (try glueing on torn pieces of colored tissue paper) is applied to bisque-fired clay, it is advisable to add a protective coating to the piece. To achieve a subtle sheen rather than a hard gloss, try liquid floor wax. Sometimes several coats of wax are necessary. Clear glossy polymer is also suggested as another coating agent.

The use of stains—oils, acrylics, gouaches, and oil pastels—on bisqueware must be sensitively and discriminatingly handled. *Restraint* is the key word. In all instances the color decoration or glaze should enhance, rather than detract from, the clay creation.

Top left and right: Shallow clay containers decorated with pellets and ribbons of clay. Grade 5, Campus School, University of Wisconsin, Oshkosh. Bottom right: Attractive clay plaque using many ceramic design elements. Jimmy Morris, Fine Arts Consultant, Clarke County Schools, Athens, Georgia.

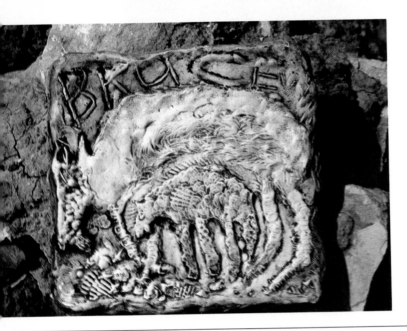 

Two attractive plaster reliefs by middle school youngsters. Notice especially how composition fills the space and how the metal patina brings out the relief highlights. "Animals and Their Young" is a popular theme chosen by many students for this challenging three-dimensional project.

Animals, birds, fish, and insects lend themselves beautifully as subjects for plaster-relief projects. Suggest that students limit the oil stains to neutral colors at first in order to achieve unity. Be sure to apply one or two coats of shellac or white glue to the plaster relief before staining it. Allow the stain to flow into incised lines.

PLASTER RELIEFS

Youngsters in the upper elementary grades and middle school are often self-critical concerning their drawing ability and need the satisfaction and challenge of creating in an art medium not always dependent on drawing or painting skills. Plaster-relief making is such an adventure. The technique, involving manipulative skills with special tools, materials, and surprise effects, whets their expressive appetites. Even though a preliminary sketch is generally recommended, the fact that it can be freely interpreted and changed in the ensuing process ensures the youngsters' approval.

Other art projects that belong in this general hands-on, craft-centered category are metal repoussé, ceramics, papier mâché, stitchery, weaving, and mobiles.

For a plaster-relief project the following materials and tools are required: moist clay, plaster, a plastic or rubber dishpan, a container for the clay mold (shoe box, cigar box, half-gallon or gallon, waxed-cardboard milk carton); an assortment of discarded and found objects of all kinds—spools, nails, wire, cogwheels, lath, screws, keys, clothespins, buckles, rope, bolts, cord, reed, dowel sticks, bottle caps, jar lids, coins, printer's letters, combs, plastic forks and spoons, and natural objects such as twigs, pine cones, acorns, nuts, seashells, and bark; a plaster-sealing medium such as white glue or shellac; a 1- or 2-inch utility brush; and staining liquids (wood stains, turp-diluted oil paints, commercial patina finishes such as Rub'n'Buff and Treasure Gold). In middle school the students need not be limited by a box mold. They can create larger free-form-shaped reliefs by using a sheet of tempered Masonite as their working surface and building a clay wall around their slab of clay.

The clay negative mold and the completed plaster relief. Because a reverse image results, letters and numerals must be impressed backwards into the clay mold to read correctly in the final relief. Shapes pressed into the clay bulge out in the plaster version. A seashell was employed for the elephant's ears. Other effective imprinting objects include beads and discarded costume jewelry, plastic forks and spoons, crumpled heavy-duty aluminum foil, heavy cord, reed, and wire.

The first step in the project is to prepare the box for the clay mold. In the case of a shoe box, simply reinforce the box with a strip of masking or strapping tape around the entire box. Put the lid under the box to reinforce that area. The inside of the box may be sealed with melted paraffin or lined with wax paper. Milk cartons should be cut in half lengthwise. If the open end is resealed, both halves of the carton may be used. No protective coat is needed. In the case of the cigar box remove the lid and seal the box with wax paper or paraffin.

Two methods of making the basic clay layer are suggested. In the simplest procedure the clay is rolled out in a

slab approximately ½ to 1 inch thick, cut to the size of the box, and placed in the bottom of the box ready for the next stage of the process. In the second method the clay is placed in the bottom of the box, pellet by pellet, until the bottom is filled with a clay layer ½ to 1 inch thick. If a very flat surface is desired, the clay may be stamped down with the end of a 2 × 4-inch woodblock.

Before the students begin their incisions and impressions in the clay mold, they should practice relief designs and textural effects on a sample slab of clay using the various imprinting tools. Discussion and demonstration will reveal that impressions made in the clay will be reversed in the plaster cast. Designs pressed or incised in the clay will bulge out in the plaster version. Letters, numbers, and names must be imprinted backwards in the clay to read correctly in the final product.

By building a clay wall around a student's practice clay relief on a square of Masonite or a pie tin, the teacher can create a quick casting to show the class what happens in the process. Knowing the limits and the possibilities of this exciting medium frees the student to be more expressive, more innovative.

There are a number of ways to create the clay negative mold. A very free and natural approach involves the use of the hands and fingers. Commercial ceramic tools may also be employed. Coils, pellets, and ribbons of clay cut out from a thin slab may be applied with water or slip.

Subject themes for plaster-relief projects are legion. Here animals, both real and imaginary, provided motivation for the top and center illustrations. The Bible story "Jonah and the Whale" inspired the interpretation in lower relief.

With younger children it might be wise to limit the design or subject matter to those ideas that can be best expressed with impressions of available found objects. In this approach, instead of scratching or incising lines in the clay with nail or stick, which often produces sharp and hazardous edges in the final plaster cast, the children press their designs into the clay rather than dig them out of the clay. For straight lines they may employ applicator sticks, popsickle holders, or the edge of a thick cardboard piece. For curved lines they may use bent reed, cord, and edges of round containers.

Recommended subject-matter themes for plaster reliefs include birds of plumage, fish, insects (butterflies), animals in their habitat, flowers, theater or clown faces, heraldic devices, personal insignia, monograms, and nonobjective designs.

When the impressions, the bas reliefs, and incised designs are completed, liquid plaster of Paris is poured over the clay mold to approximately ½ to 1 inch thickness. Before the plaster sets, bent paper clips may be inserted into it to provide hanging hardware for the completed plaster reliefs. For an explanation of plaster-mixing procedures see "Sculpture," below. Allow sufficient time for the plaster to set. This may vary from 1 to 2 hours. Some teachers recommend letting the plaster dry overnight. It is recommended that the teacher make a sample plaster mold a day or two before the project to test the hardening qualities of the plaster on hand.

When the plaster is hard, the student pries open the cardboard container or carton and separates the plaster from the clay. If this separation is handled carefully, most of the moist clay in the mold can be salvaged for a future project.

To prepare the plaster relief for the staining or glazing phase, students should file away or sandpaper the excess edges and any sharp points that may be abrasive. The relief should then be washed with water. A discarded toothbrush works best to clean the clay out of recessed areas. A nail or nut pick also may prove helpful. Before staining it, give the plaster relief a generous coat of clear shellac or slightly water-diluted white glue. Allow this coating to dry thoroughly.

The most successful stains for plaster reliefs are wood and shoe stains as well as turp-diluted oil paints; recommended oil colors are raw umber, burnt umber, raw sienna, burnt sienna, ochre, and earth green. If only high-intensity, bright hues are available they should be dulled with their complementary colors. Apply the stains with a brush, allowing the paint to flow into the indentations and incisions. Before the stain dries, wipe off raised areas with a cloth or paper towels to bring out highlights. Be careful not to wipe off all of the stain. For further embellishment try the Rub'n'Buff and Treasure Gold patinas in gold or silver. Apply with facial tissue, Q-tip, or fingertip. Turpentine is the solvent and cleanser.

For situations where color staining of the reliefs is not practicable, the dry plaster may be tinted by mixing it with neutral-colored powder paint before sifting it into the water preparatory to casting.

Plaster reliefs might be a good solution for teachers and students in upper elementary and middle school grades who are looking for a different creative challenge. For many youngsters this project will remind them of the sand sculptures they may have created at the beaches.

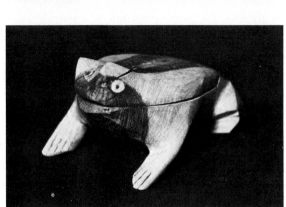

SCULPTURE

There is a wealth of sculptural projects in a host of challenging techniques, both subtractive and additive, that awaits those upper elementary grade and middle school students and their teachers who are ready and willing to make a serious, time-consuming commitment to a painstaking yet adventurous task. Too often sculpture in the elementary school has been presented as a therapeutic, hands-on activity with minor emphasis on its expressive potential. If sufficient time cannot be allotted in the schedule for the youngsters to become thoroughly involved in the sculptural process, it should be postponed until the middle-school years when more studio time is budgeted for art and when the students' perseverance and constructive skills are more developed. There is no doubt that young adolescents enjoy working with semihard substances they can chisel and carve as well as with the new found materials they can build and assemble. However, if the elementary-school teacher of art understands the limitations and possibilities of the various sculptural media and the students can be sufficiently motivated to tackle the assignment and carry it through to a rewarding culmination, the sculpture experience can be one of the most fulfilling in the upper-elementary-grades art program.

The major consideration of these three-dimensional projects is often not so much one of motivation as it is a matter of material resources, preliminary planning, special techniques, cleanup, and storage. A class of 25 or more stu-

Facing page, subtractive sculpture: clockwise beginning top right, are monkey, woodpod, Malaya; rooster, cryptomeria, Japan; elephant, ivory, India; bird, boxwood, Indonesia; elephant, wood, Africa; horse, ivory, China; and, in center, frog, wood, Mexico. This page: Plastic sculpture, grade 6.

dents working on additive or subtractive sculpture poses a number of organizational problems that must be resolved.

Teachers must decide beforehand whether they want the entire class to engage in the same technique or to allow the students to work in the material of their choosing. If instructors can control a large class where some youngsters are working on toothpick or balsa-wood construction, some on plaster block carving, and some on wire or metal sculpture, it is a tribute to their teaching skill, provided that the resulting products show evidence of the students' growth in sculptural design. If, as is often the case, the teacher becomes merely the dispenser of various materials and tools and has little time to evaluate the work in progress with the youngsters, it is much wiser to limit the offering to one sculptural technique or medium with the entire class participating. In such instances the teacher can organize materials, tools, and storage space more effectively, while building a rich motivational arsenal to benefit everyone in class. In addition, the teacher's evaluations will have meaning for all students, who in turn will learn from one another.

Recommended and readily obtainable materials for subtractive sculpture (carving) include plaster-of-Paris molds, leather-hard clay molds, lightweight firebrick, and economy-sized bars of soap. Commercially available products specifically intended for subtractive sculpture include Featherrock, Crea-stone, and balsa wood. Sandcore is highly recommended.

Subject ideas for subtractive sculpture that youngsters can handle successfully include fish, nesting birds, animals

Subtractive sculpture in a variety of materials has appealed to artists of all cultures throughout the ages. Wood in its multitudinous forms has probably proven the most popular medium for sculptors; but exquisite creations have been carved in a host of materials, including jade, ivory, bone, marble, soapstone, and alabaster.

Sculpture in elementary and middle schools is an important part of the art program encompassing a host of techniques and projects in cast plaster, wood, wire, sandcore, porous firebrick, scrap metal, soap, discarded boxes, and papier maché. It is essential, however, that sufficient time be allotted for the students to become thor- *oughly involved in the sculptural process. **Facing page:** Steps in an applied plaster sculpture show the basic armature of woodsticks, wire, and reed. Newspaper may be used for stuffing. In plaster projects such as these, mix only a small amount of plaster at a time. Lots of newspapers on hand will protect work areas.*

(especially those in repose), portrait heads, organic or nonobjective free forms, including motifs based on rocks, shells, nuts, pods, and other natural or biomorphic forms.

If plaster is selected as the sculptural material it should be mixed with additives such as fine-grain zonolite or white sand to give it a texture and make it easier to carve. Approximately one part additive to one part dry plaster will produce a fairly porous and workable carving block. A half-gallon or quart-size wax-paper milk or juice carton makes a sturdy, leak-proof container for the plaster mold.

While the students are making preliminary sketches (optional) for their sculptures on newsprint or manila paper, cut into size to fit the plaster block they plan to carve, the teacher can supervise two or three youngsters at a time in the making of their plaster molds. On a newspaper-protected table or counter near the sink (if possible) all necessary materials and tools for making the plaster block should be on

hand: molding plaster, zonolite or sand, scoops or cups, wax-paper milk cartons opened wide at the top, water, small-size rubber or plastic dishpan, wood stick or paddle, dry tempera colors (if desired), and lots of newspapers. Newspapers should cover the floor around the plaster-mixing area and line the nearby wastebaskets.

Fill a milk carton three-fourths full with water. Pour this water into the dishpan. Sift plaster into the water slowly, using hand, cup, or scoop. When islands of plaster appear above the water, add zonolite or sand. Stir gently yet swiftly with hand, squeezing the lumps until thoroughly mixed. The mixture thickens very quickly, so be ready to pour it immediately into the milk carton. Tap the plaster-filled milk carton on the table to remove trapped bubbles or stir quickly with stick or paddle. Excess plaster left in the dishpan should be scraped into the newspaper-lined wastebasket. *Never pour plaster down the sink.* Allow the plaster mold or block to dry

*The sculpture on this and the facing page is by middle school students. **This page, top:** Plaster of paris; **bottom:** Foamglass. **Facing page, top left:** Driftwood; **top right:** Stained plaster of paris block; **bottom left:** Plaster of paris mixed with vermiculite; **bottom right:** Softweight firebrick.*

completely. This may take several hours. In most cases teachers let it dry overnight. If color is desired in the plaster block, dry tempera powder color may be used to tint the dry plaster before it is mixed with water. Neutral colors such as umber, ochre, sienna, and earth green are recommended. These colors may have to be mixed.

Students may transfer preliminary pencil sketches to the block using carbon paper or draw directly on the block with pencil or ink marker. They may prefer to carve directly into the block using their sketch as a reference only. If they use their sketch, they first cut, file, rasp, or chisel away the excess plaster to delineate a profile view. Next they may refer to their top, front, and rear sketches and carve away to define those contours. They should proceed slowly and cautiously as they remove the plaster, turning the block around to define all forms consistently. The recommended tools for this process are the Sloyd or Hyde knife with the 2-inch blade or a small plaster rasp. Working areas should be covered with newspapers to expedite cleanup. One teacher counteracted the messiness by having the students hold the plaster block inside a large cardboard grocery carton as they cut away the excess plaster. In fair weather the class can do the carving outdoors on a sidewalk or similar area that can be swept.

Teachers should help the students evaluate their sculpture in process: to be aware of large masses contrasting with small forms; to capture the characteristic stance or action; to emphasize a significant feature such as the beak or claws of a bird, the mane of a lion, the horns of a bull; and to enrich the surface of their creation through texture and pattern.

When sculpting animals, heads, or human figures, youngsters should be guided to keep the base of the sculpture undefined during most of the carving process so that the piece does not become top heavy, topple, and break, unless the student plans a supplementary support of a metal rod or

Wood sculpture of turtle and its young by an unknown Japanese   *artist. Late nineteenth century.*

dowel set in a wood base. Appendages such as hands, ears, horns, tusks, beaks, tails, and other jutting forms should be kept undefined until the basic shape is well established.

The sculpture should be conceived to ensure the fullest use of the block. Youngsters should be cautioned against subject-matter themes that are too intricate and complex and that might be more easily expressed in wood, wire, metal, or clay. Textural or decorative details will be delineated during the final stages of the sculpture, but students should be reminded that no amount of texture, detail, or pattern will redeem or enhance the work if the basic form is weak in design.

Nails, discarded dental tools, and nut picks are very effective for incising texture and descriptive detail. When the carving and delineative embellishment are completed, the sculpture may be stained, glazed, waxed, or metalized. To provide a working surface for the stain or patina, the plaster sculpture should be coated or sealed with an application of shellac or slightly water-diluted white glue. Allow this coating to dry thoroughly.

Perhaps the simplest method of staining the plaster sculpture is to apply one of the many wood stains commercially available. They come in a variety of subtle shades including a new dark earth green. Apply the stain freely with a brush and let it penetrate into the incised, textured areas of the plaster. Allow the stain to set briefly and then wipe off raised areas with a cloth to bring out highlights. If the stain has dried, the cloth may have to be moistened with turpentine. If the stain did not penetrate the incised designs, reincise those lines and stain again. Tube oil paints diluted with turpentine to a liquid consistency may also be employed as a staining agent.

A complementary base for a sculpture in plaster, firebrick, or sandcore is generally recommended. Driftwood, discarded blocks of wood from a lumberyard or dismantled building, and sections of tree trunks with the bark remaining can give presence and distinction to the youngster's finished carving. The blocks of wood can be stained or painted to either contrast with or complement the sculpture.

Papier maché. *Youngsters in upper elementary grades and middle school generally possess the necessary technical and manipulative skills that the papier maché process demands. All necessary materials and tools for the project should be organized beforehand: newspapers, string, wire, masking tape, wheat paste, paper towels, plastic containers, liquid laundry starch, tempera paint, colored tissue paper, yarn, scissors, wire cutters, wood bases, and found objects. Storage for papier maché projects in process must also be assigned. Steps in one popular papier maché technique are illustrated below: the basic wire and newspaper and paper-towel padding and finally the painting with tempera including characteristic details. In the illustrations, right, of projects by interning classroom teachers, the students drilled holes in a woodblock base and secured their wire and newspaper armature into these holes, making the ensuing construction much easier to control. Notice the effectively color-coordinated printed designs on both base and sculpture. Photos courtesy of Oliver Coleman, professor of art, University of Georgia, Athens.*

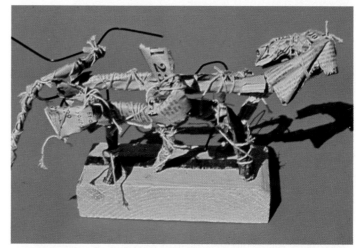

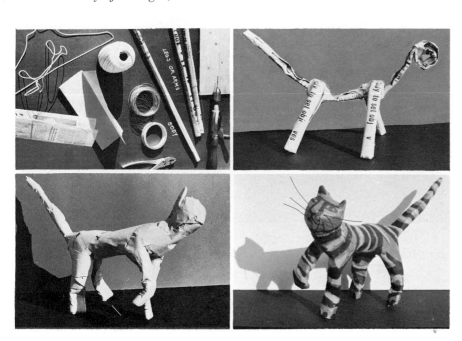

Photograph by W. Robert Nix, professor of art, University of Georgia, Athens.

CONSTRUCTIONS IN SPACE

An exciting new world of additive sculpture has opened up with the burgeoning exploitation of found materials such as applicator sticks, drinking straws, thin dowels, assorted toothpicks, reed, discarded game parts (for example, Tinkertoy) pick-up sticks, scrap lumber, and plastic packing materials. Whatever one may label the resulting constructions—stabiles, mobiles, space modulators, combine art, or assemblage—they definitely attract and hold the interest of today's space-conscious youngsters and add an adventurous dimension to elementary- and middle-school art programs.

The teacher's first consideration in the implementation of these construction projects is to see that sufficient materials and tools are on hand. A letter to the parents listing found materials especially effective in the three-dimensional construction will help build a store of discards, scraps, and remnants that can get the project going. (See Appendix E for specific suggestions.)

In many instances children will be eager to create non-objective, abstract, and geometrically oriented constructions, allowing the materials to dictate the form. This is particularly true when straws, applicator sticks, toothpicks, and reed are the building elements. The design grows, stick by stick, straw by straw, dowel by dowel.

Unless the construction itself has a stable footing, it is advisable that an auxiliary support or separate base of wood, plywood, or Masonite be employed. Determine the number and placement of supports required and then drill or hammer holes into the base at these points. Begin the structure by inserting and glueing the initial supports into these holes. The number will vary depending upon the complexity and size of the completed structure.

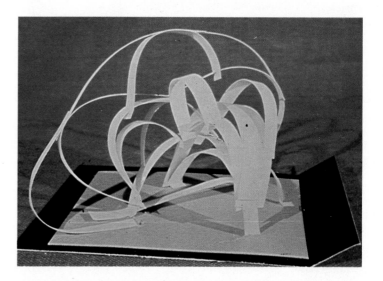

*Top: Construction using reed, construction paper, and fast-drying glue. Grade 5. **Bottom:** Space modulator created with construction-paper strips and school paste. Grade 6, Milwaukee.*

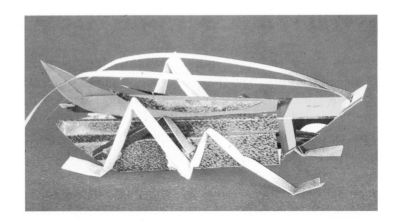

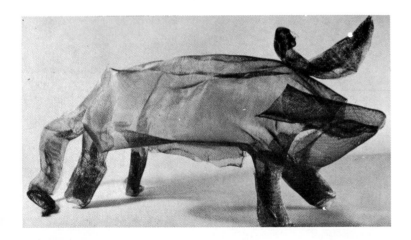

Students and teachers will discover, too, a host of affinitive materials to enrich and embellish the stick or straw constructions. Experiment, for example, with bottle corks, thread spools, beads, cord, Ping-Pong balls, small rubber balls, pegboard pegs, construction paper, mailing tubes, colored cardboard, cardboard spools from tape dispensers, miniature cardboard boxes, assorted plastic pieces, wood or plastic buttons, and tiny film canisters.

The completed constructions may be given a coat of spray paint. Black or white is especially effective in unifying the different segments of the structure and creating a striking visual impact. Always apply spray paint in a well-ventilated area.

Wood scraps, rope and yarn remnants, dried corn husks, discarded metal screen, and spools from thread can be creatively recycled in today's school art programs, as the illustrations on these pages prove. Let the youngsters' imaginations soar.

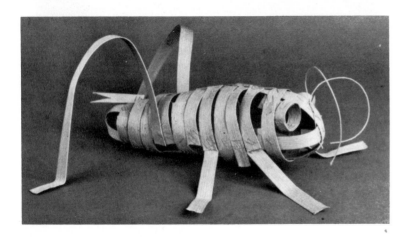

There are many avenues open to youngsters in upper elementary grades and middle school who want to explore more challenging aspects of additive sculpture. Wire and metal sculpture has a special appeal for boys. Wire can be combined with found metal pieces and objects to create exciting three-dimensional constructs. Toothpick and applicator-stick constructions can be dipped into melted crayon, wet plaster, or liquid metal. Corrugated cardboard can be cut into varisized shapes and then slotted, joined, and glued together into a stabile. Cardboard mailing tubes can be cut into multi-sized cylinders and rings and then assembled into animals, insects, and figures. It is recommended that a vibrating jig-saw be used to cut heavy cardboard, chipboard, Masonite, and heavyweight cardboard tubes.

A metal construction by a middle school student. Some soldering skills are necessary for this type of assemblage. Another example of the adage "The whole is greater than the sum of its parts."

BOX SCULPTURE

Older, more mature children often need a change of pace sparked by new challenges, materials, and techniques to keep them growing and interested in art. Imaginative constructions using cardboard boxes, mailing tubes, and assorted found objects give upper-elementary-grade and middle school youngsters a rare opportunity to express their individual ideas in a unique three-dimensional form; recycle discarded materials into new, exciting configurations; struggle with a problem in complex construction until it is solved; and prove once again the adage that "the whole is greater than the sum of its parts" in a truly individual and creative way.

At least two to four weeks before the project begins, the students should be reminded to start collecting discarded boxes of all sizes and shapes from grocery, stationery, drug, and department stores. This early personal involvement on the part of the youngsters builds mounting interest in the expressive adventure ahead.

All of the accumulated boxes and found objects can be stored until needed in a giant cardboard carton, or, if desired, students can store their personal collections of items in paper grocery sacks hand-printed with their names.

Equipment, tools, and special materials that contribute to the success of the venture include straight pins, masking tape, paper clips, string, double-faced tape, rubber bands, gummed tape, coping saw, vibrating jigsaw (optional), white liquid glue, contact cement, rubber cement, school paste, scissors, paper punch, nails, wire, old magazines, and coloring materials. X-acto knives and single-edge razor blades (taped with masking tape so that only one small point is visible) are necessary to cut cardboard boxes, but they must be used with extreme caution and only under strict supervision by the teacher.

Several problems unique to this project should be resolved before the class begins the box construction. These problems deal with adequate storage for the found objects and for the constructions in progress, as well as a sufficient supply of fastening devices and materials.

Imaginative themes and subjects for box sculpture are almost limitless: astronauts, spaceships, space stations, robots, creatures from another planet, engines, planes, toys, rockets, homes, vehicles and computers of the future, fantastic designs for playground equipment, masks, nonobjective space modulators, and imaginative animals, bugs, birds, and fish.

One method of initiating the project is to invite the youngsters to select three or four different-sized boxes and a set of cardboard mailing tubes (toilet-tissue tubes for small constructions) from the general supply or from their individual collections and manipulate these items into various juxtapositions until one arrangement or combination triggers a subject idea. Another approach is to have a theme in mind and select boxes that will give form to this preconceived idea. After the youngsters decide on the basic shape of their creation, they may want to make some sketches (optional) to help them with their construction plans. The excitement builds as youngsters see the creation change and grow as new materials are found and added. What began first as a dream car might easily emerge in the final stages as a space station.

The most difficult part of this project is the mechanics involved in fastening the separate boxes together and secur-

---

In box sculpture allow the shape of the box itself to trigger the student's imagination. Square and rectangular boxes, which were used for the ship construction on page 256, are much easier for young children to assemble. It is not always necessary to paint box sculpture, especially when boxes have colorful printed designs.

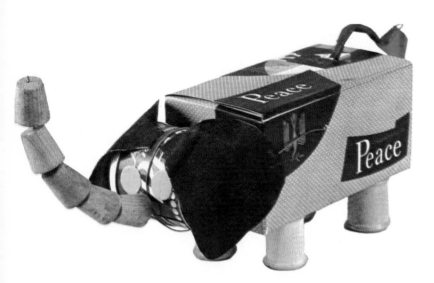

ing the appendages to the main structure. Recommended methods include glueing and securing the boxes together with string until the glue dries and fastening the boxes together with masking tape that extends around both boxes; in most instances the glue (with the exception of contact cement) should be allowed to dry overnight for a strong weld.

In the construction of standing figures, astronauts, robots, and legendary heroes, the problem of making the figure stand upright must be resolved. If necessary, a third leg or support must be created. Sometimes a tail can be added for balance, sometimes the figure can hold gear (a spear, a banner standard) that touches the ground as a stabilizer.

Plastic containers in varied sizes may be recycled into fantastic creatures. Care must be exercised when cutting into plastic. It may be prudent to reserve such construction for upper elementary grades and middle school. In the top-right illustration on the facing page, notice how the box lids, when open, become the heads of the mother and baby kangaroo.

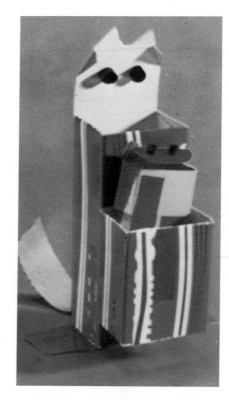

Interest in the project may be heightened by suggesting further implementation with other found materials for decorative or textural delineation. Encourage the students to exploit egg cartons, corrugated and embossed cardboard, paper drinking straws, plastic packing noodles, clothespins, plain and colored toothpicks, paste sticks, dowels, corks, pipe cleaners, reed, wooden and plastic kindergarten beads, Tinkertoy pieces, Ping-Pong balls, and game parts. Some of these materials may be purchased in quantity lots at little cost from discount stores and school supply firms.

The outcome of box-sculpture projects depends in great part on the variety of boxes and other found objects gathered by students and teachers. Sometimes an unusual box turns up that is just right for the head of a monster and triggers the design for the rest of the construction. Often a box can be partially opened and hinged to become mouth and jaws of a voracious mythical lion or dragon.

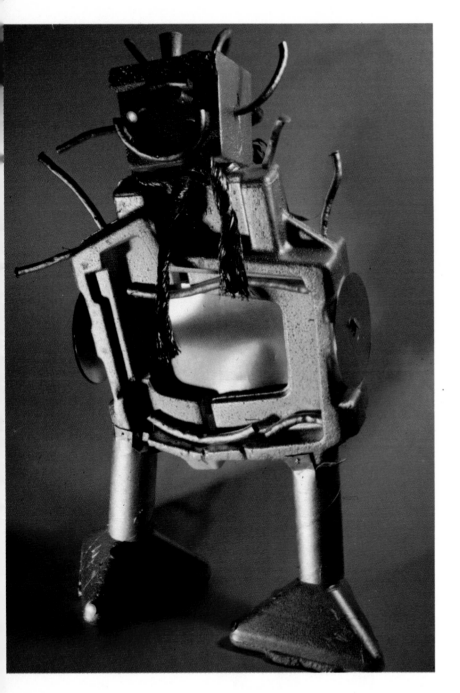

A decision must be made, too, about whether to paint the box construction. In some instances the containers with their printed designs and logos are so colorful and exciting that painting would only detract from their bold design qualities. In those instances when the sculpture is not painted, the characteristic features that give the creature or figure its unique individuality must be emphasized, especially the eyes, mouth, nose, ears, and horns.

If the constructions are to be painted, certain factors must be considered. The glossy surfaces of many boxes will resist tempera or watercolor paints. Soap will have to be added to make the paint adhere. Latex and enamel cover all surfaces effectively. If cost is not a factor, spray paint is recommended. Silver, copper, or gold spray paint may be employed for a robot, knight in armor, or astronaut. Spray paints should be applied in a well-ventilated area or out of doors.

Another possibility is to camouflage or mask the distracting areas of the boxes by covering them with colored construction paper, comic-book pages, magazine color sections, colored tissue paper, wallpaper samples, cloth remnants, or discarded gift-wrapping papers.

There are endless possibilities in box and found-object sculpture. The teacher and students who are resourceful enough, persistent enough, and patient enough to try this project have a real adventure in art awaiting them. Go for it!

A plastic container was combined with other plastic discards to produce the imaginatively constructed robot on this page. The entire sculpture was sprayed with metal paint. Caution: When spraying sculpture, do it out of doors or in a well-ventilated area. Always protect working surfaces with newspapers. Grade 6, Ann Arbor, Michigan.

Carpool, 34″ × 28″, by Robert D. Clements, professor of art, University of Georgia, Athens.

MASKS

Mask making in the elementary and middle schools has always been a popular undertaking but, unfortunately, one in which the design considerations have seldom been fully understood or effectively implemented. Too often basic compositional factors have been minimized and raw colors applied in a random, slap-dash, form-negating manner.

The most inspired and evocative masks of past centuries and cultures have almost always been based on an abstract, stylized concept rather than on natural appearance and often employing a format that capitalized on symbolic, geometric shapes such as the oval, circle, ellipse, or a subtle combination of them. Masks of various ethnological, primitive peoples often owe their impact to a semisymmetrical abstraction of the face, whether human or animal, and to psychological emphasis of significant features.

Although very young children can, on occasion, create colorful, expressively naive masks when richly motivated, mask making, because of its symbolic connotations, traditional nuances, and often complex techniques, is best postponed until youngsters reach the upper elementary grades and middle school.

A study of masks by tribal Africans and North Pacific Coast Indians, among others, reveals certain significant and recurring aspects. Facial features that capture the mood or

Colored construction-paper masks. A three-dimensional effect was achieved by cutting short slits into the borders of a square or rectangular sheet of paper and then overlapping the resulting tabs and stapling them together. Masks make highly decorative artifacts to brighten up the classroom.

spirit are emphasized or exaggerated. Characteristic elements of a face are seldom distorted to appear as something alien such as the trite asterisk-shaped eyes or mouths of stereo-typed versions.

The most expressive masks are imbued with the essence and vitality of a particular mood or emotion: astonishment, serenity, power, anger, dignity, joy, fury, frenzy, benevolence, or wonder. Continuity of facial forms and features, as exemplified by the linear flow of the nose structure into the eyebrow contour, is a recurring characteristic in primitive masks.

Facial decoration has been consistently and effectively employed to heighten the visual appeal of the mask. Students, taking a cue from mask artisans of the past, will employ lines or shapes to reinforce and emphasize the dominant features. They will create facial pattern and texture and delineate hair and beard with exquisite care. Eyes are usually emphasized by employment of highly contrasting colors and values. Color in every instance must be used judiciously, because it can either enhance or jeopardize the mask's impact or appeal. Color must be integrated with the features, not superficially applied, and it must complement rather than detract. Subtle, limited color schemes and harmonies should be encouraged. Primary colors should be employed with discretion, although they may be effectively employed to provide a necessary contrast.

Top: Giant, colored construction masks by Japanese children. Bottom: Three-dimensional masks made from corners of sturdy grocery-store cartons and painted with tempera. Additional details inserted into slots of main mask form. Upper elementary grades, Barrow School, Athens, Georgia.

Varied approaches to mask masking. **Left:** *Boxes, spools, paper cups, and yarn were employed.* **Center:** *Construction paper and raffia. Feathers could also be incorporated.* **Right:** *Papier maché over a crumpled newspaper base. Basic mask forms may also be achieved by applying newspaper strips over a mixing bowl with wheat paste or liquid starch.*

The incentive for mask making may spring just as naturally from a study of history, geography, or literature as it does from overworked Halloween sources. Youngsters should also be invited and challenged to create masks as art forms per se.

Materials and processes that result in qualitative mask making are in a sense limited. Papier mâché over a clay foundation is still the most popular and effectively controlled technique allowing for highly individualized interpretations and detailed facial modeling. Also recommended is papier mâché or plaster-impregnated gauze applied over a mixing or salad bowl, small dishpan, balloon, or beach ball. As the pasted form develops, it can be embellished with additional pieces of styrofoam, bent cardboard, and found objects to create nose, eyes, mouth, and ear shapes. String, yarn, raffia, and plastic packing material may be used for hair, beard, and other textures. These details are covered with a final layer of gauze or glue-moistened paper toweling. When dry, the mask can be painted.

A popular mask-making technique is the paper- or cardboard-construction process, but it generally requires intricate cutting and scoring of the paper to achieve effective three-dimensional quality. It has many possibilities, however, and can be pursued in the ordinary classroom because of the availability of materials and tools. Unlike papier mâché projects that involve a lengthy cleanup period and abundant storage space, paper-sculpture masks are relatively simple to manage and store.

For children in the primary grades the creation of a paper plate, paper sack, or plastic meat-tray mask is the most practical and successful technique, since it does not involve a complex three-dimensional process.

A study of early Pacific Coast Indian life provides rich motivation for a number of art projects, including the construction of a totem pole as a group effort. The youngsters choose a sheet of colored construction paper 12 × 18 inches as the background for their totem masks. With the paper placed horizontally on the desk, the 18-inch border at bottom, they draw the outline of their mask in the center of the paper using school chalk. The larger they draw it, the better, but they should leave some paper plain at each side. However, the top and bottom of their masks can touch the paper's edge. Following the custom of the Indian totem carvers, they can make their mask represent an animal, bird, human, spirit, or whatever they desire.

When the drawing is complete, the mask may be colored in various ways. They can paint it with tempera paint or color it with crayon or oil pastels. They should be encouraged to exploit unusual color combinations in their masks, including the use of black and white; repeat colors for unity; create contrast by juxtaposing light and dark colors; and emphasize important parts of their masks through a selection of vivid, dominant colors.

When the mask is colored, parts of it may be made three-dimensional by cutting slits with a single-edge razor blade around an ear or nose and folding these pieces outward

Right: A bulletin board full of colored construction paper masks by upper elementary grade children.

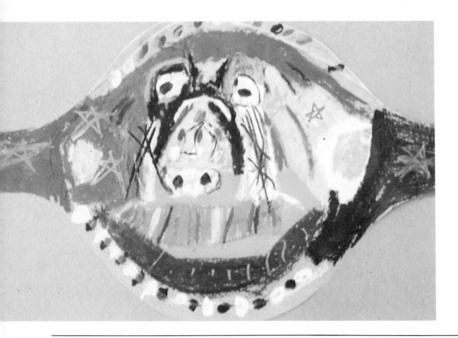

*Left: Mask designed in oil pastels on colored construction paper by first-grade child. Additional tabs were stapled on mask to provide head band. **Right**: Kindergarten children created their own Hal-* *loween costumes by recycling paper garment sacks. If such sacks are not available, secure two giant grocery bags (one with bottom cut off) with glue or masking tape.*

from the main mask or bending them back. A backing sheet of a contrasting color, 12 × 18 inches, may be added when assembling the several masks into a totem form. Youngsters may also add supplementary shapes of multicolored construction paper for teeth, fangs, horns, ears, earrings, and eyebrows.

There are diverse methods recommended for constructing totem poles out of the separate masks. One method involves the use of gallon food tins from the school cafeteria. Weight them down with sand or clay. Wrap a 24 × 36-inch sheet of tagboard around the can and secure it with masking tape, creating a 36-inch-tall cylinder. Build another cylinder above the first, if desired. Secure it again with tape. With the tagboard cylinder as a steady base, fasten the masks around it with glue, masking tape, or gun tacker. Once the basic totem pole is constructed, the youngsters may embellish it with supplemental wings, feet, and arms made out of cardboard, colored to complement the totem. Display the completed totem poles in the school foyer for everyone to enjoy.

Above: African mask. Bronze. Benin, Nigeria, nineteenth century. Reitberg Museum, Zurich. **Right:** *Masks created for a totem-pole project. Colored construction paper, 12 × 18 inches, and oil pastels were the materials employed. Completed masks were secured to discarded food tins from the school cafeteria. Slits were cut in the mask and the resulting tabs bent back to create three-dimensional ears, noses, teeth, and cheeks.*

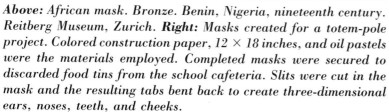

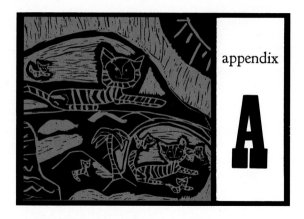

CHILDREN AND THEIR CHARACTERISTICS

Children's development follows patterns that have been identified by child study experts. There are, of course, wide variations and many exceptions, especially with special-needs children. Nevertheless, teachers of art have found the following characteristics generally applicable to children at different grade levels.

FIRST AND SECOND GRADERS: AGES FIVE, SIX, AND SEVEN

Are active and easily excited.
Enjoy working with their hands.
Exhibit strong feelings of possessiveness.
Are eager to learn.
Want to be first.
Have a limited span of interest.
Are easily fatigued.
Take great pride in their work.
Have feelings that are easily hurt.
Are alternately cooperative and uncooperative.
Usually can grasp only one idea at a time.
Delight in imaginative games, dances, stories, and plays.
Desire the approval of classmates and teachers.

*The illustrations that accompany the Appendix letters are linoleum prints by elementary grade schoolchildren. **Facing page:** Wood block print by an upper elementary grade student from Japan.*

Often live in their own secret world.
Are interested in new things to touch and taste.
Like to pretend and engage in make-believe.
Are fascinated by moving and mechanical devices.
Enjoy TV, illustrated books, movies, holidays, picnics, school field trips, new clothes, pets.

THIRD AND FOURTH GRADERS: AGES SEVEN, EIGHT, AND NINE

Have improved eye-hand coordination.
Have better command of small muscles.
Are becoming aware of differences in people.
Begin to set standards for themselves.
Are gradually learning to become responsible, orderly, and cooperative.
Begin to form separate sex groups.
May start to join gangs and cliques.
Enjoy comic books.
Are growing in self-evaluation and evaluation of others.
Are now able to concentrate for a longer period.
Are developing an interest in travel.
Are interested in the life processes of plants and animals.
Are developing a sense of humor.
Are becoming avid hobby fans and collectors.

FIFTH AND SIXTH GRADERS: AGES NINE, TEN, AND ELEVEN

Are developing a sense of values, a sense of right and wrong.

Begin to concentrate more on individual interests.

Are now interested in activities that relate to their sex grouping—especially girls.

Are becoming more dependable, responsible, self-critical, and reasonable.

Are interested in doing and making things "right."

Develop interests outside of home and school—in their community and the world at large.

Begin to criticize grownups and anyone in authority.

Are undergoing critical emotional and physical changes.

Vary in maturity. Girls are often more developed physically, emotionally, and physiologically than boys.

Become more involved in hobbies and collections.

Begin a phase of hero–heroine worship.

Often enjoy being by themselves, away from adult interference.

Are becoming self-critical, self-conscious.

Enjoy working on group projects.

Are increasing their interest-work span.

Tend to form separate gangs or cliques according to their interests, sex, color, neighborhoods, and family status.

SEVENTH AND EIGHTH GRADERS: AGES ELEVEN, TWELVE, AND THIRTEEN

Are becoming more self-conscious regarding their changing physical characteristics.

Want to be accepted by their peers. This acceptance is often more important to them than approval of parent or teacher.

May go to extremes in feelings and actions.

May develop "crushes" on the teacher.

Are often more inclined to daydream, to watch rather than to perform.

Begin to place a new emphasis on their appearance, grooming, and popularity.

Possess varying degrees of physiological and sexual maturity. Girls develop an interest in boys sooner than boys do in girls.

Are full of physical and creative energy and can exhaust their teachers unless the instructors pace their responses to the students demands.

Are in constant communication with their friends on topics of dates, parties, TV shows, movies, recordings, classmates' doings, teachers, and parents' foibles.

Are excessively influenced by a coterie of designated heroes and heroines. Girls want to be movie-star attractive. Boys want to excel in sports and be considered macho.

Do not want excessive praise in front of others unless the activity is important in the eyes of their peers.

Are often unusually sensitive to other people's problems.

Are trying to develop a code or sense of values.

Form status groups and cliques into accepted, tolerated, and rejected categories.

Have a growing desire for new and thrilling experiences.

Fluctuate between childhood and adulthood in their interests, insights, and judgments.

Facing page: Craft projects in weaving and macrame by elementary school students. Teachers are referred to the Sunset hobby and craft books. See those on leather macrame, stitchery, patchwork, ceramics, and weaving (available from Lane Publishing Co., Menlo Park, Calif., 94025).

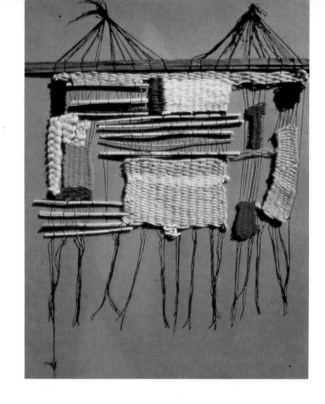

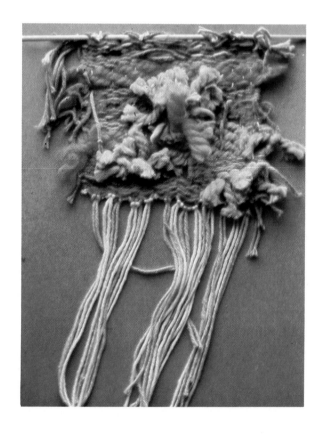

HOW CHILDREN GROW IN ART

Knowing what children are like and what their special characteristics, interests, and needs may be are important requisites for successful teaching, but a basic understanding of what youngsters do *naturally and intuitively* in art as they draw, paint, and construct is equally necessary for the essential encouragement and support of their creative growth. The children's graphic potential and the richness and complexity of their developing imagery varies with the stages of their mental, physical, psychological, physiological, and sociological development. Some fortunate youngsters may have had abundant preschool experiences in working with art materials, whereas others, culturally and economically disadvantaged, may have had limited creative opportunities. Some inquisitive children may have developed a keen interest in a particular aspect of their environment, for example, in horses, cars, trains, bikes, birds, kites, dolls, rockets, planes, insects, model building, plant, rock and shell collections, miniature models, sports, and electronic games. Consequently, their observed knowledge will often distinguish their art from that of their classmates; their work may be unique because of its complexity and richness of detail. Since youngsters express best what they know best and what they are most sensitive to or affected by, it is often possible for a discerning teacher or parent to discover through children's art what in their environment they respond to most deeply and what their attitudes, feelings, and values are.

No two children will draw the same tree in the same way. The teacher's role is to challenge them to notice trees and their varied components: trunk, bark, knots, branches, leaves, roots, twigs, buds, blossoms, and fruit. Let them touch the trees, perhaps climb them, and even pretend to be a tree swaying in the wind, feeling the rain, the snow, and the warm sunlight. Many art teachers acquire a camera to make their own color slides of nature's store of wonders to share with their students. Their photo collections grow year by year to give added visual dimensions to their motivational repertoire.

FIRST GRADERS: AGES FIVE AND SIX

Continue to draw the geometric symbols of the circle, square, triangle, oval, and rectangle, with the lines they mastered earlier, but now enhance these symbols as they respond and react to new experiences.

Employ a basic symbol, such as a circle, to depict varied visual images—the sun, the head of a person or animal, a table, a flower blossom, a tree, a body, and even a room.

Devise a variety of interpretations or schemata of the human figure, house, tree, animal, depending on their experience.

Repeat the symbols they have mastered, over and over again.

Use combinations of symbols that are very often different from those of their classmates.

Simplify their representations and are not too concerned with details.

Draw things intuitively as they know them: the sky as a band of color at the top of the page; the sun that appears in part or whole in an upper corner of almost every picture; the railroad tracks that seldom converge, the leaves that are wider where they attach to the branch or stem; the tree with a very wide trunk to make it strong; the eyes high up in the head, and the mouth as a single, curved, happy line.

Exaggerate things that are important to them and omit features that are not important; for example, children may draw themselves bigger than their parents or omit their arms and hands if they are not needed in their depiction.

Employ a baseline as a foundation on which to place objects such as a house, tree, or figure. Sometimes the bottom of the page substitutes for the baseline. Later they may use a second or third baseline higher on the page.

Use color in a personal or emotional context without regard to its local use or identity; a face may be painted blue or green, for example.

SECOND GRADERS: AGES SIX AND SEVEN

Begin to use color more naturalistically, in some instances, but as a rule limit themselves to one green hue for all trees, leaves, and grass; one blue for the sky, unless motivated to note the variety and introduced to color mixing.

Change slowly, subtly, from geometric, symbolic interpretations to more specific characterization and delineation.

Begin to use more details in their depictions—hair ribbons, buttons, buckles, eyeglasses, necklaces, rings, shoelaces, purses, fingernails, patterns, and wrinkles in clothes.

On occasion or for a special assignment, draw both the outside and inside of a place, a person, or an animal in an X-ray interpretation.

May use a foldover technique to show people on both sides of the street, diners around a table or picnic lunch, people at a swimming pool, or players on a baseball field. They turn their paper completely around as they draw.

Begin to use characteristic apparel and detail to distinguish sexes, such as skirts for girls and trousers for boys and differences in hair styles.

Draw distant things the same size as those nearer them but begin to place them higher on the page.

Sometimes draw things as they know them to be rather than how they see them at the moment; for example, a table with four legs when only two are visible from their vantage point, a house with three sides when only one side is visible from their sketching station.

THIRD AND FOURTH GRADERS: AGES SEVEN, EIGHT, AND NINE

Begin to draw and compose with more consciously deliberate planning, striving for more naturalistic and realistic proportions.

Create space and subtle depth through employment of overlapping shapes.

Begin to select and arrange objects to satisfy their compositional design needs.

May in some instances introduce the horizon line to show distant space.

May draw distant objects and figures smaller as well as higher on the page.

Make repeated efforts to capture action in their drawings of people and animals but are often handicapped because of their inability to master relative proportions and foreshortening.

FIFTH AND SIXTH GRADERS: AGES NINE, TEN, AND ELEVEN

Build on earlier drawing and design discoveries.

Become increasingly critical of their drawing ability and are often so discouraged with their efforts that they lose interest in art class unless they are wisely and sympathetically motivated and guided.

Develop a growing curiosity to experiment with new and varied materials, tools, and techniques.

Experiment more with value contrasts, neutralized colors, patterns, and textural effects.

Begin to use rudimentary perspective principles in drawing landscapes, buildings, streets, train tracks, fences, roads, and interiors.

Become more interested in their environment as a source for their drawings and paintings.

Three-dimensional projects using colored construction paper appeal to children of all ages. They like to fold, fringe, and curl the paper as well as cut out little doors and windows so they can peek into secret places. The delightful bunnies were part of an Easter-fashion-parade project.

SEVENTH AND EIGHTH GRADERS: AGES ELEVEN, TWELVE, AND THIRTEEN

Incorporate all of the color and design discoveries mastered in previous grades in their art expression.

Choose subject matter for their art expression that relates to human-interest activities, community and worldwide events, and current projects in ecology, medical research, space, and undersea exploration.

Attempt shading and crosshatch techniques to make their drawn forms appear solid, cylindrical, and believably realistic. Hone their perspective drawing skills.

Are self-conscious and self-critical about their drawing ability but with supportive instruction become increasingly skillful in figure and animal drawing through employment of contour and gesture drawing techniques.

Are ready to interpret successfully complex compositions such as richly orchestrated still lifes and multifigured events and celebrations.

Are mature and skillful enough to handle a variety of challenging crafts: photography, glazed ceramics, metal repoussé, plaster reliefs, sculpture in hard materials, and printmaking employing metal, wood, or X-ray plates.

The self-portraits on this page are contour drawings, patiently delineated, by upper-elementary-grade children in Iowa City, Iowa. They reveal once again what youngsters are capable of achieving in drawing skills whey they are encouraged to become aware, to notice characteristic features and details.

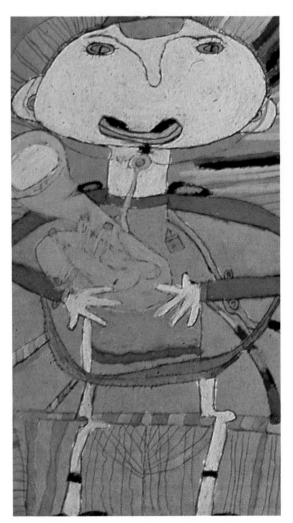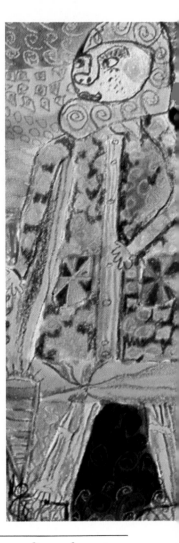

The human figure expressed and interpreted in a variety of art materials and techniques. **Left to right:** *Mixed media, tempera, oil pastels, and crayon-watercolor resist. Intermediate elementary grades.*

c

RECOMMENDED READINGS

BOOKS FOR CHILDREN

These books were chosen for their inspirational potential as motivational enrichment. They deal with art history, art fundamentals, subject-source material, perception, and art skills. The letter following each book listed indicates its suitability for (P) primary grades, (U) upper elementary grades, (M) middle school, (A) all grades.

Anno, Mitsumasa. 1977. *Anno's Journey*. Cleveland: Collins-World. (U)

Barlowe, W. D., and Summers, I. 1979. *Barlowe's Guide to Extra-Terrestrials*. New York: Workman. (U) (M)

Baskins, Leonard. 1981. *Hosie's Zoo*. New York: Viking Press. (U) (M)

Bauman, Hans. 1954. *The Caves of the Great Hunters*. New York: Pantheon Books. (U) (M)

Baylor, Byrd. 1972. *When Clay Sings*. New York: Scribner. (U) (M)

Blythe, Richard. 1977. *Dragons and Other Fabulous Beasts*. New York: Grosset & Dunlap. (U) (M)

Browner, Richard. 1962. *Look Again!* New York: Atheneum. (P)

Deny, Norman, and Filmer-Sankey, Josephine. 1966. *The Bayeux Tapestry*. New York: Atheneum. (U) (M)

Fenton, Carrol L., and Fenton, Mildred E. 1963. *In Prehistoric Seas*. Garden City, N.Y.: Doubleday. (A)

Haban, Tana. 1970. *Shapes and Things*. New York: Macmillan. (A)

Hammond, Penny, and Thomas, Katrina, 1963. *My Skyscraper City*. Garden City, N.Y.: Doubleday. (A)

Harkoven, Helen B. 1964. *Circuses and Fairs*. Minneapolis: Lerner. (A)

Hay, John, and Strong, Arline. 1962. *A Sense of Nature*. Garden City, N.Y.: Doubleday. (U) (M)

Hutchins, Pat. 1982. *I Hunter*. New York: Greenwillow Books. (U) (M)

Janson, H. W., and Janson, D. J. 1963. *The Story of Painting for Young People*. New York: Abrams. (U) (M)

Kablo, Martin. 1963. *World of Color*. New York: McGraw-Hill. (P)

Katz, Herbert, and Katz, Marjorie. 1969. *Museum Adventures*. New York: Coward, McCann & Geoghegan. (U) (M)

Kirn, Ann. 1959. *Full of Wonder*. New York: World. (A)

Law, Joseph. 1962. *Adam's Book of Odd Creatures*. New York: Atheneum. (A)

Leander, Ed. 1973. *Here's Looking at You!* New York: Dial Press/Delacorte. (U) (M)

Top: Linoleum print, 12 × 12 inches, grade 5. Teachers of art should bring this recommended list of books to the attention of their school librarians for possible purchase. Children who complete their projects earlier than their classmates should be encouraged to read more about art and artists through a perusal of selected books borrowed from the school library.

Lerner, Sharon. 1964. *The Self-Portrait in Art*. Minneapolis: Lerner. (U) (M)

Moore, Janet Gaylord. 1968. *The Many Ways of Seeing*. New York: World. (U) (M)

Munari, Bruno. 1963. *Bruno Munari's Zoo*. New York: World. (P)

Nickel, Helmut. 1969. *Warriors and Worthies*. New York: Atheneum. (U) (M)

O'Neil, Mary. 1961. *Hailstones and Halibut Bones*. [Poems about colors.] Garden City, N.Y.: Doubleday. (A)

Paine, Roberta M. 1968. *Looking at Sculpture*. New York: Lothrop, Lee and Shepard. (U) (M)

Piatti, Celestino. 1965. *The Happy Owls*. New York: Atheneum. (A)
———. 1966. *Piatti's Animal ABC*. New York: Atheneum. (P)

Provensen, Alice. 1967. *What Is Color?* New York: Golden Press. (U)

Provensen, Alice, and Provensen, Martin. 1973. *Roses Are Red, Are Violets Blue?* New York: Random House. (P) (U)

Rieger, Shay. 1971. *Animals in Clay*. New York: Scribner. (U) (M)

Rockwell, Ann. 1968. *Glass, Stones, and Crowns*. New York: Atheneum. (U) (M)

Ruskin, Ariane. 1964. *Story of Art for Young People*. New York: Pantheon Books. (U) (M)

Scheele, E. William. 1954. *Prehistoric Animals*. New York: Harcourt Brace Jovanovich.

Schissler, Barbara. 1965. *Sports and Games in Art*. Minneapolis, Minn.: Lerner. (U) (M)

Schlein, Miriam. 1958. *Shapes*. New York: William R. Scott, Inc. (P)

Smith, William Jay. 1962. *What Did I See?* New York: Macmillan. (P)

Swinton, William Elgin. 1961. *The Wonderful World of Prehistoric Animals*. New York: Garden City Books. (U)

Weisgard, Leonard. 1956. *Treasures to See*. New York: Harcourt Brace Jovanovich. (A)

Wolff, Janet, and Owett, Bernard. 1963. *Let's Imagine Colors!* New York: Dutton. (A)

Wolff, Robert J. 1968. *Feeling Blue, Seeing Red, Hello, Yellow!* New York: Scribner. (A)

Ylla. 1969. *Whose Eye Am I?* New York: Harper & Row. (A) (U)

Young, Mary. 1962. *Singing Windows*. (The stained glass wonders of Chartres cathedral.) New York: Abingdon Press. (U)

Zuelke, Ruth. 1964. *The Horse in Art*. Minneapolis, Minn.: Lerner. (U) (M)

Highly recommended for the school's art library are the following books by Shirley Glubok. Published by either Atheneum or Macmillan, New York City.

Art and Archeology	*The Art of Ancient Mexico*
The Art of Ancient Egypt	*The Art of Colonial America*
The Art of the Etruscans	*The Art of the Old West*
The Art of Ancient Greece	*The Art of the Plains Indians*
The Art of Ancient Rome	*The Art of the Vikings*
The Art of the Lands of the Bible	*The Art of the Spanish*
The Art of India	*The Art of China*
The Art of Africa	*The Art of Photography*
The Art of the Eskimo	*Discovering Tut-ankh-Amen's*
The Art of the North American Indian	*Tomb*
The Art of Ancient Peru	*Digging in Assyria*

An excellent reference book for teachers of handicapped youngsters is *The Handicapped Student in the Regular Classroom*, by Bill R. Gearhart and Mel. W. Weishawn, second edition. St. Louis: Mosby, 1980.

BOOKS FOR TEACHERS OF CHILDREN WITH SPECIAL NEEDS

Alkema, Chester J. 1971. *Art for the Exceptional*. Boulder, Colo.: Pruet.

Anderson, Frances E. 1978. *Art for All Children: A Sourcebook for the Impaired Child*. Springfield, Ill.: Thomas.

Art Educators of New Jersey. 1982. *Insights: Art in Special Education*. Reston, Va.: National Art Education Association (distributors).

Clements, Claire B., and Clements, Robert D. 1983. *Art and Mainstreaming: Art Instruction for Exceptional Students in the Regular School Classroom*. Springfield, Ill.: Thomas.

Kellogg, Rhoda. 1970. *Analyzing Children's Art*. Palo Alto, Calif.: National Press Books.

Lowenfeld, Viktor, and Brittain, Lambert. 1975. *Creative and Mental Growth*. Rev. ed. New York: Macmillan.

Lindsay, Zaidee. 1967. *Art Is for All*. New York: Taplinger.

———. 1972. *Art and the Handicapped Child*. New York: Van Nostrand Reinhold.

Sussman, Ellen J. 1976. *Art Projects for the Mentally Retarded Child*. Springfield, Ill.: Thomas.

Tilley, Pauline. 1975. *Art in the Education of the Subnormal Child*. London: Pitman.

Uhlin, Donald M. 1973. *Art for Exceptional Children*. Dubuque, Iowa: Brown.

Winsor, Maryan. 1972. *Arts and Crafts for Special Education*. New York: Pittman Learning.

Steps in a fish mobile. **Top:** *Preliminary drawing on sturdy wrapping paper. When the drawing is completed, a second matching shape is cut out.* **Center:** *Painting both fish with tempera. Heads of both painted fish should face in opposite directions to assemble the mobile correctly. When paint is dry, staple both fish partially, fill with crushed newspapers, and staple to close.*

appendix

D

AUDIOVISUAL AIDS

FILMS

The letters in parentheses following each film title indicate its suitability for (P) primary grades, (I) intermediate-elementary grades, (U) upper-elementary grades, (M) middle school, (A) all grades. Closing letters refer to distributors whose addresses follow. All films are 16 mm, sound, and in color except when noted otherwise.

African Carving: A Dogon Mask. (U) (M) PSU

Alphabet. (U) (M) PSU

Anghor: The Lost City. [Glimpse of ancient Cambodian civilization.] (U) (M) PSU

Animal Habitats. (M) EBF

Around My Way. [New York City as seen through children's drawings.] (U) (M) PSU

Art: What Is It? Why Is It? (U) (M) EBF

Art in Action with Dong Kingman. [Contemporary water colorist.] (U) (M) HAR

Art in Motion. [Color and design in motion.] (U) (M) EBF

Art and Nature. (A) IFB

Art in Our World. (U) (M) BFA

Art and Perception: Learning to See. (A) BFA

Art Scene: Newton Public Schools. (U) (M) PSU

Art of Seeing. (U) (M) PSU

Arts and Crafts of Mexico. (U) (M) EBF

Arts and Crafts of West Africa. (U) (M) BFA

Arts of Japan. [B/W] (U) (M) PSU

At Your Fingertips—Boxes. (I) (U) (M) PSU

Batik Rediscovered. (U) (M) BFA

Begone Dull Care. [Color patterns set to music.] (A) IFB

Birds in the City. (A) BFA

Bonnard. (U) (M) PSU ·

Buma: African Sculpture Speaks. (U) (M) EBF

Butterfly. [Complete life cycle of swallow-tail butterfly.] (A) BFA

Calder's Circus. [Renowned creator of mobiles.] (A) PSU

Changing Art in a Changing World. (A) PSU

Chartres Cathedral. (U) (M) PSU

Children Are Creative. [Children pursuing art activities.] (A) BFA

Children Who Draw. [Japanese children drawing and painting.] (A) BRAN

Chinese, Korean, and Japanese Dance. (A) PSU

Circus. [Animated film made by children.] (A) PSU

Creating with Clay. (U) (M) BFA

Creating with Paper. (U) (M) BFA

Coils, Slabs, and Space. (A) PSU

Collage. (U) (M) PSU

Collage-Exploring Texture. (P) (U) IFB

Color. (A) PSU

Combining Clay Forms. (A) PSU

Crafts of Edo. [Japanese art from 1600 to 1860.] (M) PSU

Crayon. (U) (M) PSU

Crayon Resist. (A) BFA

Day the Colors Went Away, The. (P) EBF

Degas. (U) (M) PSU

Design to Music. [Children painting as mood music is played.] (A) IFB

Devils, Monsters, and Dragons. (A) PSU

Discovering Art Series: Color; Composition; Creative Pattern; Dark and Light; Form in Art; Harmony in Art; Ideas for Art; Line; Perspective; Texture. (U) (M) BFA

Dots. [Abstract designs set to music.] (A) IFB

Metropolitan Museum of Art
Fifth Avenue and 82nd Street
New York, NY 10028

Museum of Modern Art
11 West 53rd Street
New York, NY 10019

New York Graphic Society
140 Greenwich Avenue
Greenwich, CT 06830

Penn Prints
31 West 46th Street
New York, NY 10036

Raymond and Raymond, Inc.
1071 Madison Avenue
New York, NY 10028

Reinhold Publishing Co.
600 Summer
Stamford, CT 06901

Shorewood Reproductions, Inc.
475 Tenth Avenue
New York, NY 10018

Van Nostrand Reinhold
450 West 33rd Street
New York, NY 10001

E. Weyhe
794 Lexington Avenue
New York, NY 10021

COLOR SLIDE AND FILMSTRIP SOURCES

American Library Color Slide Co.
222 West 23rd Street
New York, NY 10011

Art Council Aids
Box 641
Beverley Hills, CA 90213

Art Institute of Chicago
South Michigan Avenue
Chicago, IL 60603

Bailey Film Associates
11559 Santa Monica Boulevard
Los Angeles, CA 90025

Dr. Block Color Reproductions
1309 North Genesee Avenue
Los Angeles, CA 90046

Grolier Enterprises
845 Third Avenue
New York, NY 10022

International Film Bureau
332 South Michigan Avenue
Chicago, IL 60604

Life Filmstrips
Time and Life Building
New York, NY 10021

Museum of Modern Art Library
11 West 53rd Street
New York, NY 10019

National Gallery of Art
Constitution Ave. and 6th St.,
N.W.
Washington, DC 20001

Prothman Associates
2795 Milburn Avenue
Baldwin, NY 11510

Sandak, Inc.
180 Harvard Avenue
Stamford, CT 06902

Society for Visual Education
1345 Diversey Parkway
Chicago, IL 60614

Warren Schloat Productions
150 White Plains Road
Tarrytown, NY 10591

appendix

E

ART MATERIALS

To develop the expertise and confidence that will help them teach art purposefully and successfully, elementary- and middle-school teachers must be familiar with the art materials and tools available to the youngsters in their classes. They should discover the art potential of these materials through actual involvement with them. For example, if they have never experienced using wax crayons in a rich and brilliant application on colored construction paper, they will not be as enthusiastic or as motivated in inspiring students to see the ordinary crayon's glowing and multiple possibilities.

The following art materials and tools are usually found in the elementary and middle schools today, furnished by either the school or the students. Teachers should learn to identify them, use them creatively, know the quality brands and available sources, order them in economy lots and sizes, and store them properly.

Expendable materials

Pencils
Wax crayons
Fingerpaint
Tempera paint
Watercolors
Colored chalk
Manila paper
White drawing paper
Newsprint
Oaktag (tagboard)
Construction paper
Fingerpaint paper
School paste
School chalk
Clay

Nonexpendable supplies and tools

Scissors
Rulers
Compasses
Watercolor brushes
Easel brushes

Hammer, saw
Paper cutter
Stapler

Generous budget supplies

Oil pastels
Art gum erasers
Felt-nib or nylon-tip pens
Rubber cement
White liquid glue
Shellac (clear)
Turpentine
Printing inks (water, oil base)
Felt-nib watercolor markers
India ink
Linoleum for block printing
Linoleum cutting tools
Brayers (rubber rollers for printmaking)
Clay glazes
Clay kiln
Tissue paper (assorted colors)
Poster board (for mats)
Polymer medium (glossy)

Found objects were used to add decorative detail to this clay elephant.

PRACTICAL SUGGESTIONS

Keep all tools and materials in order. Store them in cigar boxes, shoe boxes, freezer containers, coffee or vegetable-shortening tins, commercially available tote trays. Label the containers. Paint tool handles with an identifying color.

Keep all tools clean. Do not let metal tools get rusty. Wipe them dry if they get wet, and oil them if they are to be stored for a period of time. Do not use scissors for clay or plaster projects. Never pour plaster in any form down the sink.

Mount motivational resource photographs on oaktag (tagboard) and store them in labeled accordion folders or flat drawers, or put them in plastic loose-leaf protectors and keep them in notebook binders.

Wash brushes clean (use detergent if necessary) and store them with bristle-ends up in a jar or tall coffee can. Be sure students rinse and clean watercolor tins. Leave them open and stack them to dry overnight. Order semimoist cakes of watercolor in bulk to refill empty tins.

Store scrap construction and tissue paper flat in drawers or discarded blanket cartons. This procedure helps to prevent the paper from being crushed.

When placing orders for tempera paint, always order more white paint, because a great deal is used to mix tints of colors. You can also order crayons or oil pastels in colors needed in bulk.

Hardboard available in 4 × 8- or 4 × 10-foot pieces in ¼ inch thickness is excellent for drawing boards and working surfaces on desks or tables. For drawing boards have the lumber dealer cut the hardboard for you into either 18 × 24- or 12 × 18-inch rectangles, depending on which size works best in your situation. For longer wear, mask tape the edges of the boards.

Yarn purchased on skeins should be rewound on balls or spools for ready use. A closed cardboard carton with holes punched in it for the yarn to pass through may be used as a dispenser.

Keep school paste in jars until ready to use; then dispense it on small squares of tagboard or salvaged cardboard from store cartons. Scrape off the unused paste back into the jar at the close of class; moisten it slightly with a few drops of water and cap tightly.

Upper-elementary-grade youngsters called on their imaginative powers to produce the exciting collages on this page. Sparked by themes such as "Cities of the Future" and "A Fantasy World," they employed colored construction paper and wallpaper samples to cut, paste, and compose these make-believe, fanciful environments.

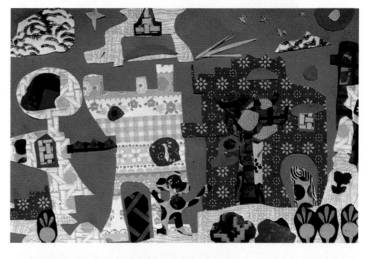

*A sixth-grade girl makes a preliminary drawing from a still-life arrangement using school chalk on colored construction paper and then employs oil pastels with deliberation and confidence. **Facing page:** Completed composition, Athens, Georgia.*

When crayons break and do not fit easily into the original carton, suggest that children store them in discarded cigar boxes, coffee or vegetable-shortening tins, or freezer containers.

Powder tempera is much easier to store than the liquid kind, but liquid tempera has definite advantages. It is always ready to use if sealed properly, and it usually has a smoother texture. The most vexing problem in tempera projects is what to do with the liquid tempera remaining in muffin tins, plastic egg cartons, or ice-cube trays. It is practically impossible to pour it back into the original containers. That is why paint should be doled out a little at a time, with refills as needed. Usually, the teacher should be in charge of paint distribution. Before closing covers on tempera jars, check plasticity of the paint. If it is too dry, add a little water to ensure moistness and then cap it tightly. To prevent liquid tempera from becoming sour add a few drops of wintergreen or oil of cloves to each container.

RECYCLING FOUND MATERIALS

When elementary and middle school teachers consider supplies for art activities, they usually consider first those materials that are available commercially. In today's productive world, however, there are a number of diverse sources they can tap, among them the discarded or junked everyday items, empty containers, scraps, remnants, and hundreds of things ordinarily thought of as worthless but that, with a little imagination and skill, can be recycled into the art program.

Most of the items on the following list can be found in basements, attics, garages, junkyards, wastebaskets, and drug or department-store disposal areas. Children and their parents should be enlisted in treasure-hunt campaigns to

build a store of the following discarded materials for use in classroom or art-studio projects. Found objects can definitely expand and enrich elementary and middle school art programs, especially when they are operating on a limited budget. Care must be taken, however, that the found objects do not end up in *lost expressions*. Selection, discrimination, restraint, and imagination must be employed so that the composition or construction becomes more than just the sum of its parts.

Acorns
Baby-food jars
Balloons
Balls (rubber, polystyrene, Ping-Pong, Jack's game)
Bark, tree
Beads
Blades (saw, broken)
Blinds (matchstick, plastic)
Blotters
Bolts and nuts
Bones
Book jackets
Bottle caps
Bottles
Boxes (grocery store, shoe, oatmeal)
Bracelets (discarded)
Buckles
Bulbs (electric, photo flash)
Burlap (remnants)
Buttons
Candles
Cardboard (corrugated)
Cards (greeting, discarded)
Carpet samples
Cartons (egg, milk, juice, ice cream, freezer, plastic)
Cellophane

Celotex
Checkers
Clock parts
Clothespins
Coat hangers
Cones (fir, paper)
Confetti
Coral
Cord
Corks
Corn, corn husks
Cotton
Dominoes
Dowel scraps
Driftwood
Earrings (discarded)
Fabric (remnants)
Feathers
Felt (assorted colors)
Foam rubber (scraps)
Foil (aluminum)
Fur
Gourds
Hat boxes
Jacks (from game)
Leather (remnants)
Linoleum (scraps)
Macaroni
Magazines

Marbles
Masonite (scraps)
Meat trays (polystyrene)
Mirrors (discarded)
Nails
Necklaces (discarded)
Neckties (discarded)
Newspapers
Nuts
Paper bags
Paper cups, plates
Paper tubes (toilet tissue, mailing)
Paper towels
Paper (shelf, gift wrap, crepe, tissue, plain, colored)
Pebbles
Pegboard (pieces)
Pie plates (paper, aluminum)
Pine cones
Pins
Pipe cleaners
Plywood (scraps)
Polish (shoe)
Popsicle sticks
Potatoes
Q-tips
Reed
Ribbon, ric rac

Rope
Rubber (innertube)
Rubber bands
Sand
Sandpaper
Sawdust
Screen
Screws
Seashells
Seeds
Shades (window)
Shingles
Spaghetti
Sponge (cellulose, metal)
Spools (thread)
Sticks (applicator)
Straws (paper, plastic)
String
Tile (acoustic, vinyl)
Tongue depressors
Toothbrush
Toothpicks
Tubes (mailing)
TV dinner trays
Wallpaper (samples)
Wood (scraps)
X-ray plates (discarded)
Yarn (remnants)

SPECIAL MATERIALS AND TOOLS

Hardboard—For drawing or sketching board, as protective coverage for desks or work tables, and for mural projects.

Brayer (rubber roller)—For inking plate in printmaking. Get the sturdy, soft, black rubber kind for longer wear (not the gelatine type).

Celluclay—Commercially available dry mixture for use in papier mâché-type projects.

Dextrin (powdered)—Add to dry or moist clay (5 to 10 percent) to harden completed work without firing.

Drywall joint cement—For creating relief effects on a two-dimensional surface; can be painted when dry.

Firebrick (porous, insulation type)—For upper-elementary-grade and middle-school three-dimensional and relief-carving projects.

Grog—Aggregate for plaster molds, clay conditioner.

Masonite (tempered)—For clay modeling boards, inking surface in print-making projects, and rinsing board in tempera or crayon resists; also practical as a portable sketching board.

Pariscraft—Plaster-impregnated gauze in varied widths for additive sculpture projects.

Plaster of Paris (molding plaster)—For plaster sculpture and reliefs.

Polystyrene—For printmaking plates, collage and craft projects, and printmaking stamps.

Posterboard (railroad board)—For multicrayon engraving project; available in several colors.

Rub'n'Buff—Paste to use as patina in sculpture projects on plaster and fired clay; also on aluminum-foil reliefs; available in metallic sheens and colors.

Shreddimix—Prepared mixture for papier maché projects.

Shellacol—Solvent for cleaning shellac brushes.

Sloyd knife (Hyde knife is similar)—All-purpose utility knife with a semi-sharp blade; excellent for carving in plaster and for delineating details and pattern in crayon-engraving projects.

Dressmaker's transfer paper—A white carbon paper useful in crayon-engraving projects.

Treasure gold—See description of Rub'n'Buff.

X-acto knife—Craft knife with sharp interchangeable blades for paper and cardboard sculpture. *Caution:* To be used by the teacher only.

These delightful prints by primary grade children were created by employing discarded styrofoam meat trays for the printing plate. Trim off the curved part of the tray. The impression is made by pressing into the tray with a blunt-pointed pencil. Water-base black printing ink may be used, rolled out on the engraved tray with a brayer. A preliminary drawing with a felt-nib pen or soft lead pencil is recommended.

appendix

F

FACILITIES FOR ART

THE CLASSROOM AS ART STUDIO

The elementary classroom or the art room can be the child's first and often most enduring art lesson. It is there, through exciting displays and eye-catching exhibits, that teachers can provide the example for good design through creative, inspiring, and stimulating surroundings. Certainly, the students should be invited to involve themselves in projects that will help make the classroom attractive and colorfully stimulating. Bulletin boards and displays should be changed regularly and often to provide evaluative and appreciatory opportunities for completed projects and to whet interest for further art endeavors. Still-life arrangements should be on view for sketching purposes. Students should be encouraged to contribute to the store of found objects and nature's treasures on constant display in the classroom or studio.

Here are some ideas for creating interest in the classroom and providing subject matter for art:

Hang a number of colorful umbrellas from the ceiling. They may overlap one another, the more variety the better. Umbrellas from the Orient are especially attractive. Also display Japanese, Chinese, Indian, and Indonesian kites, balloons, and banners. *Caution:* Don't hang anything from light fixtures.

When nothing else is available for a still-life arrangement, stack a number of chairs or stools on top of one another—some sticking out at different angles. For more interest weave some drapery or beach towels in and out of the openings. In middle school, following a contour drawing of the setup, you might suggest that the students paint the negative shapes instead of the positive shapes as a possible design approach.

Drape different kinds of fabric, plain and patterned, against a cork bulletin board. Arrange and pin the material so that you create bunches or knots of fabric balanced by draped swags. Pin some old hats of many colors against the drapery. This makes an excellent study for line, value, and color compositions.

Bring into the classroom a fairly large, dead tree branch. Mount it against a light-colored wall area or bulletin board. It provides unmatched subject inspiration for contour- and linear-drawing projects and is also ideal for display of paper sculpture or papier mâché birds, butterflies, painted eggs, fish, planes, kites, sailboats, and abstract mobiles.

Invite upper elementary grade and middle school students to remove their shoes and stack them in the middle of a table, on a chair, or on the floor for a still-life arrangement. If they object to this, have them bring an extra pair of boots or shoes to use in the still life. In a pinch use your own shoes. Boots, shoes, shoulder pads, hats, caps, helmets, and gloves provide interesting organic shapes for drawing, because they conform to the human form, which is the ideal drawing inspiration.

Arrange bottles of different colored glass on windowsills or against a light source. Fill some of them with dried flowers or branches, some clear ones with colored water, and others with strips of aluminum foil. Bleached animal bones make excellent studies for line drawings and value interpretations. Also use them as inspiration for clay-modeled forms.

Build a color environment as a motivation for painting in tempera and watercoloring. Make it a class "happening." Have students collect colored tissue paper, crepe paper, colorful fabrics, beach towels, ribbons, colored streamers, fans, banners, balloons, posters, party hats, beach balls, and fluorescent Day-Glo materials. If you arrange the display near a window you can incorporate colored cellophane and stained-glass segments as well.

Large potted plants of assorted foliage and blossoms make ideal sketching, painting, collage, and printmaking subject themes. They also give *joie de vivre* to a classroom, especially in those schools in which the demands of air conditioning have made windowless rooms an architectural necessity.

Keep on hand some large colorful examples of fabric, old bedspreads, quilts, and afghans to use as drapery on class models and in still-life arrangements. Students respond more readily to costumed models and unusual backgrounds. Set up an exciting still life against a wall or on a counter and then pose a student in costume against it. The model may be standing, sitting, or reclining. Have students take turns modeling.

Contact or write to travel agencies here and abroad to secure large, colorful travel posters. Display them in the classroom for color and design inspiration.

The qualitative art program in the elementary or middle school depends, in part, on adequate and functional instructional facilities. Some schools boast a multipurpose art room, but the majority of elementary art projects take place in the self-contained classroom. This often places a limitation on the number and variety of art experiences that can be programmed successfully. However, if certain minimal art-facility requirements are met in the planning of the classrooms destined for future construction, the climate for growth in art in tomorrow's elementary and middle schools will be more favorable and productive. Basically, the changes that need to be made are in the strategic areas of storage, display, and cleanup.

Illustrations on this page show easily constructed plywood storage facilities for both two- and three-dimensional art projects. The sturdy plastic trays are available commercially.

LOCATION

If a multipurpose art room is planned, it should be on the first or ground floor, adjacent to the stage of the auditorium or to the cafeteria, and near a service entrance. An outdoor court, easily accessible from the art room, can provide excellent auxiliary space for sketching, mural making, paint-spraying projects, ceramics, and plaster sculpture projects in favorable weather.

SPACE ALLOTMENT

Sufficient space should be provided to allow students to work on individual projects with some flexibility of movement, to permit rearrangement of furniture for group projects, and to ensure a regular flow of student traffic to the teacher's desk and storage and cleanup areas or stations.

The self-contained classroom should be planned to provide adequate space at the rear of the room and along one or two walls for storage, a cleanup (sink) facility, and counter working space. There should be sufficient room at the rear of the class for one or two large, sturdy tables suitable for craft activities and group projects.

FURNITURE

In both the self-contained classroom and the special multipurpose art room, desk, table, and counter surfaces of nonglare, waterproof, and scratch-resistant materials are recommended. Light-colored Formica working surfaces have many advantages, but they must be protected during projects involving linoleum or woodblock cutting, carving in semihard substances, or sawing and hammering on wood constructions. Tables and desks should be adjustable for height and easily movable for special projects. In the special art room, stools that can be recessed under tables during cleanup can ease the traffic problem. In the primary grades free-standing easels can effectively augment the limited desk space.

STORAGE

Effective, adequate storage facilities are a major asset in expediting a multiproject art program. There should be sufficient storage for art supplies, tools, visual aids, work in progress, and completed art projects held over for future display.

Supply storage should be provided for various-size art papers (drawers or slots should have inside measurements slightly larger than the paper itself), tempera paint, watercolors, crayons, oil pastels, inks, paste (adjustable shelves are recommended for these materials), yarn, wood scraps, found materials (large cardboard cartons painted in bright colors serve well), clay (bin-type storage, mobile metal-lined clay cart—both commercially available), tote tray cabinet, and galvanized or sturdy plastic waste containers for clay, plaster, zonolite, and sand.

A cabinet or movable cart with shelves and pegboard panels is suggested for small tool storage. A simple pegboard panel secured to a wall with the necessary accompanying hardware will alleviate the most pressing tool-storage problems. Painting an identifying shape or outline of each tool on the pegboard will help expedite storage and provide a ready inventory of tools. A hollow box made of Masonite with holes drilled in the top provides an excellent scissors container and inventory device.

Since so much of the youngsters' art centers around

What can one say about these exquisite sunflower oil pastels except to express the hope that children everywhere could have the experience of studying with an art teacher who brings out the best in them, as was the case with the students who drew these. Indeed, there is hope for the future of art education when creations such as these are discovered and documented.

painting, there should be adequate horizontal storage spaces for paintings in process. This is especially true in the special art room, where one class follows another and painting stations must be cleared quickly. There are some excellent horizontal storage facilities available commercially, but too often the limited school budget does not allow for their purchase. A simple, economical, yet serviceable flat work-storage unit can be constructed employing a framework of 2 × 4's and ¾-inch-thick plywood, with pull-out shelves of Masonite. A clothesline and spring clothespins can be used as a drying facility for in-process and completed vegetable, collograph, and linoleum prints, but do not use it for tempera paintings, or you'll have a lot of drippy problems.

A critical problem in the self-contained classroom is the storage of three-dimensional projects in progress such as clay sculpture and pottery, papier mâché, paper sculpture, box sculpture, and plaster carvings. Counter space above storage cabinets, the floor along the baseboard, and closet shelves are some possibilities. Tote trays now commonly available in discount stores provide another solution.

CLEANUP FACILITIES

To minimize traffic problems, sinks should be easily accessible from all parts of the room. They should not be located in a closet or in a corner. They should be stainproof and easily cleaned. Multiple-mixing faucets, heavy-duty drains, sink traps, and spray attachments are recommended. Sinks should be large enough to allow two or three youngsters to use them at the same time. They should be low enough so that children can reach faucets with ease; if not, they should be provided with step-up platforms. For special art-studio rooms in the middle school, peninsula or island sinks are recommended.

DISPLAY FACILITIES

A generous amount of space should be allotted for display purposes and instructional bulletin boards. This holds true for either the special art room or the self-contained classroom. Display-panel backgrounds should be neutral in color: Subtle, nonglare whites, grays, umbers, and blacks are recommended. Surfaces, in most instances, should be matte finish in cork or celotex, which provides for easy pinning, stapling, or tacking of artwork. Random-punch, butt-end acoustic tile can be glued directly to wall surfaces or to Masonite or hardboard panels to provide a simple yet effective display facility. Cork-surfaced doors on cupboard, closet doors, and storage cabinets will augment display space. One-foot-square mirror tiles with adhesive backing could be the solution to encourage self-portrait drawing projects.

OTHER SPECIFICATIONS

Floors should be of nonskid materials, hard, yet resilient and easily cleaned. Neutral-colored asphalt or plastic tile is recommended. Ceilings should be acoustically treated and of a color that provides maximum light reflection. Lighting should be of sufficient kilowatt intensity to provide students with adequate light and minimum glare. Room-darkening shades or blinds should be installed to ensure the successful projection of color slides and films. A permanent video screen should be part of the room's facilities. White-surfaced slate boards can aid effectively in presenting art lessons in a more realistic context. These boards can also serve as screens for film and slide projection. Electric outlets should be provided at intervals around the room. Check with an electrician on voltage needed if a kiln is to be installed. Electric outlets should not be positioned too close to sink areas.

SPECIAL EQUIPMENT

Whether in the self-contained classroom or the multipurpose art room, special furniture and equipment can often be a deciding factor in implementing a qualitative program. The following items are generally recommended: clay bin or cart, vibrating jigsaw, color slide projector, projection screen, workbench with vises, large-size paper cutter, electric heating plate, utility cart, ceramic kiln, drying rack for flat work in progress, tote-tray facility for 3-D projects, gun tacker, stapler, large scissors, yardstick, and a number of wastebaskets or large-sized trash containers.

What a vivid impression "a visit to a doctor" must have made on this young Japanese child. Notice how much he remembered and recorded in his watercolor painting.

appendix

G

ART EDUCATION IN THE UNITED STATES: A CENTURY OF PROGRESS, 1870–1970

1870—Industrial Drawing Act passed by Massachusetts legislature requiring that drawing be taught to all students over fifteen years of age in communities of 20,000 or more inhabitants.

1871—Metropolitan Museum of Art, New York City, established.

1873—Massachusetts Normal Art School established, the first training school for the preparation of teachers of industrial drawing in the country. Walter Smith was the founder and first principal. As the Boston schools' art instructor, he wrote *Teachers's Manual of Freehand Drawing Designing*.

1874–1877—Walter Smith organized Massachusetts Art Teachers Association, first professional art-teachers group. Also published a series of graded art lessons for grades one through normal school, designed to teach geometrical drawing. Copying encouraged to train eye and hand.

1875—Art Students' League, New York City, founded. William Merritt Chase was one of the first instructors.

1876—Thomas Eakins began teaching at the Pennsylvania Academy of Arts, Philadelphia. He relied little on cast models; emphasized nude models and anatomical studies.

1883—Department of Art Education established as an integral part of the National Education Association.

1890—Franz Cizek founded a school of arts and crafts (Kunstgewer beschule) in Vienna, Austria. Subject matter consisted of geometrical designs and pictorial compositions of children with flowers and animals.

1893—Western Drawing Teachers Association organized at World's Fair in Chicago. Forerunner of Western Arts Association.

1896—George Santayana wrote *The Sense of Beauty: Being the Outlines of Aesthetic Theory*.

1898—Arthur Wesley Dow became art instructor at Teachers College, Columbia University, New York City. Subsequently wrote textbook *Composition*, which influenced many art teachers. Design was stressed.

1899—Eastern Art Teachers Association founded, incorporating the Connecticut Valley Art Teachers group.

1901—First publication of *The Applied Arts Book*, which later became *School Arts*, with H. T. Bailey as editor. Employed picture-study units that emphasized the storytelling aspects of paintings and the design content.

1904—John Dewey, author of *Art as Experience*, joined faculty of Columbia University, New York City.

1908—*The Eight* exhibition in New York City. Eight artists, among them George Luks, John Sloan, Robert Henri, William Glackens, Maurice Prendergast, and Everett Shinn, painted revolutionary-realistic themes of slums, aged people, and shop girls. Their choice of subject matter and style greatly influenced art-school content.

Arthur Wesley Dow wrote *The Theory and Practice of Teaching Art*.

1911—Eastern Art Education Association founded.

1912—Paintings by children exhibited in Steiglitz Gallery, New York City.

1913—A. H. Munsell introduced *A Color Notation*, which established a structure by which color theories can be taught. Provided color wheel, color terminology, and color harmonies.

Armory Show opened in New York City, introducing the paintings of the Fauvists (Wild Beasts), Futurists, Cubists, and Postimpressionists to the United States art community.

Composition, a text by Arthur Wesley Dow, was published. Contained exercises in line and value using black and white illustrations. Color introduced subsequently but remained a minor element.

Clive Bell wrote *Art*, a treatise that emphasized *significant form* as an underlying element of all great works of art.

1916—Walter Sargent and Elizabeth Miller wrote *How Children Learn to Draw*.

1919—Western Arts Association, the largest of the regional art-education associations, founded.

Pedro J. Lemos became editor of *School Arts*. Drawings from natural sources were emphasized.

1920—Pedro J. Lemos wrote *Applied Art*.

1922—*Everyday Art*, an art-resource periodical, was published by the American Crayon Company and made available to teachers at no cost.

1923—Jay Hambidge wrote *Dynamic Symmetry in Composition*.

Robert Henri wrote *The Art Spirit*.

1924—Margaret Mathias, art teacher in Cleveland, Ohio, wrote *The Beginning of Art in the Public Schools*.

Belle Boas, director of fine arts, Horace Mann School, Teachers College, New York City, wrote *Art in the School*.

1925—H. and V. Goldstein wrote *Art in Everyday Life*, an art-appreciation textbook.

Pacific Art Education Association formed.

1927—C. Valentine Kirby of Pennsylvania wrote *The Business of Teaching and Supervising the Arts*.

1928—Leon L. Winslow of Baltimore wrote *Organization and Teaching of Art*.

Sallie Tannahill of New York wrote *Fine Arts for Public School Administrators*.

1929—Museum of Modern Art, New York City, incorporated. Present building erected in 1938–1939.

William G. Whitford of Chicago wrote *An Introduction to Art Education*.

1930—Southeastern Art Education Association organized.

1933—Walter H. Klar, Leon L. Winslow, and C. Valentine Kirby wrote *Art Education in Principle and Practice*.

Joseph Albers, author of *Interaction of Color*, introduced the German Bauhaus design philosophy and techniques at Black Mountain College, North Carolina.

The Owatonna, Minnesota Community Home Art Project commenced and continued through 1944. Edwin Ziegfeld, coordinator; Carnegie Corporation, sponsor.

1934—Works Progress Administration (WPA) provided employment for many artists. Scores of murals in state and federal buildings resulted.

Index of American Design, an illustrative guide covering three centuries of American folk art, crafts, and design, initiated.

John Dewey wrote *Art as Experience*.

1939—Leon L. Winslow wrote *The Integrated School Art Program*.

1940—The Progressive Education Association published *The Visual Arts in General Education*. Victor D'Amico was committee chairman.

Natalie R. Cole wrote *The Arts in the Classroom*. Painting, drawing, printmaking, lettering, taught creatively by a classroom instructor.

1941—Harold Gregg, California, wrote *Art for the Schools of America*. 40th Yearbook of the National Society for the Study of Education, *Art in American Life and Education*, published. Thomas Munro was committee chairman.

Kimon Nicolaides wrote *The Natural Way to Draw*, which emphasized contour and gesture drawing.

Ray Faulkner, Edwin Ziegfeld, and Gerald Hill wrote *Art Today*, an art appreciation textbook.

1942—Victor D'Amico, educational director at the Museum of Modern Art, New York City, wrote *Creative Teaching in Art*.

Wilhelm Viola wrote *Child Art*, documenting the teaching methods of Franz Cizek, Vienna, Austria.

1943—Herbert Read wrote *Education through Art*.

National Committee on Art Education formed. Victor D'Amico was chairman. The committee urged teachers to seek closer ties with practicing artists.

1944—Georgy Kepes wrote *Language of Vision*.

R. R. Tomlinson wrote *Children as Artists*.

1946—Edward Warder Rannells of the University of Kentucky wrote *Art in the Junior High School*.

1947—Viktor Lowenfeld, professor at Pennsylvania State University, wrote *Creative and Mental Growth*.

Moholy Nagy wrote *Vision in Motion*.

Rose H. Alschuler and LaBerta Hattwick wrote *Painting and Personality*, a psychological approach to understanding the visual expressions of children.

1947–1948—National Art Education Association (NAEA) was established and gradually assumed the administrative functions heretofore held by the four regional art associations. Annual conventions were held alternately by NAEA and the regional associations for a number of years.

1948—Henry Schaefer-Simmern wrote *The Unfolding of Artistic Creativity*, which emphasized the therapeutic uses of studio art.

1951—Florence Cane wrote *The Artist in Each of Us*.

1952—Charles and Margaret Gaitskell of Ontario, Canada, wrote *Art Education in the Kindergarten*.

Olive L. Riley wrote *Your Art Heritage*, an art-appreciation text for secondary schools.

1954—NAEA published the first yearbook devoted to research in art education.

1955—Manuel Barkan of Ohio State University wrote *A Foundation for Art Education*.

Rudolph Arnheim wrote *Art and Visual Perception*.

1957—National Endowment for the Arts and Humanities established.

1958—Ralph A. Beelke became first executive secretary of NAEA.

Charles D. Gaitskell wrote *Children and Their Art: Methods for the Elementary School*.

Italo DeFrancesco wrote *Art Education: Its Means and Ends*.

1959—NAEA published volume 1, number 1, of *Studies in Art Education*.

Howard Conant and Arne Randall wrote *Art in Education*.

1961—Louis F. Hoover wrote *Art Activities for the Very Young*.

June King McFee wrote *Preparation for Art*.

1965—Title V of the Elementary and Secondary Education Act was enacted, providing federal funds for strengthening state departments of education and making it possible for 36 states to fund state art directors.

Frank Wachowiak and Theodore Ramsay, both teaching at the University of Iowa, wrote *Emphasis: Art, A Qualitative Program for the Elementary School*.

1970—Edmund B. Feldman, professor of art, University of Georgia, wrote *Becoming Human through Art, Aesthetic Experience in the School*.

Frank Wachowiak, University of Georgia, and David Hodge, University of Wisconsin, wrote *Art in Depth: A Qualitative Program of Art for the Young Adolescent*.

Facing page: Linoleum print, actual size, middle school, Japan. How effectively the light and dark areas of this composition are balanced and how successfully the varied sea-life forms fill the space!

GLOSSARY

Appliqué decorative design made by cutting pieces of one fabric and applying them by glueing or stitching to the surface of another fabric.

Armature framework (of wood, wire, and so on) employed to support constructions of clay, papier mâché, or plaster.

Balance a principle in art. May be formal or informal, symmetrical or asymmetrical.

Balsa a strong, lightweight wood used for model building and stabiles.

Baren a device made of cardboard and bamboo leaf that is used as a hand press in taking a print (of Japanese derivation).

Bat a plaster block used to hasten drying of moist clay.

Batik a method of designing on fabric by sealing with melted wax those areas not to be dyed.

Bench hook a wood device secured to a desk or table to stabilize the linoleum block during the gouging process.

Bisque clay in its fired or baked state (unglazed).

Brayer a rubber roller used for inking in printmaking processes.

Burnish to make smooth or glossy by a rubbing or polishing action.

Ceramic a word used to describe clay constructions and products thereof.

Charcoal a drawing stick or pencil made from charred wood.

Chipboard sturdy cardboard, usually gray, available in varying thicknesses, used for collage, collograph, sketching boards, and in construction projects.

Clay a natural, moist earth substance used in making bricks, tile, pottery, and ceramic sculpture.

Collage a composition or design made by arranging and glueing materials to a background surface.

Collograph a print made from a collage. Relief plate created with an assortment of pasted or glued items such as pieces of papers, cardboard, cord, string, and other found objects.

Color an element of art. Also referred to as "hue."

Color, monochromatic all of the tints and shades of a single color plus its neutralized possibilities.

Colors, analogous colors closely related; neighbors on the color wheel: green, blue-green, yellow-green, for example.

Colors, complementary colors found opposite one another on the color wheel: red and green, for example.

Colors, primary red, yellow, blue. Three basic hues.

Colors, secondary green, orange, violet. Achieved by mixing primary colors.

Construction paper a strong, absorbent, semitextured paper available in a wealth of colors and used for drawings, paintings in tempera, crayon, oil pastel, printmaking, collage, and paper sculpture. A staple item in the school art program.

Contour drawing a line drawing delineating the outer and inner contours of a posed model, still life, landscape, or other selected subject matter.

Domination a principle in art. Opposite term is "subordination." They complement each other.

Easel a wood or metal frame to support an artist's canvas during painting. Found in many kindergartens for use in tempera painting but in a simpler version.

Embossing creating a raised or relief design on metal or leather by tooling or indenting the surface.

Emphasis a principle in art. Important elements in a composition are emphasized.

Encaustic a painting process employing hot beeswax mixed with color pigment. Sometimes used to describe melted-crayon creations.

Engobe clay slip, colored or white, used to decorate greenware before firing.

Engraving a process of incising or scratching into a hard surface to produce a printed image, as in copper engraving or crayon engraving.

Findings metal clasps, hooks, loops, and so on used in jewelry making.

Firing in ceramics, the baking of clay in a kiln or an outdoor banked fire (middle-school students might try Japanese raku-style pottery firing).

Fixative a commercial preparation employed as a spray to protect easily smudged creations in chalk, pastel, or charcoal (also known as "fixatif").

Found objects discards, remnants, samples, leftovers, and throwaways that are exploited in collages, junk sculpture, assemblages, and as stamps in printmaking projects.

Frieze a decorated, horizontal band in paint or in relief along the upper part of a building (see photos of the Parthenon) or a room.

Glaze a transparent or semitransparent coating of a color stain over a plain surface or another color used in oil painting, plaster sculpture, or ceramicware.

Greenware unfired clay in leather-hard stage, firm but not completely dry. Recommended stage for digging cavities in understructure to prevent firing explosions.

Grout a crevice filler such as the conditioned plaster sealed between clay, glass, or vinyl tesserae in a mosaic.

Gum eraser a soft eraser used in drawing. Available in cube or rectangle form.

Hue another appelation for "color."

India ink a waterproof ink made from lampblack. Used for drawing, designing, and in tempera-painting resists.

Kiln an oven used for drying, firing, and glazing clay creations.

Kneaded eraser a gray eraser made of unvulcanized rubber that must be stretched and kneaded to be effective. Used most often in charcoal drawing.

Line an element in art. The basic skeletal foundation of a design or composition.

Loom the supporting framework for the crisscrossing threads and yarn in weaving.

Children love to draw animals. They are even more enthusiastic when the subject is "animal families"—a pride of lions, a herd of buffalo, a school of fish, a covey of quail, a swarm of bees, a tangle of snakes, or a pack of wolves. Oil pastel on colored construction paper was the medium employed. Grade 5.

Macramé lacework made by tying, knotting, and weaving cord in a pattern.

Manila paper a general-purpose drawing or coloring paper, usually cream color.

Masonite a pressed board made of wood fibers. Used for clay-modeling boards, inking surfaces in printmaking, and rinsing boards in tempera and crayon resists.

Mat board a heavy poster board used for mounting or matting artwork. Available in many colors and textures.

Mobile a free-moving art construction in space. Alexander Calder's gift to the art world.

Monoprint one-of-a-kind print. Usually made by incising or marking on an inked glass plate and taking an impression.

Mosaic a design or composition made by arranging and glueing tesserae or geometric pieces of material next to one another, but not touching, on a background surface.

Mural a monumental artwork on the inside or outside walls of a building. Executed in paint, mosaic, metal repoussé, or a combination of materials.

Newsprint newspaper stock used for sketches, preliminary drawings, and prints.

Oil pastel a popular coloring media. A combination of chalk and oil available in a host of exciting colors.

Papier mâché name given to paper crafts that use newspaper moistened with wallpaper paste or laundry starch. Also paper pulp constructions.

Patina originally the color produced by corrosion on metal—the antique sheen of old age—now artificially obtained through use of patinalike pastes such as Rub'n'Buff and Treasure Gold.

Pattern design made by repeating a motif or symbol (allover pattern).

Perspective the creation of a three-dimensional space illusion on a two-dimensional surface by means of vanishing points, converging lines, and diminishing sizes of objects.

Plaster a white, powdery substance that when mixed with water forms a quick-setting molding or casting material (sometimes referred to as "plaster of Paris").

Positive-Negative Positive shapes in a composition are the solid objects—the people, trees, animals, buildings. Negative shapes are the unoccupied empty spaces between positive shapes. Atmosphere, sky, and earth considered negative space are sometimes designated as "foreground" and "background" space.

Radiation lines, shapes, or colors emanating from a central core. Sun rays, fan leaf, ripples around a pebble thrown into a stream.

Relief a projection from a surface. Low relief as in a coin is called "bas relief."

Repetition (rhythm) a principle of art. Repetition of lines, shapes, colors, and values in a composition creates unity.

Repoussé a design in metal art in which tooling and hammering are employed to achieve relief effects.

Rubber cement a clean, fast-drying latex type of adhesive. Excellent for paper projects.

Scoring (clay) to make rough indentations in clay with a nail or similar tool as a step in cementing two pieces of clay together. Also used to describe the guiding indentation in paper-sculpture curved-line folding.

Selvedge the edge of a fabric where the weft returns to weave its way to the opposite edge.

Shade refers to the darker values of a color or hue. Maroon is a shade of red; navy blue is a shade of blue.

Shellac a kind of lacquer used to seal and sometimes to protect certain art creations. Clear shellac is generally recommended.

Shellac solvent solution for cleaning shellac brushes: Shellacol, methanol, alcohol.

Sketch usually a preliminary drawing made with pencil, pen, crayon, charcoal, brush, pastel, or similar tool.

Slip clay diluted with water to a creamy consistency. Used as a binder joining two pieces of clay in ceramic construction.

Stabile a construction in space usually with no moving parts (Chicago's Picasso.) Sometimes referred to as "space modulator."

Still life an arrangement of objects, usually on a table as a subject for drawing, painting, collage, and so on.

Subordination a principle of art in which parts of the composition are subordinated so that others may dominate and be emphasized.

Tagboard sometimes referred to as "oaktag." A glossy-surfaced, pliable cardboard used in collage, collographs, glue line prints, and paper constructions.

Tempera paint an opaque, water-soluble paint available in liquid or powder form. Also referred to as "showcard" or "poster paint."

Tessera a small segment of paper, cardboard, vinyl, ceramic, and so on (usually, in geometric shape: square, rectangle) that is fitted and glued to a background surface to produce a mosaic (plural: *tesserae*).

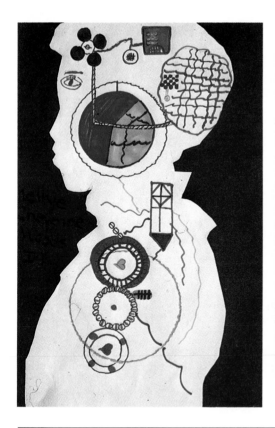
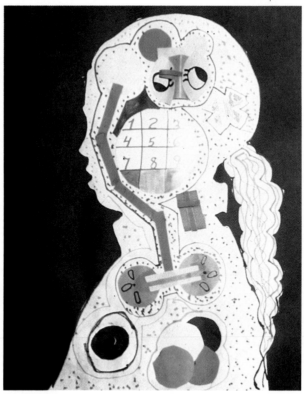
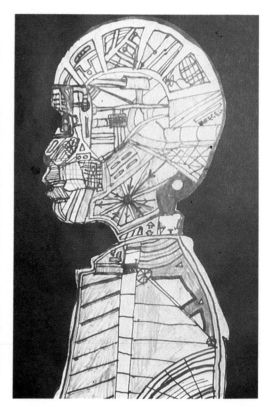

The bionic X-ray silhouettes illustrated above are the creations of fifth-grade youngsters, Timothy Road Elementary School, Athens, Georgia. Materials employed were 18″ by 24″ white construction paper, watercolor markers and/or crayons in assorted colors, wallpaper samples, scissors, pencils, and paste. The silhouette was drawn by outlining the student's profile in pencil on the white paper, utilizing a high-intensity light (film projector lamp) to create the student's shadow, then drawing around it. Motivations consisted of a discussion of various technological and electrical devices such as radio transistors, automobile motors, batteries, watchworks, cameras, computers, and television set components. TV shows such as "The Bionic Woman" and "The 6,000,000 Man" were also discussed. The completed drawings were cut out and mounted on 18″ by 24″ assorted, dark-colored construction paper.

Texture the actual or visual feel of a surface—bark on a tree, fur on an animal, sand on a beach.

Tint the lighter values of a color or hue. Pink is a tint of red.

Unity a principle of art. When everything in a composition falls into place through use of fundamental principles of art, unity is achieved.

Value in color terminology, the lightness or darkness of a hue.

Warp the thread or yarn that supports the weft in weaving.

Watercolors water-soluble colors, generally transparent or semitransparent. In common usage. Can be employed thickly to become opaque. Available in semimoist cakes or tubes.

Wedging a method of preparing moist clay by kneading and squeezing it to expel the air pockets and make it more plastic.

Weft the thread that goes across the warp from side to side in weaving. Also refers to the yarn used as weft.

INDEX